MILITARY BRATS AND OTHER GLOBAL NOMADS: GROWING UP IN ORGANIZATION FAMILIES

Edited by
MORTEN G. ENDER

2025 Reissue Edition with a New Introduction by
MORTEN G. ENDER

To Axel,
for reminding me the journey is just as important
as arriving…

DEFINITIONS

brat \ 'brat, *usa -ad.* +V \ n -s [perh. fr. ¹*brat*] 1: CHILD, OFFSPRING <an army ~ whose father was a colonel>

Webster's Dictionary (1993; p. 269)

B*R*A*T British Regiment Attached Traveler

U.S. Department of Defense website

Global Nomad aka glomad

Global Nomad Guide

Third Culture Kids (TCK) are Military Brats, Missionary' Kids, Foreign Service Dependents, and International Business Kids

Interaction International

CONTENTS

PART 2: GROWING UP ABROAD IN ORGANIZATION FAMILIES

TABLES, FIGURES, AND CHARTS

TABLES

FIGURES

CHARTS

NEW INTRODUCTION FOR THE REISSUE EDITION

MORTEN G. ENDER

The approaching silver anniversary of the publication of *Military Brats and Other Global Nomads* (2002) is the perfect time for a reissue. I conceived the idea for the initial volume in the mid-1990s. As a PhD graduate student at the University of Maryland at the time, I began collecting data on Adult Third Culture Kids (ATCKs) while finishing my coursework and writing my doctoral dissertation on soldier and spouse communication during military deployments. Though I did not think I had enough information to write an entire book about TCKs (including military brats), I knew plenty of others researching military children and adolescents, foreign service kids, Amerasians, missionary kids, and international business children such as ARAMCO brats. I solicited them for contributions, and they came through extraordinarily to produce the original volume. However, my day job kept me busy: I finished my dissertation, graduated, moved to the Midwest, started a new position at the University of North Dakota, and began our family. It took a few years, but the book finally hit the market in 2002.

In those interim years between the idea of the book and publication, my family and I spent a semester teaching at the American College of Norway in Moss, just south of Oslo, before moving back to the American East Coast, where I started a new position at the United States Military Academy at West Point, New York. As the book was going to press, terrorists attacked the United States on September 11, 2001—with one attack hitting just 60 miles down-river from us at the World Trade Center in New York City. A new reality set in. Following graduation, cadets would enter the war. The Global War on Terror (GWOT) ensued, and the lived experiences of millions of military brats were about to change markedly. In addition to moving every few years and living abroad, their uniformed service-member parent would spend the next 20 years earning combat pay with regular deployments to places like Taji, Iraq, and Helmand Province, Afghanistan. The world became increasingly unsafe for all TCKs posted abroad with their families, and much transpired on the global stage, impacting generations of military brats and other global nomads so far in the 21st century.

While fixed first on teaching cadets at West Point during the GWOT, my secondary focus turned to research less on military children and more on the people connected to the wars in Iraq and Afghanistan. Yet. I kept brats in the back of my mind.

In 2004, I traveled to Iraq to study soldiers and ultimately wrote a book—*American Soldiers in Iraq*, about their experiences in that war (Ender, 2009). We studied Iraqi adolescents (Carlton-Ford, Ender, & Tabatabai, 2008). I drew scholars from around the world, encouraging them to share their studies on Iraq and Afghanistan, which resulted in an award-winning edited volume titled *The Routledge Handbook of War and Society* (Carlton-Ford & Ender, 2009). One standout chapter in that book is by sociologist Rachel Lipari and her team. They studied military children during war deployments and uncovered the counter-intuitive statistical fact that kids coped better as the number of deployments increased.

After the book was published, my colleagues Mike Matthews, Dave Rohall, and I began a decades-long study of American undergraduate student attitudes toward a range of socio-political issues, including wars. It is the longest, continuous scholarly research of human subjects ever undertaken at West Point—running almost 25 years and comparing military academy cadets, ROTC cadets, and civilian undergraduates (Ender, Rohall, & Matthews, 2014). Follow us at genzmilitary.com. Our team also published a book in two editions that celebrated inclusion in the U.S. armed forces (Rohall, Ender, & Matthews, 2017; Ender, Kelty, Rohall, & Matthews, 2023). I proudly led an editorial team that produced a book featuring 36 chapters by 97 authors about teaching and learning excellence at West Point (Ender, Kimball, Sondheimer, & Bruhl, 2021).

Returning to the topic of brats, I concluded my research on groups impacted by the GWOT with a book on army families (Ender, 2023; see our review in Ender, Hyde, & Rashid, 2025), where I interviewed 199 army spouses about their overall deployment experience. The effort is extra special to me because I included a chapter on military children and adolescents—something others writing about military spouses during the war do only in passing. In essence, I did not lose sight of military children.

I never really lost my attentiveness to my core study group— military brats. In fact, in 2005, I published my favorite article to date—an analysis of representations of military children in 46 films across the 20th century, including *The Great Santini* and *Remember the Titans*, among others (Ender, 2005). A year later, fellow military brat and sociologist Meg Karraker at the University of St. Thomas invited me to contribute a fun essay about military children for her college-level marriage and family textbook (Ender, 2006a). That same year, I published a piece with my favorite title—"Voices from the Back Seat" (Ender, 2006b). In 2007, I had the good fortune to participate with subject matter experts on Army families, contributing a review chapter on what we knew at the time about Army children (Booth et al., 2007). A few years later, I could not pass up the opportunity to write a fun piece for the *Stars & Stripes* newspaper about military children in film (Ender, 2015). Before the end of the decade, I wrote an autoethnography about my journey as a military brat with a military mother (Ender, 2018).

The last 25 years have seen significant progress, with efforts focusing on military children expanding beyond a handful of individuals. Other examples include popular news, personal books and films, new online organizations, the establishment of research centers, and numerous studies from psychology, family studies, and sociology. Moreover, research has gone international. The following provides a brief introduction.

First, in the popular sphere, nonprofits aiding military children with free babysitting and books shuttered their operations amid backlash over the use of the term "CHAMPS" (Child Heroes Attached to Military Personnel)—essentially calling for the replacement of the term "military brats" (Bushatz, 2014). The beef went national (Gallagher, 2017). In a nutshell, a mother-daughter founding team faced ridicule as their group's language choice angered many adults who identify as "Military Brats" and who felt their cultural identity threatened by the name "CHAMPS" (an acronym). The controversy escalated into online threats and harassment, including the release of the founders' home addresses. Facing mounting hostility, the organization decided to shut down. Critics, such as Donna Musil, a film documentarian, argued that the issue reflects broader concerns about representation and the importance of lived experience in serving military communities. Military Brats kept their name.

Second, an increasing number of popular books about growing up in the military began to appear. Following on the heels of Mary Edwards Wertsch's 1991 book *Military Brats: Legacies of Childhood Inside the Fortress*, many began appearing—far too numerous to list here. The reader can search for them on their favorite search engines—try "military brats" or "TCKs" on Amazon, Google, or an AI program such as ChatGPT. The reader will find a diverse range of literature, spanning fiction (adventure, historical fiction, and mystery) and nonfiction (autobiographies and memoirs, coming-of-age stories from the U.S. and abroad, and self-help advice books for military brats). I quickly searched "military brat books" on Amazon.com and yielded 402 results. However, I must say that, despite the numerous new books available, my favorite remains *Army Brat: A Memoir* by William Jay Smith, published in 1980. Beautifully written, it chronicles the life of an army brat between World War I and World War II at one Army post, where his father played in the Army band.

One noteworthy and impressive scholarly book that I reviewed comes from colleagues up north: *Growing Up in Armyville: Canada's Military Families during the Afghanistan Mission* by Deborah Harrison and Patrizia Albanese (Ender, 2019). Published in 2016 through Wilfrid Laurier University Press, it is the best and most comprehensive study of military teens I have come across. The authors conducted in-depth research in a single military community and high school and, despite the title, concentrated almost exclusively on military adolescents.

Of course, Donna Musil has produced the best film about military brats, and not just because I am in it. Titled *BRATS: Our Journey Home*, the film captures the essence and demands of growing up in the military. It features two notable individuals: the effervescent General Norman Schwarzkopf and the iconic singer-songwriter and actor Kris Kristofferson. The film is available on Donna's website, https://bratswithoutborders.org. More recently, popular television has featured military brats either as the direct plot, such as Fox's *Going Dutch* or my personal favorite, HBO's *We Are Who We Are*, or the subplot, such as Lifetime's *Army Wives* or Fox's *Enlisted*.

The amount of scholarly research paid to military children and adolescents in the past 25 years is groundbreaking, impressive, and heartwarming. The subfield has expanded both in breadth and depth—too extensive to list here. "TCK" is a searchable term on Google Scholar, yielding a rich result. I leave it to the reader to explore specific topics in more detail. I have an extensive review in the notes section of my book *Army Spouses* (Ender, 2023). Other practitioner-oriented books provide a wealth of sources on a range of topics. *Serving Military Families* by Karen Rose Blaisure and her colleagues (2015) is a good place to start.

Several organizations have surfaced that support, celebrate, or connect military-connected children, adolescents, and adults. They include the Military Child Education Coalition, Salute the Kids, Brats Without Borders, Museum of the American Military Family & Learning Center, Our Military Kids, Tragedy Assistance Program for Survivors (TAPS), and Camp Corral, among many others. Similarly, some organizations support TCKs, including TCKidNOW,

Interaction International, the Foreign Service Youth Foundation, ARAMCO Brats, and Team Expansion. Some college campuses offer counseling and support services for both TCKs and military-affiliated youth, such as Lewis and Clark College and Texas A&M University. Likewise, many schools and programs now buoy adults from military families, including the American Overseas Schools Historical Society (AOSHS) and a whole host of social media pages and discussion groups for the American military, TCK, and like-affiliated adults, youth, and children like Brats: Honoring our Heritage and the University of Maryland Munich Campus groups on Facebook.

Additionally, students and scholars can visit new centers that advocate for military families. Some examples include the Military Family Research Institute at Purdue University, the Clearinghouse for Military Family Readiness at Pennsylvania State University, the Center for Innovation and Research on Veterans & Military Families at the University of Southern California, and the D'Aniello Institute for Veterans & Military Families at Syracuse University.

Finally, the knowledge about military children and adolescents has gone global. As more countries became part of the counterterrorism efforts of the Global War on Terror (GWOT), more research followed. Studies emerged from Coalition Force nations, including the UK, Germany, France, Canada, Australia, Italy, the Netherlands, Denmark, Slovenia, Turkey, and others. My colleague, Rene Moelker at the Netherlands Defence Academy, has led two research efforts, some of which center on armed forces-affiliated children (Moelker, 2015; 2019), and is currently working on another project.

That brings us to this reissue. I am totally stoked to reissue the book for two interconnected reasons. First, the book was widely popular upon its initial release. Beyond the traditional market of researchers, research centers, and university libraries, there was great interest among teachers and administrators who served military families, such as the now-named Department of Defense Education Activity (formerly DoDDS, now DoDEA). Moreover, that made me proud because I am married to a high school teacher and Army brat herself, Corina Morano-Ender. Second, the original book was expensive. With only a hardback version selling at almost $100.00, it was prohibitive to folks interested in smart books about military brats, Third Culture Kids (TCKs), and global nomads. Despite this, the book continued to sell. Now, the price is right, and it is available in paperback, e-book, and hardback versions.

I would like to close by acknowledging and thanking my colleague, collaborator, and friend Jess Dawson for her inspiration, mentorship, and assistance in producing this reissue of the book. Thank you, too, to the folks on the military brats' Facebook pages who suggested their elementary school class photographs as a cover. Unsure of the legalities of photographing children and teachers without consent, I opted for the dandelion cover (a free online downloadable image). The dandelion is the adopted official flower of military children and is renowned for its ability to thrive in diverse environments. I hope you enjoy the book and learn something along the way. Follow me at https://mortenender.com.

Morten G. Ender
Highland Falls, New York, USA
Memorial Day Weekend 2025

REFERENCES

Blaisure, K. R., Saathoff-Wells, T., Pereira, A., Wadsworth, S. M., & Dombro, A. L. (2015). *Serving military families: Theories, research, and application*. Routledge.

Booth, B., Segal, M. W., Bell, D. B., Martin, J. A., Ender, M. G., Rohall, D. E., & Nelson, J. (2007). *What we know about Army families: 2007 update*. U.S. Army Family and Morale, Welfare and Recreation Command.

Bushatz, A. (2014, December 10). CHAMPS nonprofit shutters after battle of Military Brat name. *Military.com*. https://www.military.com

Carlton-Ford, S., & Ender, M. G. (Eds.). (2010). *The Routledge handbook of war and society: Iraq and Afghanistan*. Routledge.

Carlton-Ford, S., Ender, M. G., & Tabatabai, A. (2008). Iraqi adolescents: Self-regard, self-derogation, and perceived threat in war. *Journal of Adolescence, 31*(1), 53–75. https://doi.org/10.1016/j.adolescence.2007.04.002

Ender, M. G. (2006a). Military brats: Growing up on the move. In M. W. Karraker & J. R. Grochowski (Eds.), *Families with futures: A survey of family studies for the 21st century* (pp. 295–296). Lawrence Erlbaum.

Ender, M. G. (2006b). Voices from the backseat: Growing up in military families. In A. Adler & C. Castro (Eds.), *Military life: The psychology of serving in peace and combat (Vol. 3: The military family)* (pp. 138–166). Praeger Security International.

Ender, M. G. (2009). *American soldiers in Iraq: McSoldiers or innovative professionals?* Routledge.

Ender, M. G. (2015, April 24). Military brats in films. *Stars and Stripes (Asia Edition)*.

Ender, M. G. (2018). Mom wore combat boots: An autoethnography of a military sociologist. In S. Hampson, U. Lebel, & N. Tabor (Eds.), *Mothers, military and society* (pp. 157–187). Demeter Press.

Ender, M. G. (2019). [Review of the book *Growing up in Armyville: Canada's military families during the Afghanistan mission*, by D. Harrison & P. Albanese]. *Res Militaris: The European Journal of Military Studies, 9*(1).

Ender, M. G. (2023). *Army spouses: Military families during the Global War on Terror*. University of Virginia Press.

Ender, M. G., Hyde, A., & Rashid, M. (2025). "Til death do us part?: Military power, marriage, and family life in Pakistan, the U.S., and the UK. *Journal of Media, War & Conflict*. https://doi.org/10.1177/17506352241302232

Ender, M. G., Kelty, R., Rohall, D. E., & Matthews, M. D. (Eds.). (2023). *Inclusion in the American military: A force for diversity* (2nd ed.). Lexington Books.

Ender, M. G., Kimball, R. A., Sondheimer, R. M., & Bruhl, J. C. (Eds.). (n.d.). *Teaching and learning the West Point way: Educating the next generation of leaders* (1st ed.). Routledge.

Ender, M. G., Rohall, D. E., & Matthews, M. D. (2014). *The millennial generation and national defense: Attitudes of future military and civilian leaders.* Palgrave Pivot.

Gallagher, B. J. (2017, December 1). Military BRATS = Bright. Resilient. Active. Talented. Successful. *HuffPost.* https://www.huff-post.com

Moelker, R., Andres, M., Bowen, G., & Manigart, P. (Eds.). (2015). *Military families and war in the 21st century: Comparative perspectives.* Routledge.

Moelker, R., Andres, M., & Rones, N. (Eds.). (2019). *The politics of military families: State, work organizations, and the rise of the negotiated household.* Routledge.

Rohall, D. E., Ender, M. G., & Matthews, M. D. (Eds.). (2017). *Inclusion in the American military: A force for diversity* (1st ed.).

Smith, W. J. (1980). *Army brat: A memoir.* Persea Books.

Wertsch, M. E. (1991). *Military brats: Legacies of childhood inside the fortress.* Harmony Books.

FOREWORD

MADY WECHSLER SEGAL

This volume makes a unique contribution to the study of children who grow up in military families, as well as in other organizational settings that take the families out of their home country. These are the "brats" referred to in the title, a label that many actually prefer (which is surprising to me because of its pejorative connotations). Some are labeled "global nomads" (by themselves and researchers). The term "expatriate children" is also used, as is "internationally mobile kids." Third Culture Kid (TCK) has become the label to describe children growing up in their non-passport country. Their parents are in occupations such as business, government work, foreign service, or missionary work. Morten Ender, the editor of this volume, is himself a military "brat."

Most early research on military children was focused on clinical populations. The studies reported by mental health professionals, showed negative effects of the military family lifestyle on children. In the past 20 years there has been a burgeoning of empirical research, both qualitative and quantitative, covering more typical military children. This new research tends to show that the earlier clinical studies over-represented the proportion of children nega-tively affected by aspects of the military lifestyle. The research reported in this book is balanced in its presentation: it shows, via both small and large scale research, theoretical and empirical, the positive and negative effects on individuals growing up in military and other "organizational" families.

Almost all chapters were written especially for this book. Those reprinted from other publications make unique contributions to our knowledge and/or the original publications are difficult to obtain. The chapters cover varied topics and populations and use a range of research methods.

This is a book from which we learn about many facets of growing up in an organizationally determined lifestyle. Many of the chapters provide recommendations for families themselves, for policy makers, and for service providers, either explicitly or implicitly through the implications of their findings. We learn about child development, including the effects of maternal absence for Navy deployments on children's behavior and parental bonding. We learn about Navy mothers' feelings about leaving their children and their attitudes toward their jobs as a result. We learn about the adjustment of teenagers moving to Germany and the conditions that help their adjustment. Many American servicemen in Vietnam left behind their children born to Vietnamese mothers; we learn about the experiences of these Vietnamese Amerasian children, both in Vietnam and after they were able to enter the United States. We are also treated to an analysis of the portrayals of internationally mobile children in children's literature and the messages conveyed by the "hidden curriculum." The application of attachment theory provides insights into potential developmental problems for internationally mobile children and ways to avoid them.

From research on adult members of "brat" organizations, we gain an understanding about the sense of identity and belonging that "organization children" have with others who have shared the same organizationally determined lifestyle of frequent moving and living overseas and the effects of that lifestyle on their feelings about family, as well as their advice for military families and service providers. Their motives to reconnect as adults, including via their electronic community, range from positive reactions to the lifestyle—

such as missing the opportunity to move to new places, to more negative concerns—such as not having a feeling of belonging to any place or other group of people and wanting to communicate with others who share that need.

The readers of this volume could be anyone desiring to understand childhood and adolescent experiences in organization families and how these experiences shape adult perspectives, feelings, and desired lifestyles. If you are a researcher or policy maker, you will find much of this material is useful to you. And those of you who grew up in such families will find resources here: you may find that reading about others with similar experiences gives you a sense of shared lives and belonging, just as others derive from membership and communication in the "brat" organizations. It may provide you with a helpful perspective with which to reflect on your experiences and a strategy to deal with your feelings about them.

This book provides insights into personal and social processes involved in transitions from one culture to another, including the adjustments required for reentry to one's "home" culture. Indeed, using the term "passport country" clues us to the fact that many "brats" and global nomads are more accustomed to another culture; that culture and country may actually feel more like home. We learn something about complex processes of cultural transitions, personal development, cross-cultural attitudes, and adult life choices and how they are affected by parental behavior, the child's gender, the home country, the organizational context, the culture of the host country, and the historical era. More research is needed to understand these processes more fully, and this book should stimulate more research on children in organization families and the adults that they become.

Mady Wechsler Segal
Center for Research on Military Organization
Department of Sociology
University of Maryland
College Park, Maryland

ACKNOWLEDGMENTS

My grandmother, Hanni Ender, saved a postcard she received in 1962 from my mother. The front of the card is a full-length, side view picture of the two smoke-stacked United States Naval Ship, *General Alexander M. Patch* (*T-AP* 122), a Military Sea Transportation Service of the U.S. Navy providing ocean transportation service to American military service members and their families stationed overseas. My mother, stepfather, and I had left Bremerhaven, West Germany, aboard the *Patch* that December bound for New York, then to Colorado for a brief vacation before moving to my new stepfather's duty station at the United States Disciplinary Barracks at Fort Leavenworth, Kansas. On the back of the postcard, mom describes herself as being seasick on the leg of the journey to England but that I was having a wonderful time in the kindergarten with the other kids.

Although I have no memory of the experience, the *Patch* journey was my first exposure to military kids. Mom tells me I fit in and the other kids accepted me. So, it is befitting that I first and foremost acknowledge and thank anyone on that voyage for treating me so well. It was my first impression of Americans, as I had been born and raised in Germany and I spoke no English.

Similar to my own experience, most of the chapters in this volume are indigenous ethnographies—people studying their own subcultures. Prior to entering elementary school and after middle school, I lived in a military family and in military communities. After high school graduation, I moved to Germany to be near both my military and extended family and to begin my freshman year of college. While attending the University of Maryland, Munich,

Germany campus, I befriended many of the kinds of people studied in this book and even married one. The experiences of my friends, classmates, and acquaintances made while studying, working, playing, and traveling throughout Europe, North Africa, and the Middle East during that time have greatly shaped my thinking about preparing this book.

After returning to the United States to complete my undergraduate studies at Sonoma State University, Bob Tellander, a sociology professor, supervised a senior level independent study where I could investigate the origin of the term "military brat." My course of study uncovered far more questions than answers, and I thank him greatly for the academic freedom to get lost in the process rather than packaging a product for some arbitrary objective grade—the best teachers know when to get out of the way of their students.

The idea for the present volume originated while I was in graduate school at the University of Maryland, College Park, and two significant sociology graduate courses: David Segal's Military Sociology and Mady Segal's Military Families. Mady's course allowed me to begin to synthesize the literature on military families and to do so in an interdisciplinary but focused manner. The structure of Mady's course in particular, especially the open-ended term paper, allowed me to explore a range of research topics in and around the military and other organization families including the TCK literature and the *Global Nomads* organization. Recognizing the commonality of many of our research findings, I made a mental note in graduate school that a common resource had not been produced that effectively linked the literature.

Almost a decade after first reviewing the literature, this volume will finally go to press. Over the past 18 months, a mental note a decade ago became a focused goal and a number of people have provided invaluable assistance in helping make it possible. First, numerous colleagues helped in shaping this volume, and I give special thanks and praises to the fellow contributors of this volume. I have never met or spoken over the telephone with many of you. In the age of the Internet, our common interests crossed in cyberspace and we became people of electronic letters and snail mail. Thank you for your trust despite our physical distances—know that I often felt your telepresence through our e-communiqués. For all of you, thanks for your low maintenance, continued commitment, collaboration, and dedication to the project, and, foremost, your passion for the topic and making your words a part of this volume. I hope I have represented your work well. Someday, somewhere, we'll share a meal together.

I want to also thank the many reviewers who agreed to blind review early editions of the chapters for this volume. They include, in no particular order, Louis Hicks, Alix Clarke, Marjorie Carroll, David Rohall, John Hawkins, Karen Davis, Annette Richardson, Brian Reed, Meg Karraker, Robert Priest, Steve Lankenau, Meg Harrell, and Corina Morano-Ender.

I am also indebted to the Office of Academic Research, United States Military Academy, and the Army Research Institute for the Behavioral and Social Sciences for providing funds through a faculty research grant to offset some administrative costs associated with this volume. Likewise, I want to recognize Casey Brower, Joe LeBoeuf , and Tom Kolditz for their leadership in the Department of Behavioral Sciences and Leadership at the United States Military Academy at West Point and for fostering an environment of interdisciplinary and current thinking in and around matters of the military. I want also to express my gratitude to my colleagues in and around the department of BS&L for their daily informal support of not only me but my family as well. In particular Scott Petersen, John Hurley, Scott Bemis, Susan Lee-Kratz, and Fran Coyle extended themselves in small but very significant ways. Without such supportive colleagues, I would have little time and even less motivation to be even marginally productive. I am also appreciative of the prompt administrative magic and computer skills wielded by Deb Butler. A special thanks to my editors Heather Staines and Emma Moore for their ongoing, prompt, sincere, and efficient support during this project.

Last, to the many adults from military families, adult Third Culture Kids, former missionary kids, and global nomads around the world who give up their time and emotional and cognitive energy to answer our open-ended questions and long questionnaires —thank you. On behalf of the researchers of the enclosed chapters and myself, thank you for your honesty, your forthrightness, and your eloquence.

Finally, it is necessary to conclude that any work representing the interests of children, adolescents, and young adults is bound to be controversial and generate heated debate. I think this is a good thing. However, know that the views of the editor and contributing authors are their own and do not purport to reflect the position of the agencies they discuss, in particular the United States Military Academy, the Army Research Institute, the Department of the Army, or the Department of Defense.

INTRODUCTION TO THE 2002 EDITION

MORTEN G. ENDER

It's been 23 years since the publication of *Children of Military Families: A Part and Yet Apart* (Hunter & Nice, 1978). This collaborative effort and edited volume, the result of a conference on military family research and sponsored by the Office of Naval Research in San Diego, California, provided the first collection of social science research on the topic of children from military families. For example, Ann Baker Cottrell (1978) contributed a chapter in that volume titled "Mixed Children: Some Observations and Speculations' (and she bridges the quarter century with a contribution in this volume). Social and behavioral science studies on children from military families did predate that volume.[1] One of the earliest studies of children of service members appeared in 1945 (Igel, 1945). Subsequent research appeared in the 1960s (see e.g., Carlsmith, 1964; Gabower, 1960; Pederson, 1966) with a broader topical range of studies coming out in the 1970s (see e.g., Carlsmith, 1973; Dahl & McCubbin 1975; Gonzalez, 1970). By the 1980s and 1990s, rich and more conceptually based research literature had developed (see e.g., Orthner, Giddings, & Quinn, 1989; Paden & Pezor, 1993; Watanabe & Jensen, 2000). Much of this research has been highly interdisciplinary, applied, undertaken, and funded under the auspices of the U.S. armed forces, and more often reactive to social and psychological problems existing in the military community and military family in general.

Maturing alongside studies of children from military families has been a similar and rich literature describing the cross-cultural living experiences of youth from organization families such as the foreign service. Pioneered by sociologists Ruth Hill Useem and John Useem in the 1960s (see Useem, 1971; Useem & Useem, 1967; Useem, Useem, & Donoghue, 1963), they developed and later elaborated on the sensitizing construct of the Third Culture Kid (TCK). Research on TCKs blossomed under the Useems and their graduate students at Michigan State University. Unlike the work on children from military families, research on the TCK emerged mostly in university settings, undertaken by mostly self-labeled adult TCK students under the supervision of their academic advisors, and resulted in a plethora of master's theses and doctoral dissertations concentrated mostly in the area of sociology and social psychology.

Organization family–raised people recognize their unique socialization experience and develop a loose network of ties by seeking out others like themselves.

In Chapter 6, my reprint from a previous book (Ender, 2000), I list some of the numerous books, magazine articles, films, and organizations that emerged during the 1980s and 1990s focusing on the experiences of growing up military. In recent years, the abundance of books on the topic of military brats, global nomads, and the TCK have helped sustain publishing houses such as Aletheia Publications and Cross Cultural Publications, Inc. Many of the resources distinguish the comparatively unique demands of the experience relative to "civilian" life.

Associations representing the common interests of Adult Third Culture Kids (ATCKs) and adult children from military families have thrived. As of March 14, 2001, some 51,949 adults claiming a military family background had registered at http://www.military-brats.com/search.cfm. Established on April 24, 1997, as an electronic network for adult children of military parents, it provides a sort of cyber-student (re)union where people can reconnect and interact with old school chums and long-lost friends. Likewise, groups and associations have formed to connect and assist adult children from foreign service, international business, educators, and missionary families (see http://globalnomads.association.com/).

In the popular press, both children and adolescents from military families and the TCK experience receive occasional attention that sets their growing up apart from their peers. Most of the press portrays atypical and nightmarish experiences of Americans living abroad:

In May 1994, 18-year-old American Michael Fay received four lashes across his bare buttocks with a rattan cane for vandalism in Singapore. Fay's stepfather was an officer with Federal Express in Singapore, and Michael attended the Singapore American High School (Tipton, 1994). The caning generated international attention when President Clinton and the *New York Times* appealed to Singapore officials on Fay's behalf.

In March 2000, three American teenagers, sons of service members stationed at a U.S. Army base in Darmstadt, Germany, and living in the military community were charged and sentenced for throwing football-size rocks from an Autobahn overpass onto the cars below. They killed two women and injured a dozen others (Komarow, 2000).

Both capture national and international attention and construct unfavorable attention on Americans living abroad. However, the events are atypical and fairly isolated experiences. A few other stories emerge and capture the more positive and generalized experiences, which are usually focused on education:

A 2000 *Reuters* article reported on the success of U.S. military child-care system (Aldinger, 2000). Serving approximately 200,000 children worldwide, the article notes how a holistic approach including childcare centers, families, childcare homes, before- and after-school programs, and other both formal and informal services make the program a success. The article quotes groups calling the system a model for the nation.

A 1999 front page *Wall Street Journal* article synthesized and reported a number of findings on the success of students attending Department of Defense Schools (DODs) relative to their U.S. civilian peers (Golden, 1999). Of noteworthy interest are a higher proportion of DODs students successfully earning higher writing scores and a higher proportion of people of color from DODs going on to college, both relative to their civilian peers.

It is common knowledge that after World War II, American and other First World countries expanded their political, military, corporate, and humanitarian responsibilities outside their national borders. What is less known and greatly misunderstood is that with families in tow, service people began to move and live, in increasing numbers, outside the borders of their host county to meet and sustain the organization's mission. Military and other service agencies in the United States and abroad imposed organizational demands on members, their spouses, and children. In addition to out-of-country service and residence, demands include in-country relocation, the risk of death or injury, family separation, normative social controls, early retirement, and relative poverty. Sometimes called TCKs (third culture kids), MKs (missionary kids), PKs (preacher kids), global nomads, and military brats, millions of children have grown up in these service families.

Estimates are that about two percent of the U.S. population grew up in a service-organization family such as the military or foreign service and lived abroad. The 2000 Census reports that 576,367 Americans, including U.S. military and federal civilian employees and their dependents, live outside of the United States (U.S. Department of Commerce, 2000). One result of this legacy is that millions of people worldwide are coming of age in the shadows of these organizations and often outside their nation of origin. Who are these people? Is there a social and psychological imprint on those coming of age in service families? The authors of this volume attempt to answer these and other questions, and within this sociohistorical context the current edited volume is published.

ORGANIZATION

This volume is organized into two parts. Part I includes chapters with data on children, adolescents, and adults who grew up both at home and abroad in (and outside) military families. Part II includes chapters addressing, and with data on, children, adolescents, and adults. The part has chapters on the experience of growing up abroad in other organization families (including military), such as the foreign service, missionary, and others. Michelle Kelley's chapter opens the volume by showing the spillover of military life demand of deployment and the impact on both parents and children. The research findings are novel for providing comparative insights between deployed fathers and mothers. The next chapter, a reprinted journal article authored by Mary Tyler, examines the experiences of American teenagers living in a military community in Germany at the end of the Cold War. The research is important because it provides one of the only qualitative studies of the period. Phoebe Price's chapter, a study undertaken for her senior under-graduate thesis, compares the behavior of civilians with military high school students in film theaters. The detailed description of her research activities should provide graduate and undergraduate students alike with a model for carrying out similar research. Vietnamese Amerasians are a special group of people not generally included in the study of military families and their children, making it an exciting contribution to this volume. Robert McKelvey gives these neglected young adults a voice through his work by describing their childhood development growing up in poverty in Vietnam (prior to and following the U.S. military exodus) as mixed-race victims of discrimination and prejudice and their relative reversal of fortune as they migrated and adopted to life in the United States.

The last two chapters of Part I investigate and report findings from studies of adult children from military families. Karen Cachevki Williams and LisaMarie Liebenow Mariglia report research findings from their study of an online group. They report five salient themes that emerge from the data and anchor the work in studies of voluntary associations. Part I concludes with my previously published chapter of an ongoing study of adults (N = 607) from primarily military families (78.5%) and also foreign-service families, international business, missionaries, U.S. government federal employees living abroad, and others. The chapter describes the findings from a scale measuring the salient life demands of organization life.

Part II has seven chapters by some of the leading scholars on the topic of ATCKs/Global Nomads. Part II begins with Barbara Schaetti's chapter on the relevance of attachment theory and its ability to explain the developmental experience of children raised internationally because of a parent's occupation—people known as "global nomads."

Next, Annika Hylmö offers up two chapters. In her first chapter she conducts a content analysis into the treatment of the expatriate experience in children's literature as a rhetorical device serving to reify romanticized conditions of international living. Richard Pearce similarly undertakes the experience of childhood in his chapter, with particular attention to international relocation and the developmental process. Adopting a pluralistic perspective and synthesizing social constructivism and symbolic interactionism, he anchors the child's expatriate experience within the social context of family and culture.

The next two chapters address adolescence. The first of these is a reprinted article by Michael Gerner and Fred Perry. In it they compare a large sample of internationally mobile adolescents by gender in Egypt and Thailand with a like age group in the midwestern U.S. for cultural acceptance, language learning, satisfaction with living abroad, attitudes toward geographic mobility, and future careers in international careers with intriguing results. Next, Annika Hylmö, in her second contribution to the volume, breaks new ground with an examination of expatriate adolescents representing countries other than the United States. Her meta-analysis of published work on global nomads and TCKs is grounded in the theoretical perspectives of postmodernism and postcolonialism where she simply challenges us with one of my favorite sentences in the book: "Expatriate youth in the diplomatic corps from Uganda have a different reality to contend with than similar youth from Great Britain."

The remaining two chapters in the book are written by pioneers in the study of TCKs—Kathleen Finn Jordan and Ann Baker Cottrell, respectfully. Their chapters are based on an extensive research project—the Adult Third Culture Kid (ATCK) Research Project—in collaboration with Ruth Hill Useem and John Useem. The study involves life histories of 696 ATCKs collected in the early 1990s. Finn Jordon's chapter examines identity formation in relation to geographic mobility, parental sponsorship, and TCK lifestyle elements. Ann Baker Cottrell's chapter brings the entire volume full circle. She examines the educational and occupational choices of ATCKs with a focus on international dimensions of higher education and occupational choices.

Morten G. Ender
West Point, New York
March 20, 2001
The First Day of Spring

NOTES

[1] Certainly, the actual experience of growing up military, or for that matter in any organization family, predates 1945. For example, historians have long written about Americans traveling and living abroad. For a recent example of early military brat experiences, see Mary Leefe Laurence's (1996) memoirs.

REFERENCES

Aldinger, C. (2000, May 16). Group praises U.S. military's child-care system. *Reuters News Service*. Available online: http://www.reuters.com/home.jhtml.

Carlsmith, L. (1964). Effect of father absence on scholastic aptitude. *Harvard Educational Review 34*, 3–21.

Carlsmith, L. (1973). Some personality characteristics of boys separated from their fathers during World War II. *Ethos*, 467–477.

Cottrell, A.B. (1978). Mixed children: Some observations and speculations. In E. J. & D. S. Nice (Eds.), *Children of military families: A part and yet apart* (pp. 61–81). Washington, DC: Superintendent of Documents, U.S. Government Printing Office.

Dahl, R.B., & McCubbin, H.I. (1975). *Children of returned prisoners of war: The effects of long-term father absence.* (Technical Report No 75-30). San Diego, CA: Naval Health Research Center, Center for POW Studies.

Ender, M.G. (2000). Beyond adolescence: The experiences of adult children of military parents. In J. Martin, L. Rosen, & L. Sparacino (Eds.), *The military family: A practice guide for human service providers* (pp. 241–255). Westport CT: Praeger Publishers.

Gabower, G. (1960). Behavior problems of children in navy officers' families. *Social Casework 4*, 177–184.

Golden, D. (1999, December 22). Pentagon's schools outrank others in academic success. *Wall Street Journal*, p. 1.

Gonzalez, V. (1970). *Psychiatry and the army brat.* Springfield, IL: C.C. Thomas.

Hill, R. (1940). *Families under stress: Adjustment to the crisis of war separation and reunion.* New York: Harper & Row (reprinted by Greenwood Press, Westport, CT, 1971).

Hunter, E.J., & Nice, D.S. (Eds.). (1978). *Children of military families: A part and yet apart.* Washington, DC: Superintendent of Documents, U.S. Government Printing Office.

Igel, A. (1945). The effect of war separation on father-child relations. *The Family, 26*, 3–9.

Komarow, S. (2000, December 1). Rock-throwing trial begins in Germany Three youths from U.S. Army families charged in deaths. *USA Today*, A.24.

Leefe Laurence, M. (1996). *Daughter of the regiment: Memoirs of a childhood in the frontier army, 1878-1898* (Thomas T. Smith, Ed.). Lincoln, NE: University of Nebraska Press.

Orthner, D.K., Giddings, M.M., & Quinn, W.H. (1989). Growing up in an organization family. In G.L. Bowen & D.K. Orthner (Eds.), *The organization family: Work and family linkages in the U.S. military.* (pp. 117–142). Westport, CT: Praeger.

Paden, L.B., & Pezor, L.J. (1993). Uniforms and youth: The military child and his or her family. In F.W. Kaslow (Ed.), *The military family in peace and war* (pp. 3–24). New York: Springer Publishing Company.

Pederson, F.A. (1966). Relationships between father absence and emotional disturbance in male military dependents. *Merrill-Palmer Quarterly, 12,* 321–331.

Tipton, V. (1994, April 20). Who is Michael Fay? Tale of 2 two families: Teen facing caning had varied background. *St. Louis Post-Dispatch,* 01A.

Useem, J. (1971). The study of cultures. *Sociological Focus, 4,* 3–25.

Useem, J., & Useem, R.H. (1967). The interfaces of a binational third culture: A study of the American community in India. *Journal of Social Issues, XXIII,* 130–143.

Useem, J., Useem, R.H., & Donoghue, J. (1963). Men in the middle of the third culture: The roles of American and non-western people in cross-cultural administration. *Human Organization, 22,* 171–179.

U.S. Department of Commerce, U.S. Census. (2000). *Overseas population of the 50 states and the District of Columbia* (December 28).

Watanabe, H. K., & Jensen, P. S. (2000). Young children's adaptation to a military lifestyle. In J. A. Martin, L. N. Rosen, & L. R. Sparacino (Eds.), *The military family: A practice guide for human service providers.* (pp. 209–224) Westport, CT: Praeger.

PART 1: GROWING UP IN MILITARY FAMILIES

1

THE EFFECTS OF DEPLOYMENT ON TRADITIONAL AND NONTRADITIONAL MILITARY FAMILIES: NAVY MOTHERS AND THEIR CHILDREN

MICHELLE L. KELLEY

INTRODUCTION

Approximately 200,000 active-duty U.S. military personnel are women. Women comprise 14.4% of active-duty military personnel. This percentage is expected to rise in the near future because, with the exception of the Marine Corps, more than 20% of all new recruits are women (Department of Defense, 2000). The steady increase in the number of female military personnel is due to the expanded role of women in nontraditional occupations within the service.

Approximately 34% of all military women are mothers (Department of Defense, 1999). For the most part, the role of military member and mother is not compatible. For instance, military jobs involve cycles of departure-absence-return, known as deployments, throughout the course of military service. Although the definition of deployment varies across branches of the service (Department of Defense, 1996), the current focus is on five-to-six-month deployments, common to U.S. military members.

We know little about the effects of deployment in nontraditional military families (i.e., families in which the woman is the military member, single military parents, or dual-career military couples). By understanding these issues, it is possible to develop programs and policies that facilitate family functioning during work-related separations, to help reduce the turnover rate for women, and, thereby, to increase military readiness.[1]

I begin with a review of the effects of deployment on adults and children in traditional families, followed by a review of the effects of separation on non-traditional military families. Importantly, little information is available on male parents who care for children during their wives' deployment. Next, findings are presented from our longitudinal study (e.g., Kelley, Hock, Bonney, Jarvis, Smith, & Gaffney, in press) examining the effects of deployment on U.S. Navy mothers and their children. Third, limitations of previous research are discussed and recommendations for future research are made. Finally, recommendations are made that may enable support programs to better facilitate family functioning during mothers' separations.

The Effects of Deployment on Traditional Military Families

Time-dependent fluctuations in individual and family functioning that are related to points in the deployment cycle have been documented cross-culturally (e.g., DeSoir, 1999) and across branches of the U.S. military (e.g., Norwood, Fullerton, & Hagen, 1996; Wood, Scarville, & Gravino, 1995).

In a study of Belgian Army families in which soldiers were deployed to Bosnia, DeSoir (1999) equates the process families' experience to an emotional roller coaster. A few days before the deployment, family members typically distanced themselves from one another. Beginning at the time of departure, tension and/or detachment were replaced by sadness and loss. Next, families began to settle into a routine and adjust to the soldier's absence; however, upsetting media reports or a lack of communication with the deployed family member could disrupt this equilibrium. A few weeks before the soldier's return, families anticipate reunion. High expectations for reunion, however, may lead to disappointment as family members may have unrealistic expectations (Amen, Jellen, Merves, & Lee, 1988; DeSoir, 1999; Norwood et al., 1996). A description of common stresses and reactions associated with deployment is presented in Table 1.1.

In an empirical study, deploying U.S. Navy personnel and their spouses reported greater emotional distress, increased life stress, and lower family functioning than did nondeploying control families. Families who reported the highest levels of stress reported less family cohesiveness, expressiveness, and organization (Eastman, Archer, & Ball, 1990).

Other research has demonstrated a cyclic pattern of depressive behavior in military wives with absent husbands (e.g., Beckman, Marsella, & Finney, 1979; DeSoir, 1999; Glisson, Melton, & Roggow, 1980; see Norwood et al., 1996). Specifically, depressive affect was higher in Navy wives immediately prior to and throughout deployment than after the spouse's return (Kelley, 1994a; Nice, 1983). Among submariners' wives, the highest level of depressive affect was reported when ships submerged and all communication ceased (Glisson et al., 1980). Clinical levels of depressive behavior have been found in wives of nuclear submariners (Beckman et al., 1979).

Many factors mediate or exacerbate the stresses associated with military-induced separation. Although the experiences, support, and stresses for World War II, Vietnam, and Persian Gulf veterans vary greatly, for all groups, the stress associated with combat (or potential combat) predisposes wives to depression (e.g., Bey & Lange, 1974; Hill, 1949; Hunter, 1986; McCubbin, Hunter, & Dahl, 1975; Perconte, Wilson, Pontius, Dietrick, & Spiro, 1993).

Table 1.1. Common Sources of Stress for Nondeployed Spouses of Military Personnel.

Phase of Deployment	Common Sources of Spouse Stress and Affective Difficulties
Predeployment	Marital stress/conflict, distancing from spouse, anger, resentment, sadness/depression, negative child behavior
Deployment	Marital problems, isolation, loneliness, anger, resentment, sadness/depression, reduced communication, stress, less social support, assuming the role of single parent, childcare difficulties, sleep disturbances, physical symptoms, home and car repairs, difficulty assessing military services, negative child behavior
Postdeployment/Reunion	Redefining responsibilities, marital stress, communication problems, anxiety, anger, resentment, parent-child attachment issues

Nineteen percent of families with a member deployed during Operation Desert Storm experienced moderate or severe family adjustment problems (Department of Veterans Affairs, 1991). More specifically, higher levels of depressive symptoms and emotional distress were found in wives with husbands deployed during Operation Desert Storm (Jensen, Martin, & Watanabe, 1996; Kelley, 1994a; Medway, Davis, Cafferty, Chappell, & O'Hearn, 1995). Pregnancy increases the risk for depression for women with deployed spouses (Light, 1992). Importantly, families experienced difficulties that were attributed to deployment for as long as one-year postreunion (Peebles-Kleiger & Kleiger, 1994).

The Effects of Humanitarian Missions on Families' Functioning

In response to continued regional conflicts throughout the world, an increasing number of United States military forces have been deployed as part of the United Nations peacekeeping or other humanitarian missions. The dangers of these missions are less foreseeable, and they are especially stressful for military families. In a longitudinal study of U.S. Army families in which (mostly) military fathers were deployed to Somalia, nondeployed spouses reported higher levels of general life stress and personal distress than their deployed spouses (Zeff, Lewis, & Hirsch, 1997). These findings, however, were based on a small and selective group of families (the military member had been in the service for an average of 16.5 years) and may not generalize to all Army families.

Families have different abilities to cope with deployment stress. Military wives with deployed husbands who exhibited secure attachment reported fewer separation concerns and less emotional distress than women with insecure attachment (Armfield, 1993; Holland, 1997). Depressive symptoms and health problems increased in a sample of Army wives with deployed husbands; however, personal hardiness moderated the ill effects of stress (Bartone & Bartone, 1999). Greater perceived support from other unit wives and unit leaders, greater connection to the military, better family relations, less financial strain, not having experienced recent relocation, and families of higher ranking soldiers report better adjustment to deployment (Bell, Tingle, & Scarville, 1991; Bourg & Segal, 1999; Coolbaugh & Rosenthal, 1992; Holland, 1997; Mozon, 1987; Rohall, Segal, & Segal, 1999; Rosen & Moghadam, 1990; Stretch, 1985; Sutker, Uddo, Brailey, & Allain, 1993; Wolfe, Brown, & Kelley, 1993).

An important exception to the above findings is Himmelman's (1995) study of Army reservists—predominantly medical personnel —who served during the Persian Gulf conflict. Many of these families may have experienced considerable economic loss, as military compensation may not have equaled presumably high-paying salaries in the medical field. Relatedly, reservists indicated that increased deployments would make it difficult to maintain civilian employment, would strain family relationships, and make recruitment and retention of reservists difficult (Schumm, Jurich, Stever, Sanders, Castelo, & Bollman, 1998). Because reservists' families may not share the same type of community and military support that active-duty families have, they may have more difficulty during times of mobilization (Rabb, Baumer, & Wieseler, 1993).

The Effects of Deployment on Children in Traditional Military Families

In response to deployment, children often experience sadness, loneliness, abandonment, anger, and exhibit acting-out behavior (e.g., Amen et al., 1988; Hobfoll, Spielberger, Breznitz, Figley, Folkman, Lepper-Green, Meichenbaum, Milgram, Chandler, Sarason, & van der Kolk, 1991). Changes in parenting behavior and couple interactions, increased time spent at work in preparation for deployment, parents' reluctance to discuss the upcoming deployment with children, children's difficulty understanding (especially in the case of younger children) or accepting the impending separation all contribute to difficulty both prior to and during the separation period (e.g., Amen et al., 1988; Hobfoll et al., 1991; Kelley, 1994b; Kelley, Herzog-Simmer, & Harris, 1994; Norwood et al., 1996).

Children's adjustment is mediated by their mothers' ability to cope (e.g., Jensen, Lewis, & Xenakis, 1986; Pedersen, 1966). Much of the previous research on school-aged or early adolescent youth, however, may not generalize to very young children (e.g., for a discussion, see Baker, Fagen, Fisher, Janda, & Cave, 1967; Jensen & Shaw, 1996). Children who exhibit preoperational thinking may believe that something they have done is responsible for the parent's leaving (e.g., Amen et al., 1988). Lack of previous experience with deployment also may limit children's adjustment (e.g., Costello, Phelps, & Wilczenski, 1994).

Children of parents deployed during Operation Desert Storm exhibited higher levels of depressive behavior than children whose parents did not deploy (Jensen et al., 1996; Medway et al., 1995; Rosen, Teitelbaum, & Westhuis, 1993). Behavior of children whose fathers experienced a routine deployment decreased over time; however, internalizing and externalizing behavior stayed the same for children whose fathers were deployed during the Persian Gulf War (Kelley, 1994a). Private admissions to a psychiatric hospital (especially for dysthymia) increased during the Persian Gulf War as well (Levai, Kaplan, Daly, & McIntosh, 1994).

In summary, school-aged American children generally experience negative behaviors in response to a parent's deployment. These behaviors generally improve over time. In contrast, children whose fathers experience a more dangerous deployment experience more difficulty, and troublesome behavior may not diminish as quickly for these children.

The Effects of Deployment on Women and their Families: Nontraditional Families

More than 7.5% of Americans serving in Desert Storm (nearly 41,000 of 540,000) were women (Holm, 1992). A Department of Defense report (1992) estimated that 37,000 children were separated from their parents due to the deployment of either a sole parent or a dual-military career couple to the Persian Gulf War. Only recently have military family researchers begun to examine alternative or nontraditional families. For instance, in a naturalistic study of Army Casualty Assistance Officers (CAOs) who assisted families of deceased U.S. Army soldiers, more than one-third of CAOs who spontaneously reported family-related information indicated that they had assisted nontraditional families (Ender & Hermsen, 1996). For the most part, however, military family researchers have not kept up with the changing dynamics of military families.

Women did not report more negative life events than men in the seven months prior to and during the Persian Gulf War. However, women reported more life events related to interpersonal factors and men reported more life events related to financial issues (e.g., Slusarick, Ursano, Fullerton, & Dinneen, 1999). Combat-deployed women reported greater levels of stress and depression than combat-deployed men. Additionally, both men and women reported greater symptomology than non-combat-deployed individuals (Perconte et al., 1993).

In an ethnography of U.S. Navy women's experiences of deployment (Godwin, 1996), a common theme at predeployment was the workload and limited time to prepare for deployment. Many respondents mentioned the benefits associated with deployment (e.g., friendships, increased independence, and increased job skills); however, many cited the day-to-day monotony of deployment and looking forward to its end. Married women talked about their concerns regarding leaving a spouse for six months and their ambivalence with being in the military. Women with children reported the difficulty associated with leaving a child. While women with families reported the importance of contact with family members at home, this was less of a concern for single women. Married women were particularly concerned with the awkwardness of being home. Although Godwin's was a descriptive study of a small number of respondents, and in-depth research may not be generalizable, her work provides a revealing look at American Navy women's concerns regarding deployment.

U.S. Navy mothers anticipating deployment reported significantly higher levels of parenting stress but reported greater sensitivity to their children than women who had recently returned from deployment (Kelley et al., 1994). Single mothers reported more separation anxiety, less family cohesiveness, and less family organization than did married mothers.

Applewhite and Mays (1996) reported few differences in the psychosocial functioning of school-aged children of U.S. Army personnel who had experienced maternal versus paternal separation. Although Applewhite and Mays conducted a seminal study of maternally versus paternally separated military children, their conclusions were based on retrospective reports of children's first extended separation.

A Longitudinal Study of the Effects of Deployment on Enlisted Navy Mothers and Their Children

The aims of the present section are to highlight some of the study goals and findings from a longitudinal study of deploying U.S. Navy mothers and their children that my colleagues and I began in 1996 (Kelley, 1999; Kelley et al., in press; Kelley, Hock, Smith, Jarvis, Bonney, & Gaffney, 1999).

Mother-child attachment was examined because military fathers reported that very young children did not recognize them at reunion (Dickerson & Arthur, 1965). Also, John Bowlby's (1980) ethological perspective of attachment stipulates the importance of a warm, sensitive caregiver that is available and responsive to the needs of the child, and able to provide comfort in times of distress. During military-induced separations, the military parent is unable to fulfill his or her role as a primary attachment figure. Ainsworth, Blehar, Waters, and Wall (1978) argued that the quality of the child's attachment to the primary caregiver depends on the mother's sensitivity and responsiveness and whether the child is able to trust in the availability of the parent.

We also examined the issue of separation anxiety, defined by Hock, McBride, and Gnezda (1989), as an "unpleasant emotional state that may be evidenced by worry, sadness, or guilt." Separation anxiety was a major concern for Army reserve nurses during Operation Desert Storm (Wynd & Dziedzicki, 1992). Holland (1997) found that older wives with deployed husbands who had been married and in the military system for over 10 years tended to exhibit lower levels of separation anxiety.

The adequacy of day-to-day care during the separation is a concern for parents as well. During the Persian Gulf War, military mothers reported childcare concerns in the event of mobilization (Wynd & Dziedzicki, 1992). Similar to previous research on traditional military families, we examined child behavior over the course of deployment.

Enlisted Navy mothers were interviewed and completed measures of child behavior, maternal separation anxiety, and mother-child attachment before and after a military-induced separation. Childcare providers completed the same measure of child behavior as mothers at similar intervals. The following research questions were examined: (1) Do children with deployed mothers exhibit higher levels of internalizing and externalizing behavior than children whose Navy mothers are not deployed, and to what extent does the point in the deployment cycle (predeployment versus postdeployment) influence child behavior? (2) Is mother-child attachment affected by deployment, and what attachment concerns do deployed military mothers report? and (3) How is maternal separation anxiety affected by a military-induced separation?

Children with deploying mothers were expected to exhibit higher levels of internalizing and externalizing behavior (especially before deployment) than children of nondeploying mothers. Deploying mothers were hypothesized to report lower levels of mother-child attachment than nondeploying Navy mothers but similar attachment concerns as those reported by deploying fathers. Maternal separation concerns were expected to be greater for deploying women than nondeploying women. Information on child-care issues and mothers' perceptions of the effects of deployment on their families was gathered from women in the deployment group as well. Deployments were scheduled, routine cruises that typically lasted five to six months.

RESEARCH DESIGN

Participants

Participants were 154 enlisted active-duty Navy mothers and their children.[2] Navy mothers were divided into a deployment group ($n = 71$) and nondeploying control group ($n = 83$). Mothers in the deployment group were facing a scheduled military-induced separation within the next 60 days. Navy mothers in the nonde-ploying group were assigned to shore duty and were not anticipating deployment in the next 12 months.

Mean age of the Navy mothers was 27.2 years ($SD = 5.1$ years). Forty-seven percent ($n = 72$) were married. Fifty-three percent of the Navy mothers were Caucasian, 36% were African American, 4% were Hispanic, 1% were Pacific Islander, and 6% reported racial/ethnic identity other than one of these categories. On aver-age, women had been in the military for 7.7 years ($SD = 4.2$ years; Range 5 months to 19.6 years). The rank of most participants was E-4 or E-5 in both groups (Range = E-1 to E-8). The majority of Navy women had one child (92 of 154 or 59.7%); however, women with more than one child were asked to answer the questions with their youngest child in mind. The mean age of the target child was 3.1 years ($SD = 1.8$ years). There were 79 boys and 75 girls.

Women in the deployment condition were recruited from five destroyers, two carriers, two oilers, two amphibious ships, or a salvage ship.[3] Women were recruited from all ships but one ship with mixed gender crews that deployed from the summer of 1996 to the summer 1998 stationed in the Hampton Roads area (southeastern Virginia, U.S.).[4] Women in the nondeploying control group were recruited from one of four shore commands ($n = 52$), a daycare center that serves military families ($n = 10$), or an advertisement in a local Navy newspaper ($n = 17$).

Measures

Child Behavior Checklist (CBCL; Achenbach, 1991, 1992). Mothers and the child's childcare provider completed the Child Behavior Checklist 2/3 or 4-18 (depending on the child's age) twice. Both the CBCL 2/3 and the CBCL 4-18 (Achenbach, 1991, 1992) provide indices of children's internalizing behavior (i.e., fearful, sad, over-controlled) and externalizing behavior (i.e., aggressive, noncompliant, under-controlled). Childcare providers had cared for children an average of 12.5 months ($SD = 12.7$ months) at the initial assessment.

Attachment Behavior Q-Set (Q-Set; Waters & Deane, 1985). Mothers and interviewers completed the Attachment Behavior Q-Set scale at both the initial and final interview. The Q-Set consists of 90 statements such as "Child will accept and enjoy loud sounds or being bounced around in play, if mother smiles and shows that it is supposed to be fun." At the pre- and postinterview, the mothers and the experimenter sorted the 90 statements into 9 piles of 10 statements each, from the most characteristic to least characteristic of the child. Mothers and experimenters' scores were correlated with the Q-Set definition of security provided by Waters and Deane.

Maternal Separation Anxiety Scale (MSAS; DeMeis, Hock, & McBride, 1986). Mothers also completed the Maternal Separation Anxiety Scale (DeMeis et al., 1986; Hock et al., 1989), a 35-item, self-report inventory. The scale measures the following three dimensions: (1) Maternal Separation Anxiety (e.g., "Only a mother naturally knows how to comfort a distressed child"); (2) Perception of Separation Effects (e.g., "My child will benefit from group experience since they will provide him/her with social experiences that he/she could not get at home"); and (3) Employment Related Concerns (e.g., "I would resent my job if it meant I had to be away from my child").

Mothers in the deployment condition were asked the following question at the predeployment interview, "Who will be your child's primary caregiver during your upcoming deployment?" At the post-deployment interview mothers were asked: "How comfortable were you with the quality of care your child received from their primary caregiver while you were on deployment?" and "Did you ever feel guilty about leaving 'child's name' to go on deployment?" If the mother answered yes to the previous question, they were asked: "How much guilt did you feel about leaving 'child's name' to go on deployment?" Additionally, at the postdeployment interview, deploying mothers were asked: "What effect do you think the long-term deployment had on your immediate family?" and "Did your child's primary caregiver change during the course of deployment?" Women who reported that their primary caregiver changed during the course of deployment were asked, "Prior to deployment, did you suspect that your child's primary caregiver might not work out?"

Procedure

Data collection for Navy women in the deployment group took place at predeployment (approximately 3-6 weeks before the deployment) and postdeployment (approximately 3-6 weeks after the deployment ended). The majority of women were deployed for five or six months. Data collection took place approximately eight months apart. With the exception of a few mothers who were interviewed after duty hours on base, participants were individually interviewed and administered the standardized questionnaires in their homes. Prior to and after deployment (and at similar intervals for the control group), childcare providers were mailed the CBCL questionnaire along with a prestamped envelope and asked to return the questionnaire within one week.

RESULTS

Child Behavior Checklist. In order to examine the above hypotheses, several repeated measures of Analyses of Variance (ANOVAs) were conducted. Both Navy mothers and their childcare providers reported that children whose mothers experienced deployment exhibited higher levels of internalizing behavior than children with mothers who were assigned to shore duty during the same time period, $F(1, 124) = 5.5, p < .05; F(1, 124) = 4.8, p < .01$.

Additionally, childcare providers (but not Navy mothers) reported that children of mothers in the deployment group exhibited slightly higher levels of externalizing behavior than childcare providers of nondeployed Navy mothers, $F(1, 102) = 4.9, p < .05$.

As a second method of examining differences between Navy and civilian children's behavior, mothers' CBCL scores were dummy coded. Children received two scores. The first score reflected whether the child's mean internalizing t score across time was in the normal range (coded as 1) or clinical range (coded as 2); the second score reflected whether the child's mean externalizing t score across time was in the normal (coded as 1) or clinical range (coded as 2). Two Mann-Whitney U tests were performed to determine whether differences existed in the percentage of children in each group (children with deployed Navy mothers, children with nondeployed Navy mothers) whose scores were in the clinical range (defined by Achenbach as a t score of 60 or above) as reported by their mothers. Analyses revealed a significant difference between groups for internalizing behavior, $Z(127) = 2.5, p < .05$. Specifically, 12% (6 of 52) of the children with deployed Navy mothers had mean internalizing t scores in the clinical range, whereas 1% (1 of 75) of children with nondeployed Navy mothers exhibited mean scores in the clinical range. The number of children exhibiting clinical levels of externalizing behavior did not differ between groups as reported by their mothers. No other main effects or interactions were significant.

Attachment Behavior Q-Set. Both mothers and interviewers Attachment Behavior Q-Set (Waters & Deane, 1985) scores did not differ as a function of group or time ($ps > .05$).

Maternal Separation Anxiety. Separation anxiety was higher for single versus married women, $F(1, 115) = 6.4$, $p < .05$, and at the initial versus final assessment, $F(1, 115) = 7.5$, $p < .05$. Women in the deployment group perceived nonmaternal care (i.e., Perception of Separation Effects) as less beneficial for children than women of children in the nondeployment group, $F(1, 121) = 8.8$, $p < .01$. The highest level of employment-related separation concerns (e.g., "I would resent my job if it meant that I would have to be away from my child") were reported by married women at the initial assessment, $F(1, 123) = 10.8$, $p < .01$.

Results from Interview Data. Women in the deployment group most often reported that the child's father (46.5%) or maternal grandmother (31.0%) would serve as the child's childcare provider during the deployment. Respondents reported that they were very comfortable with the quality of care their children received during deployment ($M = 5.4$, $SD = .7$, Range = 1 to 7). However, 87% of women who experienced deployment reported that they felt guilty about leaving the child to go on deployment. The majority of respondents who reported that they felt guilty leaving, reported considerable guilt about leaving the child to go on deployment ($M = 5.7$, $SD = 1.7$, Range = 1 to 7). When asked about the effects of deployment on family members, the most common responses were: (1) deployment was stressful for family members (38%); (2) the child had difficulty emotionally (25%); (3) mother-child attachment difficulties (24%); and (4) the child exhibited negative behavior (22%). However, 32% of deployed mothers reported that the deployment had a positive effect, and 15% reported that the deployment had no effect (see Table 1.2).

DISCUSSION

Summary of the Present Study and Comparison to Previous Research

Child Behavior. Similar to research on children with deploying fathers (e.g., Jensen et al., 1996; Kelley, 1994a; Rosen et al., 1993), our findings suggest that young children with deployed mothers are susceptible to anxiety and sadness. Importantly, approximately 12% of young children may experience clinical levels of internalizing behavior.

In contrast to older children with deployed parents whose behavior may be expected to improve, in the present study, young children's behavior did not improve over time. Deployments often require mini cruises (which may last from a few days to a few weeks) prior to departure. Although an older child may understand that these brief separations are in preparation for the deployment (i.e., in essence part of the deployment), a young child may treat each of these separations independently. Thus, the younger child is continually adjusting to the parent's absence. As suggested by others (e.g., Jensen & Shaw, 1996; Norwood et al., 1996), our findings suggest that the developmental level of young children may prohibit their understanding of causality, time, or explanations regarding their mothers' return or future deployments. This finding is probably due to the child's age rather than the gender of the deploying parent.

It is difficult to determine why differences in externalizing behavior were reported by childcare providers but not Navy mothers. It is possible that childcare providers have a wider range in which to observe children's interactions. Also, crew members must work long hours with little leave time in the weeks preceding deployment; thus, mothers may have had less opportunity to observe child behavior at the time of the predeployment assessment.

Mother-Child Attachment. Our findings do not demonstrate major disruptions in the security of the mother-infant attachment as a function of separation. However, mothers were reinterviewed approximately one month postdeployment. It is possible that mothers and children were in the deployment interview. Also, the standardized attachment measure may not assess the kinds of attachment issues that are common to deploying parents.

Table 1.2. Select Responses from the Question, "What Effect Do You Think the Long-Term Deployment Had on Your Immediate Family?"

Category of Response	Response
Negative Effect	
Deployment was stressful for family members (38%)	"I was very upset to leave her. I missed her terribly." "We (parents) lost contact. We were both on sea duty. We disagreed about our daughter." "It was very stressful for my husband."
C had difficulty emotionally (25%)	"His grandmother thought he was depressed."
M-C attachment difficulties (24%)	"She wouldn't come near me when I first got home." "I felt like a stranger in my own home." "She follows me from room to room and doesn't want to be alone. She wants to be with mom all the time."
C exhibited negative behavior (22%)	"He became disobedient to get attention." "She's not behaving as well as before. She's very angry, clingy, and temperamental."
Positive Effect	
Positive effect on C (16%)	"He matured in the last six months. It helped him grow up."
Positive effect on F (16%)	"He was able to spend time with his grandparents."
No effect (15%)	"I don't think it (deployment) had any effect. We were able to communicate via e-mail."

Approximately one-quarter of deploying mothers mentioned attachment concerns at the postdeployment assessment. Similar to research on military fathers (Dickerson & Arthur, 1965), several mothers mentioned that children did not recognize them at reunion. Others mentioned that the child would cry when she left, and duty days were especially difficult. Another concern was that the child's primary attachment figure changed during the course of deployment. This particular concern may be unique to military parents who are children's primary caregivers.

Maternal Separation Anxiety. Similar to previous research (Kelley et al., 1994), separation anxiety was higher for single versus married women. There may be a number of reasons for this finding. Some married women were able to rely on their spouses for day-to-day childcare. Additionally, dual-income couples were more likely to rely on licensed, presumably higher quality childcare. This may reduce daily separation concerns. Also, for married women, the child's father generally served as the child's primary caregiver during deployment, which may increase continuity and reduce separation concerns.

Women were concerned about the impact that deployment would have on children. Specifically, women in the deployment group perceived nonmaternal care as less beneficial for children and perceived that children would be less comfortable during the departure, adapt less positively to nonmaternal care, and benefit less from mother-infant separation.

Interestingly, married women about to deploy reported greater resentment about work-related separation concerns. In contrast to single women who may have less choice, married women may have a greater degree of control over whether to stay in the military or not. This is similar to Godwin's (1996) finding that some married women reported ambivalence about being in the military.

Future Research

Much of the literature reviewed was cross-sectional, based on retrospective reports, and sample sizes were small to moderate. Longitudinal research with carefully selected control groups and multiple raters of child behavior are needed. Even with longitudinal research it is difficult to know whether improved behavior over the course of the deployment reflects children's typical level of functioning or regression to the mean. Ideally, a study is needed that follows families prior to the notice of deployment.

The findings from several important but unpublished theses or dissertations were reported in the present chapter. While students have constraints that make publication difficult, more effort is needed to disseminate findings from student research to the larger psychological community.

Most of the recent research has examined the short-term effects of a single deployment. It is not known, however, whether deployment results in elevated behavior over the long-term. Related to this issue is the need for more ongoing, programmatic research that identifies factors that may mediate or exacerbate a family's ability to cope with deployment. At the same time, it is important to realize that not all deployments affect families in the same way, and military members experience different types of deployment with different frequency.

Also, research has examined traditional families with school-aged children in which fathers generally represented career military personnel. For the most part, families were recruited from a single military base and remained in that area during the father's absence. Families residing on base, in other government housing, in a largely populated military area, or in a politically conservative area of the country should experience greater military and community support. More globally, sample selectively has taken place in previous research.

Researchers have attempted to homogenize the stages and effects of deployment across branches of the military. Clearly, the nature of deployments is unique to the branch of the service being considered.

Due to shortages in manpower and changing gender roles, the military must increasingly rely on female recruits (Kaslow, 1993). There are important differences in the family dynamics between male and female military parents. Similar to national reports (see Reynolds, 1991), our study found that Navy mothers appear more likely than Navy men to be never married or dual-career Navy men. In contrast to military men who generally rely on their wives for childcare during deployment, this is not the case for many military mothers. Approximately one-half of children of enlisted U.S. Navy mothers live with someone other than their fathers during their mothers' deployment. For many children, deployment meant the loss of their mothers, leaving their homes and childcare providers, developing relationships with new caregivers and childcare providers, new schools, routines, and so forth. Also, many children were unfamiliar with their caregivers prior to the deployment. Clearly, the experiences of very young children and children of single parents are different from those of school-aged children of intact, father-deployed families (i.e., the typical family examined in previous deployment research). Related to this is whether continuity of care affects children's adjustment to deployment.

Family supportive policies and practices are important ways for the military to retain military personnel (see Bourg & Segal, 1999; Coolbaugh & Rosenthal, 1992). Although some research has begun to address this issue (e.g., Kelley et al., in press), the degree to which family factors affect women's decisions to remain in the military has not been examined. Young children increase the stress associated with deployment (Coolbaugh & Rosenthal, 1992). Clearly, research is needed that examines coping in male spouses and nonparental caregivers during the deployment period.

Implications for Support Services

Based on the literature review and findings from the present study, the following suggestions are recommended:

* Information needs to be included into existing deployment programs regarding the cyclic nature of deployment for school-aged/adolescent children and spouses of deployed military members.

* Information needs to be included in deployment materials describing common responses of very young children, helping children during this time, and obtaining professional assistance. Cognitive limitations that limit the child's understanding of deployment should be included.

* A pamphlet should be developed for nonparents who serve as caregivers during separations. Importantly, these individuals may have less knowledge of deployment and military services. Because these caregivers may not reside in an area with military support services, a 1-800 should be included.

* Military leaders should provide military parents with time off without losing pay or vacation time for relocating children prior to and after deployment.

* A pamphlet should be developed for support service

personnel who work with military mothers. The pamphlet should include information on deployment guilt, attachment issues, and childcare concerns.

* Women who had access to e-mail during the deployment often commented that it was very beneficial. Ensuring that crew members have access to computers and e-mail during deployments is very critical.

* More globally, military and civilian mental health professionals need to offer additional support for families and caregivers experiencing separations.

Similar to the private sector, the military force must increasingly rely on women. Thus, comprehensive family programs that recognize changes in military families, including the increasing diversity of servicemembers, and improving policies regarding childcare are necessary to maintain combat readiness and to continue to recruit and retain highly skilled military personnel.

NOTES

[1] Readiness is the standard for measuring how well an individual or unit is likely to perform when called to combat or other military missions.

[2] Very few female commissioned officers assigned to ships surveyed had children and essentially none of these commissioned officers had small children. Thus, a decision was made to survey enlisted mothers only.

[3] There was the possibility that recruiting women from the briefings or contacting them individually (in a few cases) may have compelled them to sign up for the study. We believed, as did the participating commands, that this was the most efficient and effective way to inform all potential respondents about the study. We do not know whether some women felt compelled to sign up for the study. However, 87% of women who met the criteria (174 of 199) agreed to participate. When contacted by phone to set up the first interview, however, 11% of these women (20 of 174) declined to

participate. Thus, 154 women participated at the initial assessment.

[4] The Hampton Roads area of Virginia is a primary Naval station. In 1999, 107 ships were stationed, and more than 81,000 active-duty Navy personnel (over 225,000 military personnel and dependents) were assigned to the Hampton Roads area (Personal Communication, (1999), Public Affairs Office, Norfolk, Virginia).

REFERENCES

Achenbach, T.M. (1991). *Manual for the Child Behavior Checklist and Revised Child Behavior Profile.* Burlington: University of Vermont Department of Psychiatry.

Achenbach, T.M. (1992). *Manual for the Child Behavior Checklist/2-3 and 1992 Profile.* Burlington: University of Vermont Department of Psychiatry.

Ainsworth, M.D.S., Blehar, M.C., Waters, E., & Wall, S. (1978). *Patterns of attachment: A psychological study of the strange situation.* Mahwah, NJ: Erlbaum Associates.

Amen, D.J., Jellen, L., Merves, E., & Lee, R.E. (1988). Minimizing the impact of deployment on military children: Stages, current preventive efforts, and system recommendations. *Military Medicine, 153,* 441-446.

Applewhite, L.W., & Mays, R.A. (1996). Parent-child separation: A comparison of maternally and paternally separated children in military families. *Child and Adolescent Journal, 13,* 23-39.

Armfield, L.L. (1993). *Deployment separation and patterns of attachment.* Unpublished doctoral dissertation, The California School of Professional Psychology, Alameda, CA.

Baker, S., Fagen, S., Fisher, E., Janda, E., & Cave, L. (1967). Impact of father's absence on personality factors of children. *American Journal of Orthopsychiatry, 37,* 269.

Bartone, J.V., & Bartone, P.T. (1999, August). *Those left behind: Stress and health in U.S. Army wives.* Paper presented at the meeting of the American Psychological Association, Boston, MA.

Beckman, K., Marsella, A.J., & Finney, R. (1979). Depression in the wives of nuclear submarine personnel. *American Journal of Psychiatry, 136*, 524-526.

Bell, D.B., Tingle, R.B., & Scarville, J. (1991). *Army Family Research Program: Select preliminary findings on Army family support during Operation Desert Shield (ARI Research Product 91-20)*. Alexandria, VA: U.S. Army Research Institute.

Bey, D.R., & Lange, J. (1974). Wailing wives, women under stress. *American Journal of Psychiatry, 131*, 283-286.

Bourg, C., & Segal, M.W. (1999). The impact of family supportive policies and practices on organizational commitment to the Army. *Armed Forces & Society, 25*, 633-652.

Bowlby, J. (1980). *Attachment and loss: Vol. 3*. New York. Basic Books.

Coolbaugh, K.W., & Rosenthal, A. (1992). *Family separations in the Army*. (ARI Research Product-964). Alexandria, VA: U.S. Army Research Institute.

Costello, M., Phelps, L., & Wilczenski, F. (1994). Children and military conflict: Current issues and treatment implications. *The School Counselor, 41*, 220-225.

DeMeis, D., Hock, E., & McBride, S. (1986). The balances of employment and motherhood: Longitudinal study of mother's feelings about separations from their first-born infants. *Developmental Psychology, 22*, 627-632.

Department of Defense. (1992). *Military manpower statistics: December 31, 1991*. Washington, DC: U.S. Government Printing Office.

Department of Defense. (1996). *Military readiness: A clear policy and better oversight are needed to guide management of frequently deployed units: Report to congressional requesters*. GAO/NSIAD-96-105B-271135.

Department of Defense. (1999). *Fact sheet: Women in the military*. Alexandria, VA: Defense Manpower Data Center.

Department of Defense. (2000). *Navy personnel statistics* (March 25, 1999). Available: http://www.navy.mil.

Department of Veterans Affairs, VA Persian Gulf Returnees Working Group. (1991). *War zone stress among returning Persian Gulf troops: A preliminary report.* West Haven, CT: National Center for PTSD.

DeSoir, E.J.L. (1999, August). *Systemic view on psychosocial support during peace operations: Belgian experience for peacekeepers and their significant others.* Paper presented at the annual meeting of the American Psychological Association, Boston, MA.

Dickerson, W.J., & Arthur, R.J. (1965). Navy families in distress. *Military Medicine, 13,* 894-898.

Eastman, E., Archer, R.P., & Ball, J.D. (1990). Psychosocial and life stress characteristics of Navy families: Family Environment Scale and Life Experiences Scale findings. *Military Psychology, 2,* 113-127.

Ender, M.G., & Hermsen, J.M. (1996). Working with the bereaved: U.S. Army experiences with nontraditional families. *Death Studies, 20,* 557-575.

Glisson, C.A., Melton, S.C., & Roggow, L. (1980). The effect of separation on marital satisfaction, depression, and self-esteem. *Journal of Social Service Research, 4,* 61-76.

Godwin, S.A. (1996). *An ethnography of women's experience with military deployment.* Unpublished doctoral dissertation. Department of Psychology and Family Studies, United States International University, San Diego, CA.

Hill, R. (1949). *Families under stress: Adjustment to the crises of war separation and reunion.* Westport, CT: Greenwood Press.

Himmelman, T.L. (1995). The Persian Gulf conflict: The impact of stressors as perceived by Army reservists. *Health & Social Work, 20,* 140-145.

Hobfoll, S.E., Spielberger, C.D., Breznitz, D., Figley, C., Folkman, S., Lepper-Green, B., Meichenbaum, D., Milgram, N. A., Chandler, I., Sarason, I., & van der Kolk, B. (1991). War-related stress: Addressing the stress of war and other traumatic events. *American Psychologist, 46,* 848-885.

Hock, E., McBride, M.T., & Gnezda, M.T. (1989). Maternal separation anxiety: Mother-infant separation from the maternal perspective. *Child Development, 60,* 793-802.

Holland, M.A. (1997). *Separation anxiety in Army wives with deployed husbands*. Unpublished master's thesis, Department of Counseling Psychology, Loyola University, Chicago, IL.

Holm, J. (1992). *Women in the Military*. Novato, CA: Presidio Press.

Hunter, E.J. (1986). Families of prisoners of war held in Vietnam: A seven-year study. *Evaluation and Program Planning, 9,* 243-251.

Jensen, P.S., Lewis, R.L., & Xenakis, S.N. (1986). The military family in review: Context, risk and prevention. *Journal of the American Academy of Child Psychiatry, 25,* 225-234.

Jensen, P.S., Martin, D., & Watanabe, H. (1996). Children's response to parental separation during Operation Desert Storm. *Journal of the American Academy of Child and Adolescent Psychiatry, 35,* 433-441.

Jensen, P.S., & Shaw, J.A. (1996). The effects of war and parental deployment upon children and adolescents. In R.J. Ursano & A.E. Norwood (Eds.), *Emotional aftermath of the Persian Gulf War: Veterans, families, communities, and nations* (pp. 83-109). Washington, DC: American Psychiatry Press.

Kaslow, F. (Ed.). (1993). *The military family in peace and war.* New York: Springer.

Kelley, M.L. (1994a). Military-induced separation in relation to maternal adjustment and children's behavior. *Military Psychology, 6,* 163-178.

Kelley, M.L. (1994b). The effects of military-induced separation on family factors and children's behavior. *Journal of Orthopsychiatry, 64,* 103-111.

Kelley, M.L. (1999). *The impact of deployment on Navy women and their families.* (Final Technical Report, DAMD 17-96-1-6300). U.S. Army Medical Research and Materiel Command, Fort Detrick, Frederick, MD.

Kelley, M.L., Herzog-Simmer, P.A., & Harris, M.A. (1994). Effects of military-induced separation on the parenting stress and family functioning of deploying mothers. *Military Psychology, 6,* 125-138.

Kelley, M.L., Hock,E., Bonney,J.F.,Jarvis, M.S., Smith, K.M., &

Gaffney, M.A. (In press). Reenlistment intentions of enlisted Navy mothers experiencing deployment. *Military Psychology.*

Kelley, M.L., Hock, E., Smith, K.M., Jarvis, M.S, Bonney, J.F., Gaffney, M.A. (1999). *Internalizing and externalizing behavior of children with enlisted Navy mothers experiencing military-induced separation.* Unpublished manuscript, Old Dominion University, Norfolk, VA.

Levai, M., Kaplan, S., Daly, K., & McIntosh, G. (1994). The effect of the Persian Gulf Crisis on the psychiatric hospitalizations of Navy children and adolescents. *Child Psychiatry and Human Development, 24,* 245-254.

Light, D.W. (1992). *Prevalence of depression among pregnant spouses of deployed servicemen.* Unpublished master's thesis, Department of Health Services, University of Washington, Seattle, WA.

McCubbin, H.I., Hunter, E.J., & Dahl, B.B. (1975). Residuals of war: Families of prisoners of war and servicemen missing in action. *Journal of Social Issues, 31,* 95-109.

Medway, F., Davis, K.E., Cafferty, T.P., Chappell, K.D., & O'Hearn, R.E. (1995). Family disruption and adult attachment correlates of spouse and child reactions to separation and reunion due to Operation Desert Storm. *Journal of Social and Clinical Psychology, 14,* 97-118.

Mozon, A.L. (1987). *Marital satisfaction, stress and coping patterns among wives of deployed Navy men.* Unpublished doctoral dissertation, California School of Professional Psychology, Alameda, CA.

Nice, D.S. (1983). The course of depressive affect in Navy wives during family separation. *Military Medicine, 148,* 341-343.

Norwood, A.E., Fullerton, C.S., & Hagen, K.P. (1996). Those left behind: Military families. In R.J. Ursano & A.E. Norwood (Eds.), *Emotional aftermath of the Persian Gulf War: Veterans, families, communities, and nations* (pp. 163-196). Washington, DC: American Psychiatry Press.

Pedersen, F. (1966). Relationships between father absence and emotional disturbance in male military dependents. *Merrill-Palmer Quarterly, 12,* 321-331.

Peebles-Kleiger, M.J., & Kleiger, J.H. (1994). Re-integration stress for Desert Storm families: Wartime deployments and family trauma. *Journal of Traumatic Stress,* 7, 173-194.

Perconte, S.T., Wilson, A.T., Pontius, E.B., Dietrick, A.L., & Spiro, K.J. (1993). Psychological and war stress symptoms among deployed and non-deployed reservists following the Persian Gulf War. *Military Medicine, 158,* 516-521.

Rabb, D.D., Baumer, R.J., & Wieseler, N.A. (1993). Counseling Army reservists and their families during Operation Desert Shield/Storm. *Community Mental Health Journal, 29,* 441-447.

Reynolds, V.L. (1991). *Issues surrounding the deployability of single and dual-service parents in the Navy.* Unpublished master's thesis, Naval Post-graduate School, Monterey, CA.

Rohall, D.E., Segal., M.W., & Segal., D.R. (1999). Examining the importance of organizational supports on family adjustment to Army life in a period of increasing separation. *Journal of Political and Military Sociology,* 27, 49-65.

Rosen, L.N., & Moghadam, L.Z. (1990). Matching the support to the stressor: Implications for the buffering hypothesis. *Military Psychology,* 2, 193-204.

Rosen, L.N., Teitelbaum, J.M., & Westhuis, D.J. (1993). Stressors, stress mediators, and emotional well-being among spouses of soldiers deployed to the Persian Gulf during Operation Desert Shield/Storm. *Journal of Applied Social Psychology,* 23, 1587-1593.

Schumm, W.R., Jurich, A.P., Stever, J.A., Sanders, D., Castelo, C., & Bollman, S.R. (1998). Attitudes of reserve component service-members regarding the consequences of frequent overseas deployments. *Psychological Reports, 83,* 983-989.

Slusarick, A.L., Ursano, R.J., Fullerton, C.S., & Dinneen, M.P. (1999). Life events in health care providers before and during Persian Gulf War deployment: The USNS Comfort. *Military Medicine, 164,* 675-682.

Stretch, R. (1985). Posttraumatic stress disorder among U.S. Army Reserve Vietnam and Vietnam-era veterans. *Journal of Consulting and Clinical Psychology,* 53, 935-936.

Sutker, P.B., Uddo, M., Brailey, K., & Allain, Jr., A.N. (1993).

War-zone trauma and stress-related symptoms in Operation Desert Shield/Storm (ODS) Returnees. *Journal of Social Issues, 49*, 33-50.

Waters, E., & Deane, K. (1985). Defining and assessing individual differences in attachment relationships: Q-methodology and the organization of behavior in infancy and early childhood. In I. Bretherton & E. Waters (Eds.), *Growing points of attachment theory and research* (pp. 41-65). Monographs of the Society for Research in Child Development, 50 (1-2, Serials No. 209).

Wolfe, J., Brown, P.J., & Kelley, J.M. (1993). Reassessing war stress: Exposure and the Persian Gulf War. *Journal of Social Issues, 49*, 15-31.

Wood, S., Scarville, J., & Gravino, K.S. (1995). Waiting wives: Separation and reunion among Army wives. *Armed Forces & Society, 21*, 217-236.

Wynd, C.A., & Dziedzicki, R.E. (1992). Heightened anxiety in Army Reserve Nurses anticipating mobilization during Operation Desert Storm. *Military Medicine, 157*, 630-634.

Zeff, K., Lewis, K.A., & Hirsch, S.J. (1997). Military family adaptation to United Nations operations in Somalia. *Military Medicine, 162*, 384-387.

2

THE MILITARY TEENAGER IN EUROPE: PERSPECTIVES FOR HEALTH CARE PROVIDERS

MARY P. TYLER

INTRODUCTION

Though the well-being of American teenagers in Europe is of concern to military leaders and care-giving professionals, the topic has received little scholarly attention. Recent research by Orthner, Giddings, and Quinn (1986) has investigated the adjustment of Air Force youth within the United States, but the special problems associated with teens' residence abroad remain unexplored in the current literature. In an effort to provide needed information, the United States Army Medical Research Unit, Europe, is carrying out an investigation of the European tour as experienced by adolescents in the military community. The first phase of the research took place in a larger Army community in West Germany [Germany]. The community includes 15,500 military members, 11,500 family members, and 2,000 other American civilians. Sometimes referred to as a "troop town" because of the large proportion of combat-arms elements, the community has a slightly higher proportion of lower-ranking soldiers than USAREUR [United States Army Europe] as a whole. It is also large geographically, covering a total of 1,750 square miles and including 10 major installations. The community has a single high school, with some students commuting by bus from more than an hour away.

A random sample of 60 adolescents was selected from the high school registrar's role. Eight were unavailable because they PCSed [permanent change of station with their parents]; one was unavailable because of suspension from school; in four cases the student or parent refused to give consent. The remaining 47, 21 boys and 26 girls, were interviewed. The average age of the respondents was 16 years 4 months, with a range of 14 years 3 months to 18 years 7 months. The majority of participants (24) were sponsored by senior NCOs [noncommissioned officers] in [military ranks] grades E7-E9. Another nine had sponsors in grades E4-E6, eight were sponsored by civilian employees, and six, by officers. In addition, 16 adult professional people were recommended to the investigator on the basis of their expertise with teenagers and agreed to be interviewed on their perceptions of teens in the community.

After written consent was obtained from both teenager and parent or guardian, each adolescent was interviewed privately for about an hour (one-class period). Interviews were semistructured. Open-ended questions guided the respondent to areas of general concern, but there was also the opportunity for the teenager to bring up points of personal interest. Results were recorded as near verbatim as possible and later transcribed. Data were analyzed by asking questions of the data set, developing categories of responses and computing percentages.

RESULTS

Initial Adjustment

The first year emerged as a difficult period for most teenagers. Interviews with teens in their first year and the reminiscences of longer-term residents presented a consistent picture:

For about three months I hardly left my room. It was hard
on my parents and family. After school started and I started
to make friends, I started to enjoy myself and not put myself
down. (17-year-old girl)

At first I had a problem, not the teachers, just me. I didn't
want to be here and wasn't trying. (17-year-old boy)

Feelings of sadness, withdrawing from others, excessive TV
viewing, overeating, and poor school performance seemed to be
common responses to the stresses of the first year. The underlying
problem did not seem to be "culture shock," commonly mentioned
in the professional literature as a hazard for the American teens
abroad (Bower, 1967; Nice and Beck, 1978; Shaw, 1979). The teens
presented the practical challenges of learning to get around and
mastering the currency, measurement systems and the non-English
environment as "no big deal." What loomed large in their lives was
grief over separation from friends and relatives back home and the
painful, lonely period before a new peer group could be formed.

But it's not "Germany," it's more moving's...hard on
teenagers. If you just moved you don't have friends to talk
over problems with, cry on their shoulders. (16-year-old girl)

Two naturally occurring processes seemed to facilitate the resolution of teenagers' grief. One was talking it over, usually with
understanding parents.

I talked to Mom; she was going through the same stuff; we
stuck together and survived it. (14-year-old girl)

The other healing process was the formation of a new friendship group.

When I got here and met new people, the feelings (of
sadness) went away. I still write, we're still friends, but I have

new friends and they've kind of taken their place. (15-year-old girl)

Despite the commonly held belief that summer moves are best for children, teens who moved during summer vacation seemed to experience particular difficulties.

I felt really down about coming here...no friends, new school, trying to make new friends...just sat around the hotel, watched TV the whole summer. (15-year-old boy)

Their problem was that, with school out of session, it was very difficult to identify potential friends and begin to form relationships. Thus, the first summer was often a long and lonely period for the newly arrived teenager.

Friends and Social Life

In spite of their mobility, the teenagers formed friendship patterns similar to those in typical American high schools. Of the adolescents, 88% reported having either a "best friend" or a small group of very close friends. Only 4% had no friends at all. Friendship formation typically occurred at school, where classes or extracurricular activities grouped students together on the basis of abilities and interests, and a few friends could be selected from the larger affinity group. Children of officers or of NCOs tended to choose best of similar parental status, while the status of civilian employees' children seemed quite flexible. The relationship between parental rank and teenagers' friendship patterns appeared to be a source of embarrassment; 53% of the adolescents denied knowing the rank of their best friends' sponsors. Though adult respondents expressed concern that teenagers who moved so often might form "superficial" relationships, the teens' friendships seemed not only to be carefully chosen but also to be intense and important to them. Friends played key roles in one another's lives, exploring the

German environment together and supporting one another in times of trouble.

Of the teens, 55% reported that they belonged to a specific crowd or larger social group of 10 to 25 teenagers. Most crowds were characterized by particular styles of dress and behavior and often by a specific "hangout" as well.

> All pretty cool, Preps. About ten boys and we hang around with girls, about 20 altogether. Today I'm bummed out in surfing clothes. Usually we wear sweaters with little collars and Benetton shirts. (16-year-old boy)

> We're Rockers and we hang together... Like rock, wear jean jackets, the guys have long hair, they smoke. (**How many?**) 25 boys and girls. More in the school but they don't hang out where we hang out. (**Where's that?**) Before and after school we go to the smoking area and have a couple of cigarettes and talk and on the weekend we go to a special club and meet there. (17-year-old girl)

Like the "special club," some hangouts were off [the military]-post bars or discos, which many teenagers' parents did not allow them to visit, so the role of the hangout was often more symbolic than real.

Though the crowds themselves were similar to what might be found in a stateside high school, living in Germany added an interesting dimension to crowd membership. Most of the clothing items and accessories needed to signal one's crowd membership often could be purchased only on the German economy, giving teenagers a powerful impetus to master the skills necessary for shopping downtown.

Education

Most teenagers believed that, in the classroom, they were getting an education as good or better than they would in the United States. Achievement test scores and the result of a recent accreditation visit supported their positive evaluation of their school. Of the students, 75% participated in at least one organized activity such as a team or club. In addition, 68% could describe some way in which they were learning from living in a foreign country. For example:

How they do things…walk to the store every day and buy food for that day. The fresh flowers on sale in the morning, the smell, very clean except for the manure. Even in the city it doesn't smell like the States. (17-year-old girl)

(Learning) to communicate and socialize with other people besides Americans. I can stretch out, reach people, learn different cultures. (14-year-old boy)

Other teens appeared to be learning quite a bit without realizing it; they took for granted such accomplishments as their mastery of the metric system or their ability to function in a foreign-language environment.

Adult professional people pointed to a significant educational problem with no obvious solutions. Distance from the United States made postgraduation planning difficult for students graduating while abroad. Transitions to college or military service, though challenging, seemed easier than moving into vocational training or entry-level jobs, since local resources were limited and stateside facilities not prepared to offer housing and supervision to a young person from outside the immediate vicinity.

Travel and Other International Experiences

Echoing the professional literature, adults expressed concern about the "isolation" of teenagers and their families within the "ghetto" of the American enclave (Seiler, 1985; Wolf, 1969). Teenagers, however, reported extensive international experiences.

Of the adolescents, 69% reported participating in at least one activity outside the American community. The most popular pursuit was shopping in German stores, reported by 81% of the teens. Nearly half the shoppers regarded it as a necessity, since needed items could not be purchased in the PX [military postexchange shopping center]. Other teenagers simply preferred European clothing styles or enjoyed the greater variety available downtown. Though some adults disparaged teens' shopping as less valuable than more "cultural" pursuits, the teenagers seemed to be learning quite a bit from their experiences—to find their way around the city, use the public transportation system, understand metric measurements, manage the currency and comparison shop with fluctuating exchange rates, follow local customs, and function in a foreign-language environment.

Other activities reported by teenagers were family travel within Germany (41%), outside Germany (34%), and sightseeing or dining out in the local community (38%). All these percentages are probably low estimates. The teenagers often saw their activities, for example weekends at nearby Alpine resorts, as so mundane that they neglected to mention them to the interview. Teenagers' international experiences also included personal contact. Of the teenagers, 72% reported at least one significant relationship with a citizen of West Germany or another European country. The most common types of relationships were teen friends (36% of the total sample) or family friends, reported by 30% of the teenagers. In addition, all of the teenagers were acquainted with German or German-American students who were being educated in the American school; these teens and their families played an important role as a cultural "bridge" between the German and American communities.

My German friend is from the exchange program. I spent a week with her and she spent a week with me. I see her, not often, she lives in O—. We go there at Christmas for tea. We both like reading and horses. We went to a stable and helped out. The whole families visit together. (15-year-old girl)

We used to live farther out of town and got to know our neighbors. I didn't really meet people my own age. Also a German lady who is a good friend of my mom taught us to knit. She met her through a knitting group. (16-year-old boy)

Kids in the neighborhood. They have bikes, we go biking, play soccer, catch the bus and go somewhere. (14-year-old boy)

Though the teenagers valued their German friends, no one listed a German from outside the school as a "best friend" or as a person who would be asked for help with a serious problem. Their closest emotional ties were within their families and peer group from school. They seemed to enjoy the best of both worlds—European friends to broaden their horizons, and American friends to understand and support them in times of trouble.

The Military Community

Most teenagers seemed to feel comfortable in the military community and to appreciate its support.

I like it better with the military. We all know what each other have been through when we go from place to place. It's really close. (18-year-old boy)

Since many had known no life outside the military, they found it difficult to analyze that lifestyle and contrast it with others. The major negative aspect mentioned by teens was their minority status in a society composed mainly of young adults and small children. Teens were too old for the playground but too young for the NCO club. Few community activities were tailored exclusively for teenagers, and most teens scrupulously avoided programs that grouped them, even by implication, with younger children. They expressed the wish for a "teen center" or other meeting place, and an alcohol-free disco for teenagers.

Family Life

Adult professional people and teenagers differed sharply in their depiction of family life during a European tour. Professional people, apparently responding to their experiences and trouble families, emphasized family disorganization in response to work-related stress.

> There is stress on everybody in the family. Moving may be hard on the mother, father may be in the field [separation from family involved in military training and maneuvers] a lot. We see kids not doing homework; the mother is out of control, overloaded with marital problems. The family sometimes falls apart, with meals not prepared regularly. One parent can't cope with father in the field. Some families pull together in that kind of stress. (Adult professional)

The adolescents' responses suggested that in families not requiring treatment, "pulling together in that kind of stress" was much more common than being undone by it. Teenagers, while not denying problems, emphasized family strength and healthy coping responses.

> Dad goes TDY (temporary duty away from home station), Mom works Saturdays, but it's no big problem. I get home at 16:30 [4:30 p.m.], 17:00 [5:00 p.m.]; everybody gets home at once and we have dinner together. We take trips together. (17-year-old girl)

> In the beginning it affects you. You feel like they don't really care. But once you both talk it over and realize what they gotta do, it gets better. They will try to spend more time with you when they have it. If you talk it all over it comes around. (16-year-old boy)

In outlining their household responsibilities, most teens described a pattern in which parental expectations reflected the youngsters' development, not the parents' inability to cope.

> Yes, (I have more responsibilities now); I'm getting older and have to look out for a lot of things, make sure if I make a mess my mom doesn't have to pick up behind me. (15-year-old boy)

> We're older and do more chores. (15-year-old girl)

Of the teenagers, 43% felt that the European tour had had no significant effect on their family life; another 45% saw the experiences as having brought them closer to their families in one way or another. Most teens regarded their parents as an important source of support and guidance. Parents were, in fact, the helping resource most often mentioned by teenagers. The most common impression was of strong families in which parents were passing their own coping skills on to their adolescent children.

Problems and Helping Resources

Teenagers and professional people agreed that the problems of the teen years were similar whether the teen lived in Germany or in the United States. The problem most often mentioned by adolescents was boredom or "not enough to do" (24% of the teenagers). Other problems noted by teenagers included alcohol and drug abuse, general misbehavior, stealing, fighting, conflicts with parents, pregnancy and other problems associated with sexuality. In general, the teens felt that these difficulties were not common, but that they were serious when they did occur. They generally agreed that none of these problems were more serious in Germany than in the United States, though 15% of the teenagers thought there might be more teen drinking in Germany (an equal number reported the opposite impression). The interviewer's impression was that "social drinking" was ubiquitous, cigarette smoking common, and that abuse of illegal drugs, though occurring occasionally, was neither practiced nor tolerated by the great majority of teenagers.

> People I've talked to say it's harder over there (in the United States). Here if you drink you drink. You'd do it anyway in the States, but it's made a bigger deal of. Friends say drugs are worse there. People drink here—I do sometimes, but only one, no problem. (17-year-old girl)

The combined resources of the school, community, and a major medical center allowed teenagers access to a wide array of outpatient services, while good communication networks within the professional community facilitated referrals and multi-disciplinary intervention. However, professional people regretted the scarcity of inpatient resources for emotional or substance-related problems and the absence of an American-style juvenile justice system for teenagers who needed it. When asked where a teenager would go with a problem, adolescents most often mentioned parents (58%), peers (53%), or a counselor or other caregiving professional inside school (49%).

CONCLUSIONS AND RECOMMENDATIONS

Since the investigation was conducted in only one military community, care must be taken in generalizing the findings. Teenagers' concerns might, for example, be somewhat different in a smaller community or one without easy access to a major medical center. Additional research is now being conducted to explore the generalizability of the findings. Nevertheless, results of this intensive study of the one military community suggest several recommendations for professional people working with adolescents:

1. It is important to remember the positive opportunities afforded by life in a military community in Europe. Teens

have the chance to explore foreign culture without leaving the security of their families and the American educational system.

2. Experience with the minority of teens who need special services can lead professional people to "miss the mark" in identifying stresses that affect the majority of teenagers. Though adults worry about culture shock and overtaxed families, most teenagers do not seem to fund cultural differences overly stressful, nor do they "run wild" in a foreign environment. The average teenager's family is note overwhelmed by the difficulties of life in Europe; on the contrary, parents are a major source of support and guidance.

3. For the nonclinical population, the most serious problems seem to involve the initial transition to Germany, grief over separations from friends and family, and the period of loneliness preceding the formation of a satisfactory peer group. The first year is a high-risk period for academic difficulties, acting out, and other problems whose underlying roots in grief and depression might not be immediately apparent to concerned adults. Contrary to conventional wisdom, adolescents who move during the summer seem to suffer most.

4. Development of programs to welcome new teenagers and incorporate them into the community might be helpful as a preventive measure. Such programs will, however, fail if they do not reflect the complexities of the teen social structure. Program planning can be enhanced by taking into account the results of empirical studies normally functioning teens and their families, and by involving responsible teenagers in the planning process.

SUMMARY

There is little information available on the effects of a European tour on military adolescents. As the first step of a comprehensive investigation, a random sample of 47 teenagers from one military community was interviewed. Results of the study suggest that most teenagers adjust well, with strong support from family, school, and community. Most appreciate the opportunity to learn from living in a foreign country and participating in its activities. The most significant problems tend to occur during the first year, when new peer relationships must be formed while the teen struggles with grief over friends and relatives left behind. Adults who work with teenagers and their families need to beware of two pitfalls—overgeneralizing from problem situations and designing programs that are insensitive to the complexities of the teen social structure.

NOTES

[1] EDITOR'S NOTE: This chapter is reproduced from a noncopyrighted journal: Mary P. Tyler. 1989. "The military teenager in Europe: Perspectives for health care providers." *Medical Bulletin of the U.S. Army Medical Department, Professional Bulletin 8-89-1/2*, January/February, 13-17. Reprint permission obtained from the editor and the author. The comments in brackets are made by this editor.

REFERENCES

Bower, E. (1967). American children and families in overseas communities. *American Journal of Orthopsychiatry, 37*, 787–796.

Nice, D.S., & Beck, A.L. (1978). *Cross cultural adjustment of military families overseas.* Bethesda, MD: Naval Medical Research and Development Command, Report 78–58.

Orthner, D.K., Giddings, M.M., & Quinn, W.H. (1986). *Youth in transition: A study of adolescents from Air Force and civilian families.* Athens, GA: University of Georgia, Center for Work and Family Issues.

Seiler, S. (1985). *Die GIs: Amerikanische soldaten in Deutschland* [The GIs: American soldiers in Germany]. Reinbek bei Hamburg, Germany: Rowalt Taschenbuch Verlag.

Shaw, J.A. (1979). Adolescents in the mobile military community.

In S.O. Feinstein and P.O. Giovacchini (Eds.), *Adolescent psychiatry: Volume 7. Developmental and clinical studies* (pp. 191–198). Chicago, IL: University of Chicago Press.

Wolf, C. (1969). *Garrison community: A study of an overseas American military community.* Westport, CT: Greenwood Press.

3
_____

BEHAVIOR OF CIVILIAN AND MILITARY HIGH SCHOOL STUDENTS IN MOVIE THEATERS

PHOEBE EVELYN PRICE

INTRODUCTION

This study was undertaken and designed to isolate the variables of military and nonmilitary family backgrounds, film genre, and group size, on high school–aged student behavior.[1]

Family Background

Previous research shows that there are many differences between military and nonmilitary organizations, including the family (Nebecker, 1994). Military families are addressed as a "unique population" and there are many elements that create this distinctiveness (Saxe & Cross, 1997). Of these, frequent relocations, or the mobility required of a military family, seem to have the most significant impact, especially on children (Plucker & Yecke, 1999; Segal, 1989;).

Military families are not only a unique population, but also one of the most rapidly changing (Knox & Price, 1999; Norwood, Fullerton, & Hagen, 1996). Some of these changes include the aging enlisted force and thus the increasing number of military families as well as from a high-post Cold War deployment rate.[2] Another change in the last 20 years has been the increase of women in the military and thus the increasing number of military mothers and "dual military families," in which both parents wear a military uniform. While this dynamic is not shown to affect children differently based on the gender of the child or whether the separation is mainly maternal or paternal, it has been shown to affect parent-child relationships in general (Schumm, Bell, Rice, & Samders, 1996). However, while these effects are not pin-pointed, research has shown the important role a mother plays in child development and the influence a father has on a child's well-being (Applewhite & Mays, 1996). Therefore, the behavior of a child from a "dual military family" could be greatly impacted by the absence of both parents due to military involvement.

Beyond the day-to-day differences between a military community and its civilian counterpart, there are more extreme differences during wartime, which take a toll not just on the soldiers in battle, but also on military families and communities as a whole (Ursano & Norwood, 1996). Regardless of the level of United States participation, studies have shown that wartime affects the level of academic difficulties, anxiety, and aggressive behaviors in children of military families (Schwab, Ice, Stephenson, Raymer et al., 1995). It may be fair to say that any government conflict will be reflected in the behavior of military children.

Film Genre

Studies of the effects of film content on behavior are not new to the fields of psychology and sociology. Doob and Kirshenbaum (1973) studied arousal, frustration, and aggression using aggressive films as their medium for that variable. Studies among undergraduates and high school students showed that viewing aggressive films significantly increased arousal (Doob & Kirshenbaum, 1973). Another, similar study on films found that filmed violence facilitates aggressive and increased violent behaviors (Leyens, Camino, Parke, & Berkowitz, 1975). Many other studies have been done that reaffirm these 1970s findings.

In 1997, media violence became recognized as one of the key factors contributing to the rise in youth violence and the development of antisocial behavior (Huesmann, Moise, & Podolski, 1997; Withecomb, 1997). One study on adolescent self-concept addressed the fact that exposure to media violence affects both attitudes and behaviors (Funk & Buchman, 1996). In the last few years, the documented connection between violence on the screen and its impact on the behaviors of younger viewers has been strong enough to begin movements toward censorship policies (Sheehan, 1997).

As will be described later, I chose to operationalize film genres such as "action," "comedy," "drama," "romance," "horror," and "western" instead of simply examining films as violent or nonviolent. Since research on actual film genres was limited, I predicted, based on personal experience, which films I felt would elicit the most disruptive behavior. Action, comedy, and horror films were my three choices. Not surprisingly, these three film genres also tend to contain more aggressive and violent content (Zillmann, Bryant, & Huston, 1994).

Group Dynamics

Group association impacts individual self-esteem and behavior (Smith & Tyler, 1997). One study showed strong evidence that groups change notably over time (Chidambaram & Bostrom, 1997). This finding put an emphasis on more recent and generalizable studies. One study on social identity that met these criteria showed that people are more likely to act out when their identity is salient (Foster, 1999). In a social setting, while a group maintains its group identity, individual identity is usually masked by that of the group, which allows for higher levels of misbehavior because the individuals feel less identifiable.

A 1990 study showed that in peer groups, the tone of the group dictates group behavior and that a negative tone can create antisocial behaviors among group members (George, 1990). Given the idea that "one bad apple spoils the whole bunch" and the preference of youths for media that is violent in content, this finding combined with elements of hiding personal identity behind the group helps better explain the phenomena of group behavior (Funk & Buchman, 1996).

Another possibility for the increase in group misbehavior is the incentives or rewards that a large group places on misbehavior. Wageman and Baker (1997) showed that task and reward interdependence interact to increase performance. For a high school student seeking acceptance in proportion to the group he or she is in, being laughed at or cheered on, are rewards that will act as incentives to misbehave.

Another study showed that poor group decisions were increased by factors such as overestimation of the group and pressures toward uniformity (Schafer & Crichlow, 1996). Both of these elements increase as group size increases. Therefore, it follows that the larger the group, the more homogenous it would become, the more it would exert its power or exemption from rules, and the more comfortable individuals in that group would feel violating social norms.

EXPERIMENTAL DESIGN

The three research areas generated three studies examining the following variable sets: a comparison of family background to misbehavior, a comparison of film genre to misbehavior, and a comparison of group size to misbehavior. From this, I developed three hypotheses, which encompassed the scope of my study and determined the direction I expected from the results.

· *Hypothesis One*: High school students from nonmilitary families will report more disruptive behavior in movie theaters compared with students from military families.
· *Hypothesis Two*: High school students will report more disruptive behavior in action, comedy, and horror films than in drama, romance, and western films.
· *Hypothesis Three*: High school students attending films in

a group of four or more will report more disruptive behavior
than will students in a group of three or less.

The next step in designing this study was to operationalize some of
the key concepts that I would be investigating. From the first hypothesis, I found it necessary to define a military family. Recent studies
have used the quality of "at least one parent presently or recently in
the military" to define the military family (Plucker & Yecke, 1999).
Because I believe that a grandparent or sibling would create a
similar family dynamic, I extended Plucker and Yecke's definition
(1999). I labeled a family as military or not by asking the student if
they had an immediate family member (e.g., mother, father, or
someone who lives with them) in the military.

For the second hypothesis, based on personal experience and the
presence of violence in certain film genres, I defined film groups as
action/comedy/horror and drama/romance/western (Zillmann et
al., 1994). For the third hypothesis, I used previous research that
defined group size to establish a small group as three or fewer
people and a large group as four or more people (McCabe, Jenkins,
Mills, Dale, Cole, & Pepler, 1996).

Finally, for the indicators of misbehavior, I listed various behaviors that were possible in a movie theater setting and considered
those that are specifically prohibited, such as talking. With talking as
my minimum level of misbehavior, I considered the other activities
that were more disruptive as deviant in a theater setting. I developed
the following six behaviors: (1) talking, (2) shouting, (3) throwing
things, (4) activities that resulted in being asked to be quiet, (5)
actions that resulted in being told to behave, and (6) activities that
resulted in being asked to leave. The frequency of these behaviors
would determine each individual's misbehavior level.

METHOD

Participants

Ninety-four sophomores, juniors, and seniors from a small and rural high school in New York State near a military installation participated as subjects in this study. The breakdown by class, gender, and family background was as follows: 60 seniors, 29 juniors, and 5 sophomores; 44 males and 50 females; forty-three percent ($n = 41$) students from military families and 53 from nonmilitary families. Further breakdown showed 19 males and 22 females to be from military families and 25 males and 28 females to be from nonmilitary families. The head of the school's history department and the school's social psychology instructor sponsored the study.

All seniors, because they were enrolled in a history department class, had an equal chance to participate. Juniors and sophomores could participate if they were taking a history department class or social psychology. From this pool, those students who returned a signed volunteer agreement by the date that the survey was administered were allowed to participate. A total of 107 students returned the volunteer agreement and took the survey, which was 100% of those in the participating classes. Of those, 94 surveys were acceptable for research purposes. Surveys were deemed unacceptable if students had not answered all of the survey questions, circled more than one response in a multiple choice question or wrote in their own answers instead of selecting from the listed multiple choice answers.

Instructors offered extra credit to those students who returned the volunteer agreement on time and turned in a completed survey to the experimenter. All subjects were treated in accordance with the "Ethical Principles of Psychologists and Code of Conduct" (American Psychological Association, 1992).

Materials

This study required a volunteer agreement, four-page Movie Theater Survey (see Appendix 3.1) and follow-up letter for each student, and a testing area in which to administer the survey. The volunteer agreement explained in general what I was studying, the purpose of the survey, and how long it would take. It also let the students and their parents know when the survey would be conducted, when the volunteer agreement was due back to school (signed by both a parent and the student), and included my phone number and e-mail address in case questions arose. The survey consisted of a cover sheet and four parts. The cover sheet explained the purpose of the survey, contained a confidentiality statement, and reminded students not to write their names anywhere on the survey. Part I solicited demographic data, such as the student's grade, age, sex, hometown, race, and religion. Part II clarified the student's family background as military or not. Part III consisted of 19 multiple-choice questions about the student's self-report behavior in movie theaters. Part IV asked two open-ended questions: the most recent film the student had seen in a theater and the student's favorite film. The follow-up letter thanked the students for participating, again restated the purpose of the study, and gave information to the students and their parents so they could contact me if necessary. The students' normal classrooms and class times served as the survey area.

Design and Procedure

The project was designed through interest, literature, and advisor supervision. After the project was designed, including a finalized form of the volunteer agreement, survey, and follow-up letter, it was submitted to the United States Military Academy (USMA) Human Subjects Review Board. Simultaneously, I brought the same materials to the high school principal to request sponsorship. Within a few months, the research received approval from the USMA committee and the high school had chosen to accept the study. The high school arranged for a mentorship program between my study and the school history department.

I then began working with the two high school instructors involved and set up a schedule to conduct the study. Within a week, the instructors handed the volunteer agreement out to their students, explained the process, and told the students to return the volunteer agreements signed by both them and their parents as soon as possible. After two weeks, I collected all of the volunteer agreements and administered the survey. I explained the purpose again to the students, emphasized that they needed to respond truthfully to the questions, reminded them that the survey was confidential, and thanked them for their help. The survey took each student approximately 10 minutes to complete, and upon completion of the questionnaire they brought their surveys up to the front of the room where I handed them the follow-up letter.

After all of the surveys were collected, I answered specific questions from the students in an open-forum format. I provided them with greater depth about the purpose and previous literature of the study, explained the follow-up letter, and informed them that if they had any questions, they could contact me. Survey administration required five sessions, and all sessions were conducted within a five-hour time period on the same day.

Scoring

First it was necessary to relate each survey question to its respective hypothesis. One question determined family background (Part II), 3 questions pertained to film genres (Part III, numbers 14, 15, & 16), 7 questions pertained to group size (Part III, numbers 4–7 &, 11–13), and 12 questions dealt with misbehavior in general (Part III, numbers 8–19). Next, I determined a level of misbehavior for each survey to compare with the other data and prove or disprove hypothesis one and three. For each misbehavior question, I assigned a value of 0 or 1 based on the survey response (0 for no misbehavior and 1 for any positive response). The numbers were tallied, giving each survey a misbehavior level from 0 (no misbehavior) to 12 (high level of misbehavior), and compared with the demographic and group data to determine results for hypotheses one and three. For hypothesis two, I examined each individual answer to determine results. I controlled for three types of misbehavior: (1) talking, (2) shouting, and (3) throwing things and examined the frequency of different film genres.

I determined statistical significance by running a t test. I chose a p-value of less than or equal to .05 to determine significance because I felt that a 95% or more likelihood that my results did not occur by chance as reliable for this study. I then analyzed the cross tabulations to determine the direction of significance. This resulted in three conclusions but also presented other unintended relationships and conclusions.

RESULTS

The distribution of the data for hypothesis one is provided in Chart 3.1 and showed that indeed high school students from nonmilitary families reported more disruptive behavior (average misbehavior level of 5.62) in movie theaters than students from military families (average misbehavior level of 4.85). However, this finding was not statistically significant ($p = .23$).

The analysis of the data for hypothesis two showed that high school stu dents reported more disruptive behavior in action, comedy, and horror films than in drama, romance, and western films. The distribution in Chart 3.2 shows the results of the examination of talking. The findings revealed the following frequencies (Action = 8, Comedy = 48, Horror = 15, Drama = 6, Romance = 15, Western = 2). While frequency of talking was much higher in action, comedy, and horror films, the findings were not statistically significant ($p = .32$).

One variable that I did not originally control for was gender. However, after scoring each survey, I became curious about how the levels of misbehavior would distribute controlling gender—I had the means to do so. The distribution of data is reported in Chart 3.3. As might be expected, males self-reported misbehaving more than females (male average level of misbehavior = 6.16, female average level of misbehavior = 4.52; $p = .01$).

Chart 3.1.

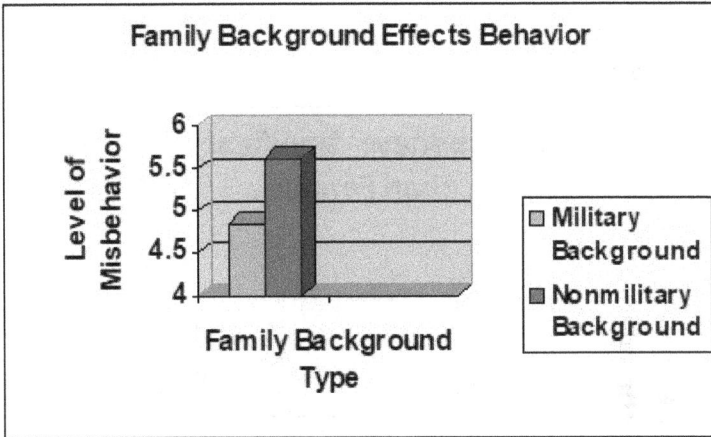

Family Background Effects Behavior

Chart 3.2.

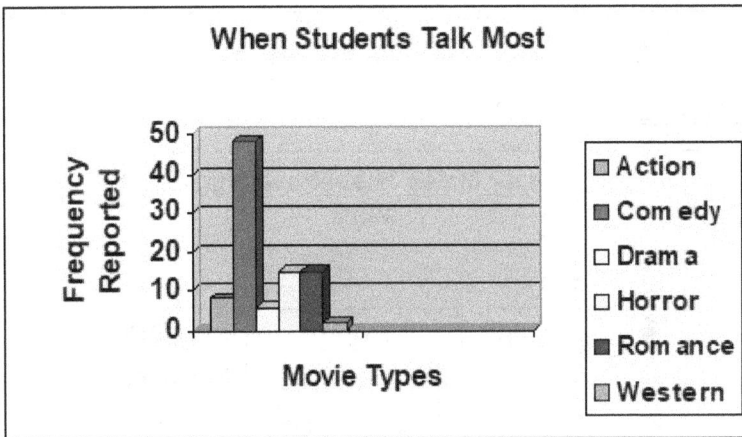

When Students Talk Most

When I controlled for both gender and family background together, I found that nonmilitary males misbehaved more than any other group. The distribution in Chart 3.4 shows each group's mean level of misbehavior followed by Table 3.1 and the significance levels in comparison to the nonmilitary males.

Chart 3.3.

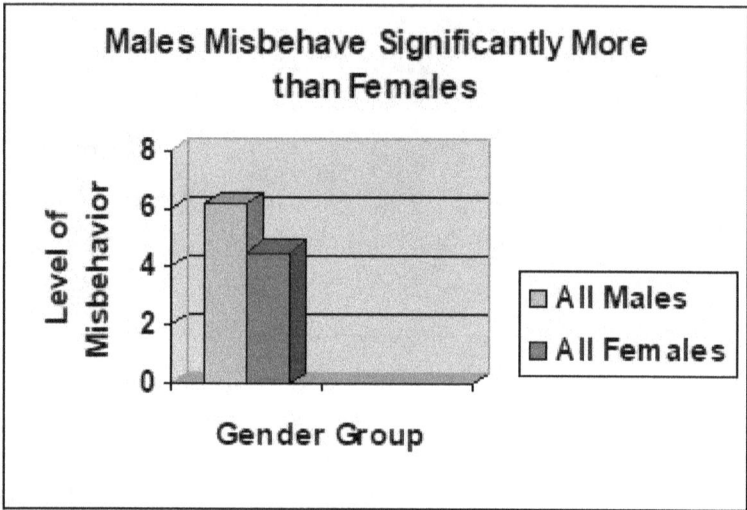

Males Misbehave Significantly More than Females

- All Males
- All Females

Level of Misbehavior / Gender Group

Chart 3.4.

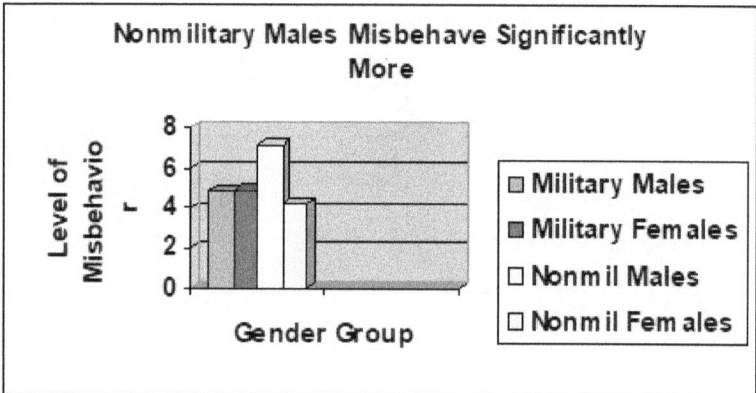

Nonmilitary Males Misbehave Significantly More

- Military Males
- Military Females
- Nonmil Males
- Nonmil Females

Level of Misbehavior / Gender Group

Table 3.1 Gender Group Comparison.

Gender Group	Military Males	Military Females	Nonmilitary Males	Nonmilitary Females
Average Level of Misbehavior	4.84	4.86	7.16	4.25
Significance Against Nonmilitary Males	$p = .02$	$p = .008$	N/A	$p = .002$

DISCUSSION

One explanation for the lower levels of misbehavior among children of military families may be a result of the military family structure or of parenting in military families. A profile of military children showed that while, in general, psychological profiles of military children were similar to civilian population samples, military children did show a lower level of some childhood disorders such as attention deficit hyperactivity disorder (ADHD). This is believed to be associated with a lower threshold in military parents for inattentive, hyperactive, or impulsive behaviors in their children (Jensen, Watanabe, Richters, Cortes et al., 1995). This finding can account both for the difference in overall misbehavior levels between students from military and nonmilitary families as well as the lack of statistical significance in this finding. However, because this section of the study did not control for gender, it is likely that similar gender effects existed but were not isolated.

Another possible explanation for the decreased level of misbehavior is the high degree of geographic mobility among military families. Researchers argue that geographic mobility affects families differently depending on where they are in the life cycle (Ender, 2000; Segal, 1989). Because adolescence involves a search for personal identity, which usually involves integration into a peer group, movement at this time of development can be significant. Moving not only disrupts relationships with peers, but also hampers participation in extracurricular activities and employment, which can have effects on one's self-concept (Piotrkowski, 1979). These effects may cause children of military families, especially the males, to be more reserved or less disruptive because they are not sure of themselves or of their position in peer groups.

A third explanation for lower reported levels of misbehavior among military youths may be due to normative constraints. The military organization exercises constraints on families through normative pressures on the behavior of spouses and children (Segal, 1989). Family members learn that their behavior is under scrutiny and that the degree to which it conforms to normative prescriptions can affect the military member's career. Violations of such norms "by children that come to the attention of military authorities [may] result in pressure on the service-members to control their family members" (Segal, 1989). Therefore, one can conclude that another reason military youths may misbehave less in movie theaters is because of the normative expectations of their behavior and the resulting consequences if they do not conform to such expectations.

Previous studies on group dynamics also lent to the explanation of family background and gender differences. Research showed that those in groups whose social identity is based on stereotypes are less active, or would score lower on the misbehavior level, than those with a social identity based on social experiences (Foster, 1999). It is possible that while nonmilitary students form groups based on social experiences, military students see themselves as a stereotype and their behavior follows the findings of Foster (1999). Additionally, it is possible that males from military families versus males from nonmilitary families have an intensified version of this effect that would account for their dramatically lower level of misbehavior in comparison.

While I was examining group size, other studies on the subject of group behavior examined its basis in cultural norms and peer pressures (Cummings & DeHart, 1995). These elements are usually magnified in the high-school age groups. Group behavior that may contribute to risk-taking activities or the misbehavior that I studied can be found in certain demographics and institutions such as the family or gender (Cummings & DeHart, 1995). Further study in this area would attempt to control for combinations of gender, group size or tendencies, family background, or other social characteristics to determine more clearly where the true differences and effects lie.

Some possible sources of error for this study included parent/guardian permission, the survey questions, variable selections, theater location, and self-reporting. While I received a very high return percentage rate on the volunteer agreements, there is the possibility that a parent with a child with a history of disruptive behavior may have opted for their student not to be surveyed on misbehavior, ultimately eliminating him or her from my subject population.

Next, while I believe that overall, my survey was a good indicator of misbehavior, some of the questions could have been improved on. For example, one subject when asked, "What kind of movie do you throw things most during" answered "a bad one," instead of circling a film genre or a negative response. If the survey were to be rewritten, these ideas should be accounted for. Also, as with any question, there is always a chance that each student will interpret questions and words differently from others and this should be accounted for.

One variable in particular that may have skewed my data was that of film genre. While it was clear in my results where the highest frequency of misbehavior occurred for both family backgrounds, both genders and both group sizes may have occurred because the students surveyed predominantly attended films of such genre. Defining film groups as action/comedy/horror and drama/romance/western may have been faulty in that there are very few western and romance films in comparison to action, comedy, and horror films. So, while violent content in these films may explain my results in terms of previous research, this is perhaps the more significant limitation in the study.

Another aspect of film watching that I did not account for was whether students attended films in post or civilian theaters. Whether or not military dependents were socialized in military theaters is a possible issue for this research. While my personal experiences, especially at this location, do not show post theaters to have a consistent effect on the behavior of the young people who attend films there,

there is no empirical evidence to support this claim. Therefore, my study would have been more complete if I had worked into the survey some questions about theater location.

Finally, while self-reporting was the best method of collecting data for my purposes, past studies have shown that among high-school students, there are implications with self-reporting, especially regarding unlawful or socially undesirable behaviors (Winfree, Baecktroem, & Mays, 1994). Possibly, the students did not know or care what the survey was looking for but still reported their behaviors in a manner that reflected their ideal behaviors instead of their actual behaviors. While students from military backgrounds reported less disruptive behavior than those from nonmilitary backgrounds, there are many ways in which students may have answered that they would have inaccurately affected these results. For example, some students may have been more streetwise and thought that answering the questions would somehow get them in trouble. From being members of high-profile families, some military students may have answered how they desired their background or family to be depicted. Further, teens with bitter or rebellious attitudes about the military or their upbringing may have wanted to cast a negative shadow on the military and did so through their survey responses. Those who had deep pride in their background may have reported excessively good behavior to help out the image of them and their family. Each of these is a possibility that could account for specific results. Another idea is that those who generally misbehave or are known as troublemakers or see misbehavior as idolized, may have reported even more misbehavior. On the contrary, well-behaved students may have enhanced the reporting of this by reporting less disruptive behaviors than they actually took part in.

Regardless of these possibilities for error, I can only account for them. Given my efforts to conduct a quality study based on self-report data in the most controlled manner possible with a conscious effort to reduce any of the effects that I mentioned, I think that any error, if present, was probably negligible. Future studies should account for my limitations.

A 1987 study by Orthner and Associates allows my research to draw conclusions about aspects of military families such as their overall health. While I would tend to conclude that these subjects indicate a population of good well-being as indicated by low levels of misbehavior, it is possible that a higher level of misbehavior may be normal and that something is affecting the normal behavior of these high-school students. Conversely, the results may indicate a high level of delinquency in the other students. This could be specific to my sample population or to any population with similar demographics. This could only be proved however if the study was carried out at other high schools near military posts that bring in both students from military and civilian families.

Orthner et al. (1987) concluded that there are no major differences between the military and civilian youths regarding their overall levels of stress. This may account for the lack of a significant overall difference in misbehavior. However, females from military families do report a higher level of overall stress and that may cause their slightly increased misbehavior level in comparison with the military males (Orthner et al., 1987).

There is no doubt that this new research on the behavior of high school students in movie theaters contributes to the knowledge of society. One noteworthy contribution this study made involved my second hypothesis. While the variable of film violence has been studied often, specific film genres have never been investigated. The movie theater setting was also an uncommon addition to research. The most important explorations, however, involved family background. The authors of significant research on military families (including those contributing to this volume) clearly recognize the present need to deal with issues surrounding the military, military families, and especially the children of those families (Bowen & Orthner, 1989).

Therefore, the findings involving my first hypothesis, regardless of statistical significance, speak to the differences between military and nonmilitary families concerning behavior. These compounded with the unexpected but more statistically significant findings concerning males from nonmilitary families further support that children of military families report less misbehavior.

While this research could not conclude indefinitely the reasons for such reporting trends, it examined film genres and group size independently as well, showing students to report more misbehavior in action, comedy, and horror films or when they are attending films in groups of four or more. In addition to the above-mentioned, future research examining the connection between my three hypotheses could also prove significant. Finally, the subjects I worked with, although unique, could be considered representative of similar populations. This study not only has significance to research because of its specific findings but also could be used to draw further conclusions about similar populations.

NOTES

[1] A most recent version of this paper received the 2001 Elise M. Boulding Undergraduate Student Paper Award from the Peace, War, and Social Conflict section of the American Sociological Association. An earlier version of this paper was presented and received an undergraduate paper award at the 16th Annual Hudson Valley Undergraduate Psychology Conference, Dominican College, Orangeburg, NY, April 28, 2000. I would like to acknowledge and thank my thesis advisor, Brian Reed, for his assistance and direction. His leadership and support were instrumental in bringing this paper together. The views of the author are my own and do not purport to reflect the position of the United States Military Academy, the Department of the Army, or the Department of Defense (Paragraph 4-3; AR 360-5).

[2] These facts were provided by an anonymous reviewer on previous drafts of the manuscript. The author wishes to thank this family sociologist who shared his or her personal experience growing up in a military family.

REFERENCES

American Psychological Association. (1992). Ethical principals of psychologists and code of conduct. *American Psychologist,* 47, 1597–1611.

Applewhite, L.W., & Mays R.A. (1996). Parent-child separation: A comparison of maternally and paternally separated children in military families. *Child and Adolescent Social Work Journal,* 13, 23–39.

Bowen, G.L., & Orthner, D.K. (Eds.). (1989). *The organization family: Work and family linkages in the U.S. military.* New York: Praeger.

Chidambaram, L., & Bostrom, R.P. (1997). Group development (I): A review and synthesis of development models. *Group Decision and Negotiation,* 6, 159–187.

Cummings, C.M., & DeHart, D.D. (1995). *Ethnic minority psychical health: Issues and intervention.* Boston, MA: Allyn & Bacon, Inc.

Doob, A.N., & Kirshenbaum, H.K. (1973). The effects on arousal of frustration and aggression. *Journal of Experimental and Social Psychology,* 9, 57–64.

Ender, M.G. (2000). Beyond adolescence: The experiences of adult children of military parents. In J. Martin, L. Rosen, and L. Sparacino (Eds.), *The military family: A practice guide for human service providers* (pp. 241–255). Westport, CT: Praeger Publishers.

Foster, M.D. (1999). Acting out against gender discrimination: The effects of different social identities. *Sex Roles,* 40, 167–186.

Funk, J.B., & Buchman, D.D. (1996). Playing violent video and computer games and adolescent self-concept. *Journal of Communication,* 46, 19–32.

George, J.M. (1990). Personality, affect, and behavior in groups. *Journal of Applied Psychology* 75, 107–117.

Huesmann, L.R., Moise, J.F., & Podolski, C.L. (1997). *The effects of media violence on the development of antisocial behavior.* New York: John Wiley & Sons, Inc.

Jensen, P.S., Watanabe, H.K., Richters, J.E., Cortes, R. et al. (1995). Prevalence of mental disorder in military children and adolescents: Findings from a two-stage community survey. *Journal of the American Academy of Child and Adolescent Psychiatry,* 34, 1514–1524.

Knox, J., & Price, D.H. (1999). Total force and the new American military family: Implications for social work practice. *Families in Society,* 80, 128–136.

Leyens, J.P., Camino, L., Parke, R.D., & Berkowitz, L. (1975). Effects of movie violence on aggression in a field setting as a function of group dominance and cohesion. *Journal of Personality and Social Psychology, 32*, 346–360.

McCabe, J.R., Jenkins, J.R., Mills, P.E., Dale, P.S., Cole, K.N., & Pepler, L. (1996). Effects of play group variables on language used by preschool children with disabilities. *Journal of Early Intervention, 20*, 329–340.

Nebecker, D.M. (1994). *I/O and OB in the military services: Past, present, and future.* Mahwah, NJ: Lawrence Erlbaum Associates, Inc.

Norwood, A.E., Fullerton, C.S., & Hagen, K.P. (1996). Those left behind: Military families. In R.J. Ursano & A.E. Norwood (Eds.), *Emotional aftermath of the Persian Gulf War: Veterans, families, communities, and nations* (pp. 163–196). Washington, DC: American Psychiatry Press.

Orthner, D.K., Giddings M.M., & Quinn, W.H. (1987). *Youth in transition: A study of adolescents from Air Force and civilian families.* Wash-ington DC: Government Printing Office.

Piotrkowski, C.S. (1979). *Work and the family system: A naturalistic study of working-class and lower-middle-class families.* New York: Free Press.

Plucker, J.A., & Yecke, C.P. (1999). The effect of relocation on gifted students. *Gifted Child Quarterly, 43*, 95–106.

Saxe, L., & Cross, T.P. (1997). Interpreting the Fort Bragg Children's Mental Health Demonstration Project: The cup is half full. *American Psychologist, 52*, 553–556.

Schafer, M., & Crichlow, S. (1996). Antecedents of groupthink: A quantitative study. *Journal of Conflict Resolution, 40*, 415–435.

Schumm, W.R., Bell, D.B., Rice, R.E., & Samders, D. (1996). Trends in dual military couples in the U.S. Army. *Psychological Reports, 78*, 1287–1298.

Schwab, J.J., Ice, J.F., Stephenson, J.J., Raymer, K. et al. (1995). War and the family. *Stress Medicine, 11*, 131–137.

Segal, M.W. (1989). The nature of work and family linkages: A theoretical perspective. In G.L. Bowen & D.K. Orthner (Eds.). *The organization family: Work and family linkages in the U.S. military* (pp. 3–36). New York: Praeger.

Sheehan, P.W. (1997). Violence on the screen and its implications for censorship. *Australian Journal of Psychology, 49,* 164–168.

Smith, H.J., & Tyler, T.R. (1997). Choosing the right pond: The impact of group membership on self-esteem and group oriented behavior. *Journal of Experimental Social Psychology, 33,* 146–170.

Ursano, R.J., & Norwood, A.E. (Eds.) (1996). *Emotional aftermath of the Persian Gulf War: Veterans, families, communities, and nations.* Washington, DC: American Psychiatric Press, Inc.

Wageman, R., & Baker, G. (1997). Incentives and cooperation: The joint effects of task and reward interdependence on group performance. *Journal of Organizational Behavior, 18,* 139–158.

Winfree, L.T., Baecktroem, T.V., & Mays, G.L. (1994). Social learning theory, self-reported delinquency, and youth gangs. *Youth and Society, 26,* 147–177.

Withecomb, J.L. (1997). Causes of violence in children. *Journal of Mental Health UK, 6,* 433–442.

Zillmann, D., Bryant, J., & Huston, A.C. (Eds.). (1994). *Media, children, and the family: Social scientific, pychodynamic, and clinical perspectives.* Mahwah, NJ: Lawrence Erlbaum Associates, Inc.

APPENDIX 3.1

Purpose: The purpose of this survey is to gain information about the behaviors of high school students in movie theaters.

Confidentiality: All of your responses will remain confidential and will only be used to determine trends within the different groups you comprise.

Please do not write your name anywhere on this survey.

SURVEY

PART I: PLEASE FILL IN THE FOLLOWING:

Grade: Hometown:
Race: Religion:
Age: Sex:

PART II: PLEASE CIRCLE THE APPROPRIATE RESPONSE:

Do you have an immediate family member (mother, father or someone who lives with you) in the military? a) Yes b) No

PART III: PLEASE CIRCLE THE MOST APPRO-PRIATE RESPONSE:

1. How many movies have you been to in the last week?
a) 0 c) 3-4
b) 1-2 d) 5 or more
2. How many movies have you been to in the last month
a) 0 c) 3-4
b) 1-2 d) 5 or more
3. About how many movies do you go see in a year?
a) 0 d) 11-15
b) 1-5 e) 16 or more

c) 6-10

4. Who do you go to the movies with most often?

a) A family member c) A date

b) A friend d) A group of friends

5. How often do you go to the movies with a family member?

a) Always c) Sometimes

b) Never

6. How often do you go to the movies with only one or two close friends?

a) Always c) Sometimes

b) Never

7. How often do you go to the movies with three or more friends?

a) Always c) Sometimes

b) Never

8. Do you ever talk during the movies?

a) Yes b) No

9. Do you ever shout in the movies?

a) Yes b) No

10. Do you ever throw things in the movies?

a) Yes b) No

11. When do you talk most in the movies?

a) When I'm with a family member

b) When I'm with one or two close friends

c) When I'm with three or more friends

d) I don't talk in the movies

12. When do you shout most in the movies?

e) When I'm with a family member

f) When I'm with one or two close friends

g) When I'm with three or more friends

h) I don't shout in the movies

13. When do you throw things most in the movies?

a) When I'm with a family member

b) When I'm with one or two close friends

c) When I'm with three or more friends

d) I don't throw things in the movies

14. What kind of movie do you talk most during?

a) Action e) Romance

b) Comedy f) Western

c) Drama g) I don't talk

d) Horror

15. What kind of movie do you shout most during?

e) Action i) Romance

f) Comedy j) Western

g) Drama k) I don't shout

h) Horror

16. What kind of movie do you throw things most during?

a) Action e) Romance

b) Comedy f) Western

c) Drama g) I don't throw things

d) Horror

17. Have you ever been asked to be quiet in a movie

a) Yes b) No

18. Have you ever been told to behave in a movie?

a) Yes b) No

18. Have you ever been asked to leave a movie

a) Yes b) No

PART IV: PLEASE ANSWER THE FOLLOWING QUESTIONS:

1. What was the most recent movie you saw?

2. What is your favorite movie

4

VIETNAMESE AMERASIANS: IN SEARCH FOR IDENTITY IN THEIR FATHERS' LAND

ROBERT S. MCKELVEY

INTRODUCTION

Vietnamese Amerasians are the children of Americans and Vietnamese. This chapter focuses on those Amerasians who had American fathers and Vietnamese mothers and were born during the period of major American involvement in the Vietnam War (1962–1975).

The Amerasian Homecoming Act

After their defeat in 1954, the French offered citizenship, transportation to France, and educational assistance to their Eurasian offspring in Vietnam (Bemak and Chung, 1997). By contrast, the United States government maintained for many years that the Vietnamese Amerasians were not its responsibility. The Vietnamese government assumed a more ambivalent position, initially arguing that they were the sons and daughters of Vietnam and then that they were not. In September 1982, seven years after the fall of Saigon and almost nine years after the withdrawal of American forces, the U.S. government began to process Vietnamese

Amerasians and their families for immigration to the United States. Their applications were considered under the Orderly Departure Program (ODP). The ODP was established in 1979 to enable Vietnamese boat people to immigrate legally to the United States rather than to undertake perilous escapes by sea. In December 1987, the U.S. Congress, in response to media depictions of the Amerasians' plight in Vietnam and growing public pressure to intervene on their behalf, passed the so-called "Amerasian Homecoming Act" (PL 100-202, Section 584) (United States General Accounting Office, 1994). This measure offered Amerasians born between January 1, 1962, and January 1, 1976, special priority status under the ODP.

The Amerasian Homecoming Act greatly accelerated the immigration of Vietnamese Amerasians and their families to the United States. Initially, the Homecoming Act allowed Amerasians to bring along only one family member, sometimes putting them in the uncomfortable position of having to choose between, say, their mother or their spouse (Brenden, 1990). This policy was later relaxed, and they and their immediate family members were offered the opportunity to immigrate to the United States at U.S. government expense. Here they received special refugee entitlement benefits such as health care, English language instruction, job training, and assistance with housing. In the first 20 years (1979 to 1999) of ODP operations, 467,113 Vietnamese immigrated to the United States under its auspices. Of these, 89,467 (19%) were Amerasians and their family members. The remainder were reeducation camp detainees and their families (165,718) and other Vietnamese immigrants and refugees (211,928) ("Orderly Departure Program," 1999). ("Re-education" camps were detention centers where officials and officers of the former South Vietnamese government and military were subjected to brainwashing and forced labor by the Communists after the war's end).

Stages in the Amerasian Immigration Process

The Amerasian Transit Center (ATC) was built with U.S. government funds in 1989 in Ho Chi Minh City. It provided temporary housing for Amerasians and their family members who were applying for the Amerasian Resettlement Program, but who did not live in the city or nearby. The ATC offered them accommodations, food, and informal English language instruction while they awaited ODP interviews and physical examinations. From the ATC, Amerasians and their families were transported to the Philippine Refugee Processing Center (PRPC). The PRPC is a large refugee camp north of Manila administered by the United Nations High Commission for Refugees. There they remained for approximately six months receiving instruction in English language and American culture until placements were found for them at cluster sites in the United States. The cluster sites were scattered throughout the United States and were operated by voluntary nongovernment agencies under contract with the U.S. State Department. The task of the cluster sites was to assist Amerasians with the resettlement process. Like other Vietnamese immigrants and refugees before them, some Amerasians found their initial resettlement sites unsatisfactory, often because of climatic conditions or the lack of a large Vietnamese community. Many undertook secondary migrations to parts of the United States, such as California and Texas, with warmer weather and larger concentrations of Vietnamese (Forbes, 1984).

A "Golden Passport" to the United States

The possibility of free immigration to the United States if one were Amerasian or an Amerasian's relative had a profound impact on Amerasians' standing in their communities (McKelvey, 1999; Valverde, 1992). Previously despised and ostracized, they were now "golden passports" to the United States. Many unrelated non-Amerasian Vietnamese tried to take advantage of this opportunity by either marrying them, pretending to be Amerasians themselves, or pretending to be members of an Amerasian's immediate family (McKelvey, 1994; Moore, 1990; United States General Accounting Office, 1994). In the early days of the Amerasian Resettlement Program, it was fairly easy to pass as an Amerasian or an

Amerasian's relative. After the Vietnam War ended, the mothers of Amerasians tried to conceal the fact that they had had a relationship with an American. They frequently destroyed documents, such as birth or marriage certificates, military identification cards, or photographs that might connect them to the United States. As a result, few Amerasians could document their identity. Their appearance was often their only proof that they had an American father. A member of a non-Vietnamese (or *Kinh*) ethnic group, of which there are 53 in Vietnam, might claim she was an Amerasian. Her features, different from those of an ethnic Vietnamese, might persuade an ODP interviewer that she did have an American father. The increasing number of fake Amerasian cases presenting to the ODP led to growing concern about immigration fraud. Rates of acceptance into the Amerasian Resettlement Program slowed dramatically. By 1994, 80% to 90% of applications were rejected (McKelvey, 1999; United States General Accounting Office, 1994). By the end of the 1990's the resettlement program had been shut down and the Amerasian Transit Center was closed leaving an unknown number of Amerasians still in Vietnam with little hope of ever reaching "the land of their fathers" (McKelvey, 1999).

Other Amerasians

Vietnamese Amerasians are, of course, not the only "Amerasians." Pearl S. Buck first employed the word in 1930 in her novel *East Wind: West Wind* (Felsman, Johnson, Leong, & Felsman, 1989). There are many Amerasians in Korea and the Philippines, where the United States has had a significant military presence for many years. They are also found in other East and Southeast Asian countries such as Cambodia, Laos, Japan, Taiwan, and Thailand. However, only the Amerasians of Vietnam have attracted widespread political and popular interest and support in the United States. This is related in part to the ongoing American preoccupation with the Vietnam War. Also, because the United States lost the war it could be seen as abandoning its children in the hands of its former enemies (McKelvey, 1999).

POPULAR PERCEPTIONS OF AMERASIANS

The Dust of Life

The photographic images that brought Vietnamese Amerasians to the attention of the American public showed ragged and dirty street children extending their hands to passersby in Ho Chi Minh City's "April 30th Park." The park was renamed as a reminder of the date on which Saigon fell to the North Vietnamese Army. It lies behind the redbrick, French-style Roman Catholic cathedral and fronts on the former South Vietnamese Presidential Palace, the present-day Vietnamese Foreign Affairs Bureau, and the base of Le Loi Street. Half a mile away is the erstwhile American embassy to South Vietnam. Amerasians often gathered in the park to sleep, pass the time, and tell their sad stories to foreigners, hoping for a handout or for help in reconnecting with their American fathers.

Journalists during the 1980s recounted the unhappy lives of Amerasians in Vietnam. They had experienced prejudice and discrimination because of their illegitimate birth, mixed racial heritage, and obvious connection to the American enemy. They were impoverished and poorly educated. Their American fathers, and sometimes their Vietnamese mothers, had abandoned them. Some were street children, begging, stealing, and sleeping on benches and under bridges to survive. They had become a part of that nearly invisible army of the downtrodden, "the dust of life" (*bui doi*) (McKelvey, 1999).

RESEARCH ON AMERASIANS

Early Studies

Early studies of Vietnamese Amerasian children resettled in the United States did little to dispel the popular perception that their difficult early lives in post-war Vietnam had left them scarred and unhappy. In 1985 the United States Catholic Conference (USCC) reported that 10% of the Vietnamese Amerasians resettled by them in 1983 and 1984 had "serious adjustment problems" (running away, withdrawal, and depression) (United States Catholic Conference, 1985). The report identified two risk factors for these adjustment problems: not being with one's biological mother, and having no formal schooling in Vietnam. The USCC report called into question the popular belief that Amerasians were the products of brief liaisons between American soldiers and prostitutes or bar girls. It showed that their mothers had lived with their American fathers for an average of two years. Nicassio, LaBarbera, Coburn, and Finley (1986) utilized the Personality Inventory for Children to evaluate a group of 24 Amerasians resettled in Connecticut. They reported that "Amerasian youth showed greater psychological deviance than one would expect in a nonclinical American sample" (Nicassio et al., 1986). Majka reviewed information given by Amerasians to Mutual Assistance Associations (resettlement organizations developed by refugees and immigrants) (cited in Felsman et al., 1989). He noted that 83% of Amerasians reported resettlement problems during the first two years after their arrival in the United States. After four years here, 62% of Amerasians continued to report such difficulties. The following factors were correlated with resettlement problems: an unstable home environment in the United States, male gender, having an American father from a minority group, and living outside of the Southeast Asian community.

Vietnamese Amerasians at the Philippine Refugee Processing Center

In 1988, Felsman et al. conducted the first large-scale, well-designed study of Vietnamese Amerasians, evaluating a sample of 259 Amerasians awaiting placement in the United States at the PRPC (Felsman et al., 1989). They employed a background demographic questionnaire and several self-administered symptom checklists to assess subjects' levels of psychological distress and to develop a risk profile predicting those with higher levels of distress. Their results confirmed earlier research cited above that suggested Amerasians have high levels of psychological distress. They also found that Amerasian females had significantly higher levels of distress than Amerasian males. Factors placing Amerasians at higher risk of psychological distress, in addition to female gender, were Afro-Amerasian ethnicity, low scores on oral and reading tests, and fewer than nine years of school in Vietnam. In addition, higher risk was conferred by not being raised by one's biological mother, traveling unaccompanied by mother or siblings, having a history of illness and/or hospitalization, and having a history of missing school. Leong and Johnson subsequently evaluated 115 biological mothers of Amerasians at the PRPC to learn more about their backgrounds and to assess their levels of psychological distress (Leong and Johnson, 1992). As in the previously cited USCC study, most of the women evaluated had had long-term relationships with their children's fathers and had lived with them. While few were officially married (12.5%), most received financial support from the father while he was in Vietnam and expected to rejoin him in the United States. Like their Amerasian children, the mothers of Amerasians reported high levels of psychological distress.

Amerasians in Vietnam

The first assessment of Amerasians still living in Vietnam was conducted by McKelvey and associates in 1990 at the Amerasian Transit Center in Ho Chi Minh City (McKelvey et al., 1992). Based on the design of Felsman and associates' earlier work in the Philippines, this study of 161 Amerasian subjects also included an evaluation of their expectations for life in the United States. Utilizing a modification of Felsman and associates' background questionnaire and the same self-administered symptom checklists, McKelvey et al. developed a risk profile of factors related to elevated levels of psychological distress among Amerasians still in Vietnam. This risk profile confirmed a number of items similar to those in Felsman and associates' earlier risk profile. These was a history of hospitalization, of missing school, no school, and not always living with one's biological mother. However, it did not confirm Felsman and associates' finding that female gender or Afro-Amerasian ethnicity conferred risk, although Afro-Amerasian ethnicity did almost reach statistical significance as a risk factor. The study identified additional risk factors for psychological distress: negative or indifferent feelings toward one's American father, a hostile relationship with one's step or foster father, very low family income, and having symptoms of a Conduct Disorder (American Psychiatric Association, 1987). The risk factors in this study were found to be additive: the more risk factors, the higher one's level of psychological distress. In the same study, McKelvey et al. found a significant connection between Amerasians' expectations for life in the United States and their levels of psychological distress (McKelvey & Webb, 1993). High expectations for one's life in the United States were associated with lower levels of both anxiety and depressive symptoms. High expectations for receiving assistance from one's American father were associated only with lower symptom levels of depression. High expectations for receiving help from the Vietnamese community in the United States were not significantly related to either anxiety or depressive symptoms.

In a subsequent reevaluation at the PRPC of the 1990 cohort, McKelvey et al. found a significant relationship between a greater number of risk factors identified in Vietnam and higher levels of psychological distress in the Philippines (McKelvey et al., 1993). This extended the validity of the risk profile as a predictor not only of concurrent psychological distress but also of future levels.

A subsequent study conducted at the ATC in 1993 compared levels of psychological distress in a group of Amerasians about to immigrate to the United States with those in a group of like-aged, nonmigratory Vietnamese (McKelvey & Webb, 1997). Amerasians were found to have higher levels of depressive symptoms than their non-Amerasian peers. This finding was thought to relate to their more traumatic early lives in Vietnam.

Vietnamese Amerasians in the United States

The cohort of Amerasians assessed by McKelvey et al. at the ATC in 1990 was reassessed approximately 18 months after their resettlement in the United States (McKelvey & Webb, 1996b). The large secondary migration characteristic of many Vietnamese Amerasians (Forbes, 1984) made it difficult to contact most of the study's original subjects. As a result, only about 20% could be re-interviewed. However, the prospective nature of the study allowed the investigators to compare premigratory risk factors and expectations for life in the United States with postmigratory psychiatric symptoms. This permitted an assessment of the premigratory risk factors' ability to predict post-migratory mental health. The investigators found that only pre-migratory expectations for support from the Vietnamese community in the United States were significantly related to post-migratory symptoms. Specifically, high expectations for receiving support from the American Vietnamese community were correlated with high symptom levels of depression. This finding suggested that Amerasians were not receiving levels of support from the Vietnamese community comparable to those that they had hoped to receive prior to leaving Vietnam. Also implicit in this finding was that the social isolation Amerasians had experienced in Vietnam was being replicated among the Vietnamese community in the United States.

Vietnamese Amerasians Compared with Other Vietnamese

There have been two studies comparing the adjustment of Vietnamese Amerasians in the United States with the adjustment of non-Amerasian Vietnamese. In the first, a sample of 100 Amerasians was compared with a sample composed of 25 of their non-Amerasian siblings and 30 unrelated Vietnamese (United States General Accounting Office, 1994). Amerasians were found to have lower levels of education in Vietnam than the other two groups and to be less likely to pursue further education in the United States. Despite arriving in the United States with few job skills, most (65%) Amerasians were able to find employment, but usually at unskilled, low paying jobs with little opportunity for advancement. Over time, fewer unemployed Amerasians found jobs than did their non-

Amerasian siblings or unrelated Vietnamese. An important factor contributing to Amerasians' comparative difficulties pursuing educational or vocational opportunities was their lack of family support. Despite these difficulties, most Amerasians described themselves as being happy in the United States. They also reported fewer problems with employment, material need fulfillment, and discrimination than had been the case in Vietnam.

McKelvey and Webb compared the personal histories and levels of psychological distress of 140 Vietnamese Amerasians with those in 71 of their non-Amerasian siblings and 118 unrelated non-Amerasian Vietnamese (McKelvey & Webb, 1996a). Amerasians reported that in Vietnam they had more experiences of childhood trauma, fewer years of school, and more hospitalizations than the other two groups. In the United States, they reported higher levels of depressive symptoms and alcohol use. Despite these problems, the Amerasians also reported levels of social support and success at adapting to American life comparable to those of their non-Amerasian siblings and non-Amerasian Vietnamese.

THEMES IN THE LIVES OF VIETNAMESE AMERASIANS

Paternal Loss, Discrimination, and Poverty

Common to the lives of almost all Amerasians was the early loss of their American father. Very few knew their father while he was in Vietnam, and most (88%) have little or no knowledge about him (Felsman et al., 1989; McKelvey, 1999). Only about 3% were able to locate their American fathers in the United States. Many of these reunions were mutually unsatisfactory because of the huge cultural gap between father and child (McKelvey, 1999). Vietnam is a patriarchal society in which a family's status and socioeconomic level derives largely from the father. The lack of a father contributed to Amerasians' difficulties in developing a positive identity. Their mixed race and connection to the American enemy reinforced these identity problems (Bemak & Chung, 1997; United States General Accounting Office, 1994). They also led to frequent experiences of prejudice and discrimination (McKelvey, 1999). Discrimination against Amerasians was institutionalized in Vietnam. They, along with the children of other "collaborators," were forbidden by the government to continue their education beyond high school (McKelvey, 1999). The low educational levels found among Amerasians are a result of this officially sanctioned discrimination and a lack of support from their families in Vietnam. Some of their families were too poor to allow them to continue their education beyond a few years in elementary school. Others discriminated against their Amerasian step- or foster children by forcing them to care for or help support their full-blooded Vietnamese half-siblings so that the siblings could continue their education.

Maternal Loss

Along with their American fathers, the mothers of some Amerasians also abandoned them (McKelvey & Webb, 1993). Those who did not live continuously with their biological mothers were found to have higher levels of psychological distress. Maternal abandonment also contributed to Amerasians' identity problems and left them even more impoverished and often without adequate adult protection or guidance.

Identity Issues and Depression

Growing up with multiple losses, reduced educational opportunities, prejudice, discrimination, and poverty, many Amerasians came to feel depressed about their lives and futures in Vietnam and were eager to leave for the United States (Felsman et al., 1989). While their lives here are undoubtedly better than they were in Vietnam (McKelvey & Webb, 1996a); USGAO, 1994), some of the problems that plagued them there continue to follow them in the United States. Many still struggle with identity issues and are not sure to which ethnic group they belong (Bemak & Chung, 1997; McKelvey, 1999). Whatever their racial or ethnic background, they are acculturated Vietnamese. They are more likely to develop social relationships with other Amerasians or with non-Amerasian Vietnamese than with black, Latino, or white Americans. An Afro-Amerasian goatherder, for example, may superficially resemble an African American more than a Vietnamese (McKelvey, 1999). However, his life experience and cultural training make him feel more comfortable relating socially to other Vietnamese. Amerasians' lack of educational and vocational training in Vietnam, their generally poor English-language abilities, and their lack of family financial support leave them trapped in entry-level jobs with little hope for significant advancement (Nwadiora & McAdoo, 1996; USGAO, 1994). While their material circumstances are undoubtedly better here, their chances for a fulfilling career are only marginally better than they were in Vietnam. Finally, their often traumatic and neglected lives in Vietnam leave them at high risk for the development of depressive disorders and post-traumatic stress disorder (Bemak & Chung, 1997; McKelvey & Webb, 1996a).

DISCUSSION

Despite difficult and often traumatic early lives in Vietnam, Amerasians appear to be adapting to American life with relative success. Both quantitative and qualitative studies suggest that they are self-supporting, able to develop social networks, and reasonably content with their lives in the United States. Few, if any, appear to wish that they were still in Vietnam or have made plans to return to live there, although many continue to miss those family members they left behind. Compared with other recent Vietnamese immigrants, however, they have lower levels of education and job training and are probably more likely to remain in unskilled entry-level positions. They are also at greater risk of developing acculturative, identity, and psychiatric problems.

What Might Have Been

Still unanswered is the question of what might have been had the United States elected to bring the Amerasians and their mothers out of Vietnam during their early years rather than waiting until they were adolescents or young adults. Unlike the French, the United States waited eight years to begin reaching out to its children in Vietnam (Bemak & Chung, 1997) and it was a full 12 years, when Amerasians were on average in their late adolescence, before the Amerasian Homecoming Act was passed. There are no studies comparing Amerasians who immigrated to the United States as young children with those who came out much later as part of the Amerasian Resettlement Program. However, one is tempted to speculate that bringing them to the United States in their infancy or early childhood would have had a number of important and salutary effects. They would not have been exposed to years of poverty, malnutrition, prejudice, and discrimination in Vietnam. They would have developed their English-language skills at an age when they would probably be able to speak fluent and unaccented English. They would have been able to benefit from the educational system in the United States, completing high school and perhaps college and graduate school, rather than having their educational careers foreshortened because of poverty and discrimination in Vietnam. They would have been better able to develop favorable identities in a country where their mixed race, and certainly their fathers' nationality, would not have had such a negative impact on their development as it did in postwar Vietnam.

Future Research

There are some Vietnamese Amerasian children who did leave Vietnam during or immediately after the war with their fathers and grew up in the United States. It would be informative to compare their outcomes with those of the Amerasians described in this chapter. Such a study might provide objective data to reinforce future efforts to bring home the children of Americans born abroad sooner rather than later. It would also be interesting to compare the adaptive and psychological outcomes of Amerasians in Vietnam with those of Amerasians in other East and Southeast Asian countries, especially ones with a higher standard of living than Vietnam. This would help to disentangle the effects on development of prejudice and discrimination from those related to socioeconomic factors. Finally, the Amerasians are now old enough to have children of their own. Previous research has suggested that the children of parents subjected to traumatic events may exhibit certain personality characteristics or diagnoses thought to be related to their parents' experiences (Rowland-Klein & Dunlop, 1998; Sack, Clarke, & Seeley, 1995). A study comparing Amerasians' children with those of like-aged non-Amerasian Vietnamese would help us to learn more about the possible intergenerational effects of Amerasians' early adversity on their offspring.

CONCLUSION

The lives of Vietnamese Amerasians illustrate the developmental effects on children of being abandoned by one's father and his country in the land of their enemies. Vietnamese Amerasians grew up in a country that, despite being the land of their birth, ostracized and discriminated against them because of their mixed race and connection to a hated foe. Coming to the United States in their teens and twenties improved their lives, but it was too late to fully undo the effects of years of trauma and neglect. It is, perhaps, too much to expect frightened and lonely young men to remain sexually abstinent when they are sent abroad to fight. However, it is unacceptable for their country to abandon the children they leave behind.

Amerasian Voices

Asked how people in the village had treated her, Khoi [a white Amerasian] began to cry:

Life there was terrible. The people had a deep hatred for the Americans. Not many kids liked to play with me; they tried to isolate me. The teachers despised me because I was Amerasian. Sometimes the kids would chase me away from school. Even then the local security agents kept interrogating my mother because she'd had an affair with an American. (McKelvey, 1999, p. 44)

I am a Vietnamese Amerasian. Other Amerasians are allowed to go to the U.S. ; why not me? I should have that right, too. If they'll let me go, I'll work hard to make a future for my children and earn money to send back to my foster mother. She is very poor. If I stay here, I'll be too poor to help her. In Vietnam I've suffered a lot for being Amerasian. I just want to get out. Americans need to understand that Vietnamese despise Amerasians. Most of us have never experienced love and affection. Our society rejects us. As a result, many of us are angry. We get upset at what has happened to us and sometimes we misbehave. People should try to understand our situation and not blame us for being human. (McKelvey, 1999, p. 115-116)

All Amerasians want to resettle in the United States. From the day we were born, the constant discrimination in Vietnam has made our lives awful. When we go for ODP interviews they keep asking for information about our fathers and for documentation. But after Liberation Day everyone burned their papers! They were terrified about what would happen if the government knew they had been with the Americans. Now the ODP asks us all these questions. If we get mixed up, they deny our application. I have nothing at all back in my village. My mother's house has collapsed, and my relatives there are very old and can't support us. (McKelvey, 1999, p.116)

REFERENCES

American Psychiatric Association. (1987). *Diagnostic and statistical manual of mental disorders* (3rd ed. - revised). Washington, DC: Author.

Bemak, F., & Chung, R.C.Y (1997). Vietnamese Amerasians: Psychosocial adjustment and psychotherapy. *Journal of Multicultural Counseling and Development, 25,* 79–88.

Brenden, M. (1990). *Amerasian update*. Washington, DC: Office of Refugee Resettlement.

Felsman, J.K., Johnson, M.C., Leong, F.T., & Felsman, I.C. (1989). *Vietnamese Amerasians: Practical implications of current research*. Washington, DC: Office of Refugee Resettlement.

Forbes, S. (1984). *Southeast Asian refugee resettlement report*. Washington, DC: Office of Refugee Resettlement.

Leong, F.T.L., & Johnson, M.C. (1992). *Vietnamese Amerasian mothers: Psychological distress and high-risk factors*. Washington, DC: Office of Refugee Resettlement.

McKelvey, R.S. (1994). Refugee patients and the practice of deception. *American Journal of Orthopsychiatry, 64*, 368–375.

McKelvey, R.S. (1999). *The dust of life: America's children abandoned in Vietnam*. Seattle: University of Washington Press.

McKelvey, R.S., Mao, A.R., & Webb, J.A. (1992). A risk profile predicting psychological distress in Vietnamese Amerasian youth. *Journal of the American Academy of Child and Adolescent Psychiatry, 31*, 911–915.

McKelvey, R S., & Webb, J.A. (1993). Long-term effects of maternal loss on Vietnamese Amerasians. *Journal of the American Academy of Child and Adolescent Psychiatry, 32*, 1013–1018.

McKelvey, R.S., & Webb, J.A. (1996a). A comparative study of Amerasians, their non-Amerasian siblings, and unrelated like-aged Vietnamese. *American Journal of Psychiatry, 153*, 561–563.

McKelvey, R.S., & Webb, J.A. (1996b). Premigratory expectations and post-migratory mental health. *Journal of the American Academy of Child and Adolescent Psychiatry, 35*, 240–245.

McKelvey, R.S., & Webb, J.A. (1997). Comparative levels of psychological distress in pre-migratory Vietnamese Amerasians and a Vietnamese community sample. *Australian and New Zealand Journal of Psychiatry, 31*, 543–548.

McKelvey, R.S., Webb, J.A., & Mao, A.R. (1993). Premigratory risk factors in Vietnamese Amerasians. *American Journal of Psychiatry, 150*, 470–473.

Moore, J. (1990). Amerasians provide an exit. *Far Eastern Economic Review, 7*, 55.

Nicassio, P.M., LaBarbera, J.D., Coburn, P., & Finley, R. (1986). The psychosocial adjustment of the Amerasian refugees. Findings from the Personality Inventory for Children. *Journal of Nervous & Mental Disorders, 174*, 541-544.

Nwadiora, E., & McAdoo, H. (1996). Acculturative stress among Amerasian refugees: Gender and racial differences. *Adolescence, 31*, 477–487.

Orderly Departure Program. (1999, January 27). *Viet Nam News*, 1–3.

Rowland-Klein, D., & Dunlop, R (1998). The transmission of trauma across generations: Identification with parental trauma in children of Holocaust survivors. *Australian and New Zealand Journal of Psychiatry, 31*, 358–369.

Sack, W.H., Clarke, G.N., & Seeley, J. (1995). Posttraumatic stress disorder across two generations of Cambodian refugees. *Journal of the American Academy of Child and Adolescent Psychiatry, 34*, 1160–1166.

United States Catholic Conference. (1985). *In our fathers' land: Vietnamese Amerasians in the United States.* Washington, DC: Author.

United States General Accounting Office. (1994). *Vietnamese Amerasian resettlement.* Washington, DC: Author.

Valverde, C.C. (1992). From dust to gold: The Vietnamese Amerasian experience. In M.P.P. Root (Ed.), *Racially mixed people in America* (pp. 144–161). Newbury Park, CA: Sage.

5

MILITARY BRATS: ISSUES AND ASSOCIATIONS IN ADULTHOOD

KAREN CACHEVKI WILLIAMS & LISAMARIE LIEBENOW MARIGLIA

INTRODUCTION

As Hunter and Nice (1978) recognized, "No longer is a family issued if the military wants a serviceman to have one, since most military service personnel now come equipped with a family, including a child or two" (p. vii). Military families, including children, have been the focus of study for many years, with more recent work (Bowen, 1989; Paulus, Nagar, Larey, & Camacho, 1996; Wertsch, 1991) pointing out that "serviceman" is no longer the most descriptive term. Many military families are ones where Mother is in the military in addition to or instead of Dad, creating a new set of issues for the children (known as "Brats").

This chapter focuses on a study (Mariglia, 1997) designed to answer the question "Why do adults who were children in military families seek each other out?" The term "Brat" has been used in the title and throughout the chapter to follow the wishes of the participants. It is a term that they use and feel comfortable with, signifying anyone who had at least one parent in a branch of the armed forces. We will begin with a background review of the literature centering on stress in military families, identity formation within military families, and the issue of family support in the military. Next comes a description of the research study including rationale for the use of qualitative methodology, information on participants, and data collection and analysis. Family systems theory and sociological perspectives form the basis for discussion of results, with the final section as a "call to action" with implications for family and child services.

BACKGROUND

Children worldwide go through the same developmental processes, even though they are exposed to, and influenced by, different experiences (Bandura, 1977; Erikson, 1963; Piaget, 1977; Vygotsky, 1962). An abundance of research (Long, 1986; Paden & Pezor, 1993; Shaw, 1987; Ursano, Holloway, Jones, Rodriguez, & Belenky, 1989) suggests that children raised in military families deal with problems civilian children never encounter. What are these stressors and how do they affect Brats' experiences, development, and sense of identity?

Stress and Military Families

No one would question the fact that military families move a lot, often all over the world. Parents can be separated from their children for long periods, both during times of war and extended military exercises. Early studies on children of military families focused on correlation between geographic mobility, father absence, and negative attributes (Hillenbrand, 1976; LaGrone, 1978). Research associated increased irritability, depression, impulsiveness, maternal dominance, need for attention, aggression, and dependency with life as a child in a military family.

A change in the focus of research and its findings began in the 1980s with increased attention being given to resiliency and support services for military families. Morrison (1981) and Chess and Thomas (1984) found little difference between military and nonmilitary children on measures of schizophrenia. Others such as

Rodriguez (1984) looked back to and continued work done by Kenny (1967) showing that military children had lower delinquency rates, higher achievement scores, and a higher median IQ. This attention may have played a part in the Army declaring 1984 as "The Year of the Military Child" and 1985 as "The Year of the Military Family" (Jensen, Lewis, & Xenakis, 1986; Paden & Pezor, 1993). Another explanation may be the shift from a predominantly single to a predominantly married force (Bowen, 1989), the creation of the family adequacy program (FAP) in 1982, and a recognition of the needs of the military family (Albano, 1994; O'Keefe, Eyre, & Smith, 1984) with a subsequent focus on quality of life (QoL) issues and benefits to children in the military (Ender, 1996).

Identity Formation within Military Families

In order to understand the issues facing military families, it is first necessary to understand attachment theory and its impact on children in the military community. As noted in the previous section, research suggesting that parental absence can present difficulties to a child is abundant. Erikson (1968) maintained that the child must establish a basic sense of trust within the first few years of life. Bowlby (1988) argued that during the first two years of life, separation from a parent, especially a major attachment figure, could be damaging to the development of a child. Researchers demonstrated that it is imperative for attachment figures to be available to a child through each of the developmental stages (Ainsworth, 1989; Bowlby, 1988; Erikson, 1968), an availability which is much more difficult to maintain in the military. In fact, for this and other reasons, Paden & Pezor (1993) claimed that the military child was a child with special needs.

To understand this further, one must realize that all children gain part of their identity from their family. The child in a military family gains this identity from an occupational-social spectrum subsumed under the special mission of national defense (Rodriguez, 1984). Military culture is organized according to rank, military specialty, unit membership, branch of service, and residence (Dunivin, 1994), all of which affects the identity formation of a child growing up in a military family. The rank caste system of the military is visible everywhere in the military community through symbols (Truscott, 1990), and status is most visible and manifested in the military community through segregation of family housing (Ursano et al., 1989).

The highly structured society of the military requires that all members of the military family be accountable for their actions (McIntyre & Drummond, 1978). Shaw (1987) pointed out that the patriarchal military community requires soldiers and their families to follow certain patterns of conduct. The behavior of a Brat is a direct reflection on the military member, so the child's identity and self-worth are directly tied to the family (Truscott, 1990; Useem, Useem, & Donoghue, 1963). Pressure on the child and family members can be extreme. Richard Bloom (1993) researched the military family and found that developing and maintaining beliefs worth dying for may be necessary for the military family.

There is a tremendous increase in the number of American children growing up overseas (Werkman, 1979). Military families can be differentiated into two groups—those who have lived overseas and those who have not (Truscott, 1990). Overseas experienced military children and their families "living on the local economy" must learn languages; adjust their dress, behavior, cuisine; and adapt to new traditions. Culture shock ensues if the family does not adapt and acculturate (Churchill, 1984), yet families with a positive attitude who are resourceful see living abroad and relocation as an adventure (Ursano et al., 1989). These families encourage members to continue communicating with friends left behind and emphasize with feelings of loss while focusing on the predictably familiar rules and environments within the military community (Ursano et al., 1989).

Research indicates that close interpersonal relationships influence identity formation (Erikson, 1968), which can be particularly problematic for the child in the military. Bloom (1993) believed that by moving continuously, a person's self identity could be lost through the loss of those who become part of their identity.

Through these losses, a new life must be reconstructed in a new community, with new social rules and roles. Long (1986) speculated that some children in military families display typical military determination when they relocate by denying their grief. Through continued uprooting, the military child may project unresolved feelings from previous relationships into new relationships, which Freud (1961) would call "negative transference."

Voluntary Group Association

Research on the topic of those who search out organizations and their reasons for group affiliation is important in understanding why adult children of military families become members of Brat organizations. Blau (1977) contended that people associate with those who share similar social characteristics. He called this the "homophily principle." Popielarz and McPherson (1995) suggested that organizations recruit from a specific area of social space referring to it as the organization's "niche." Those in this niche are at the highest risk of being recruited because they are most like the present members.

Druckman (1994) researched group loyalty and wanted to understand why feelings of loyalty are generated in a group. His findings suggested that feelings of attachment are basic to an individual's definition of self. When a member is loyal to their group, their own identity and sense of belonging are strengthened. Most important, Druckman mentioned that the group affiliations, from an early point in their lives, have a great impact on the group to which they will later belong. Several studies have focused on the historic inadequacy of the Department of Defense (DoD) in providing supportive resources for military families (Albano, 1994; Bloom, 1993; Jensen et al., 1986; Long, 1986; Paden & Pezor, 1993; Srabstein, 1983; Ursano et al., 1989). Jensen and associates (1986) and others (Armitage, 1984; Shaw, 1987) suggested that military members may also be stigmatized if they seek out supportive services. Other studies (Cantwell, 1974; Eastman, Archer, & Ball, 1990; Paden & Pezor, 1993; Peck & Schroeder, 1976; Srabstein, 1983; Werkman, 1979) cite families not being close in proximity to health and other service facilities, which may contribute to families having difficulty in adapting to new environments. However, military Family Support Centers have been shown to make transitions easier for members of the military family (Albano, 1994; O'Keefe et al., 1984; Paden & Pezor, 1993).

METHODS

Understanding the behavior and lived experiences from the point of view of the participants required the use of phenomenology—an interpretive qualitative approach (Denzin & Lincoln, 1994). It allows for the discovery of the meanings and realities of those being studied.

Lincoln & Guba (1985) recommend purposive sampling (choosing participants in a focused, nonrandom way) as the best strategy to target participants who belong to a particular desired group for investigation. For this study, typical cases were examined through a sampling of convenience. This meant that information could be gathered from a small, purposeful, but meaningful, sample of participants who were already active in Brat organizations. Participants were identified through two sources: attendees of an annual Overseas Brats (OSB) conference, and users of an Internet site for Overseas Brats. The second author, LisaMarie Mariglia, grew up as a military Brat. This established an immediate rapport and trust, making gaining entry relatively easy. In each case, she identified herself as a researcher with an interest in Brats stemming from her own experiences. Internet users were sent consent forms only if they contacted her via e-mail, providing a further method of future data collection. Participants contacted in person were also given consent forms, and they continued their participation via e-mail as well after sending signed consent forms.

Participants were asked to respond to an initial set of questions:

1. To what organizations do you belong?
2. How did you become a member?

3. What activities do you participate in?

4. Are those activities on or off base?

5. What bases have you lived at and for how long?

6. What activities did you participate in at those bases?

7. What activities did you participate in at other bases that you are no longer active in?

8. What kinds of activities were your parents in?

9. What kinds of activities were your siblings in?

10. As an adult, did you join the military or marry someone in the military?

11. Where would you like to be stationed as an adult? Are you trying to return to previous stations? Why?

12. Can you describe your experiences as a dependent?

13. Were you ever uncomfortable at any of the bases you were stationed due to the political climate? Was that as a child or as an adult?

14. Would you recommend that others in the military have children? Why or why not?

15. Is there anything else you would like to share with me about your experiences as a military dependent?

16. Describe how you became interested in "Brat" organizations? Why were you attracted to them?

Participants were given the option to use a pseudonym or their own name for the study and could specify their choice on the consent form. They responded to the initial set of questions then were contacted again to clarify responses, answer additional questions stemming from others' responses, and as a means of member checking to be sure that the researcher was accurately reflecting their ideas, issues, and opinions (Lincoln & Guba, 1985).

Collection of data over a period of one year helped to ensure what researchers refer to as "prolonged engagement" (Bogden & Biklen, 1998; Lincoln & Guba, 1985). Collection stopped when e-mailed responses continued to duplicate previous information. Data sources allowed data triangulation (Denzin & Lincoln, 1994) and included participant observation field notes from the Overseas Brats conference, artifacts and historical materials, emailed responses to structured and unstructured questions by six participants, and reflective memos. Numbering data, notes, and artifacts chronologically allowed data to be sorted into separate computer directory files. Data were then coded for emergent categories and broken down into subcodes, which were summarized separately. Those codes also contained the reflective memos and became the major themes for the study. Further grounding of findings resulted from triangulation of themes with sociological theories about group membership and concepts about the military family. Participants and a debriefer were used in the member check process as described above. The debriefer, who was also a military Brat but not a study participant, acted as a critical friend (Lincoln & Guba, 1985) with whom to discuss the findings and get additional feedback on credibility.

DISCUSSION

Five main themes emerged from this study. Three directly related to affiliation with military Brats organizations in adulthood, and two focused on childhood experiences, which may have impacted participants' feelings about the military and therefore their reasons for joining a Brat organization. They are (1) Keeping Up as Staying Connected, (2) Others Like Me—Creating Safety, (3) Lack of Social Hierarchy, (4) Disconnected Adults: Adjustment Issues, and (5) Impact of Military Life on Feelings about Family. Each discussion includes examples to give participants a "voice."

Keeping Up as Staying Connected

Interviewees often commented that their membership in Brat organizations was important to their sense of staying connected to the past, including friends and places that had been important to them. For example, Denise felt "[Brat] organizations provide me with a method to get in touch with people I knew that [I had lost] touch with as a child because [we moved] so much. It also gives me a sense of community."

Lena liked the "connection" she felt with other Naples, Italy, alumni. Because she left Naples three days after high school graduation, she "didn't feel like [she] had the opportunity to say good-byes to friends, teachers, places, Italian friends, food" and wanted to "return for closure."

The OSB and other Brat organizations facilitated connections with other Brats by the mere existence of their homepages on the Internet where the reader could contact other alumni. Their databases include addresses, phone numbers, years of attendance, and previous names. Brats frequently left messages, which went out to all on the LISTSERV, for lost friends or acquaintances. Most of these messages identified the person being looked for, the year they graduated or attended the school, and how the sender could be contacted. Once Brats connected with each other, they began coordinating reunions to gather face-to-face. These reunions were generally organized by school or home city (e.g., Naples Brats) or by the decade (e.g., Brats attending a particular school in the 1980s).

Announcements going over the Internet targeted more than those who wanted to reconnect with old chums. Some Brat announcements told of impending marriages and births of children. They also shared memories of deceased former teachers, administrators, and Brats.

Others Like Me—Creating Safety

Participants in this study joined Brat alumni associations for a variety of reasons, but one of the most frequently cited was "the desire to make contacts with those who had shared similar experiences." Jim joined to meet others who came from "the same environment, if not the same place." He stated, "The only real 'home town' I have is my cohort of military Brats who grew up in the military culture and moved around a lot too."

Joe organized the Overseas Brats (OSB) in 1986 out of a need to "bring many people together to share similar experiences." He conceptualized OSB as a tool for reunification with his "own kind." This fit Cindi's view of the OSB. She said that she was a "unique member of a very select club" and that joining OSB gave her "a sense of roots, history and [of] belonging somewhere" that "no [one]else [could] better understand."

Brat organizations create a safe forum for sharing deep feelings and memories, resulting in a sense of security. An example is this piece of an essay submitted to an Internet site by a Brat who shares memories of a return visit to Naples:

> Crime, pollution, traffic, vibrancy, con-games, and the beauty (who can forget that view of the Bay of Naples, from downtown to Vesuvius to Sorrento to Capri back over to the tip of the Posillipo?). It's all still all there. Graduating in 1982, I didn't anticipate returning to Naples ever again. The drive in had been an almost surreal experience, not providing time for any reflection—the three years spent looking at the Bay, the walks downtown, the nights spent at Mergellina, the visits to Capri and Sorrento, the time spent in school, the friends, the teachers. Now, though, out of the car and in our room, it finally hit me: I was back in Naples—a few blocks from home and a street away from Forrest Sherman. What I miss most about Naples isn't something that you can see, hear, or even touch. It's an attitude. One which openly defies life's hardships and shrugs off any misfortune. I feel fortunate that I returned to Naples, but not just to see the city, the Bay, Via Manzoni, or Capri again; the real pleasure in returning was realizing that the Neapolitan spirit and character still thrives.[1]

Brats often commented sympathetically and added their own reflections. For example, one person commented: "Your post brought back many fine memories for me. Thank you." There was, however, an unwritten rule not to comment negatively on another Brat's writing. On September 26, 1997 one Brat commented that an item seen on the LISTSERV "everyone must have seen...in another media." This brought comments that he ought to keep his negative feelings to himself, with reminders that membership was voluntary. Brats protect Brats.

Lack of Social Hierarchy

Once Brats became adults the barriers disappeared. The clear hierarchy present in the military that even affected their childhood friendships on base (and access to some experiences, like Sunday brunch at the Officer's Club) vanished. It mattered less whether a Brat's dad had been a general or what branch of the military a parent had belonged to than all Brats sharing common memories and life experiences during their life as children and separated them from non-Brats. Although some Brats affiliated with organizations that focused on a particular branch of the service, overseas versus stateside experiences or schools, rank lost its meaning once a person was a member of a Brat group.

Members in the Brat organizations did not create hierarchical structures within those organizations. There are contact members for alumni groups and Internet mailing lists. There are also contact individuals to lead a group in organizing reunions. Nevertheless, the groups did not recognize any group structure that placed one individual on a higher status than any other. Interviews and Internet site data suggested that Brat organizations did not discourage individuality within the group, another sign that hierarchies and levels of status had changed from member experiences on the base. It is interesting to note that as children, the research participants and some family members joined organizations where conformity and sometimes "rank" was imbedded, such as the Boy and Girl Scouts and the American Red Cross.

Disconnected Adults: Adjustment Issues

Several participants in the study and some messages on the Internet indicated that Brats who were no longer in the military faced adjustment problems in civilian life. Affiliation with Brat organizations may have been a result of an unconscious desire to reconnect to a known, structured system and sometimes fondly remembered childhood.

Two examples illustrate this feeling of disconnection. Marlene voiced a longing for an attachment to life as a military Brat when she said:

> The experiences I had could never be replaced and I would love to give my son the same type of experience one day...I really miss the moving and seeing new places. It is difficult to settle down even after 18 years [of living in one place]. My restlessness gets worse after visiting my parents overseas.

On the other hand, Jim did not remember his childhood experiences as fondly. He felt as though moving every few years had prevented him from making friends and left him feeling as though he never had a home. In fact, Jim often felt as if he were an "unwelcome outsider." Both are active members of Brat organizations and frequent the Brat internet sites.

Impact of Military Life on Feelings about Family

The last theme did not directly address the research question but kept emerging from participant responses and the Internet data. Experiences as military Brats strongly influenced perceptions of their own families and whether they felt that people in the military should have families. Most participants felt that raising families in the military culture provided for an enriched childhood. Only one participant advised the military personnel not to have children. All participants had advice for those in the military with families, and some even went as far as to suggest avenues the military might take to ensure healthy families. It is not surprising that perceptions of their own experiences influenced their responses and their advice. Denise, supporting having children while in the military, said:

> Most of my time was spent outside of America—the things I learned and the traveling I got to do was just awesome. My

family tended to be adventuresome and definitely did not hang around the base. We usually lived off-base, learned the local language, and got to know the "locals" quite well...my playgrounds were the El Yunque Rain Forest...the Caribbean, the Atlantic, the Italian and French Riviera, the Mediterranean. I got to do my 7th grade play (The Merchant of Venice) in an Old Roman Amphitheater... There were many times that we would stay off the streets due to the anti-American sentiment generated during Communist rallies that sometimes led to aggressive behavior. Since we lived on the "economy" we generally blended in with the locals [and] didn't have any problems...talk about frequent uprooting issues openly and present moves as opportunities [to the children]. They should also take advantage of what the local area has to offer as much as possible and not be "base bodies."

Lena had positive memories of her experiences as a military Brat and thought that people in the military should have children, but felt the military could make things go more smoothly, commenting:

School psychologists and other psychologists [should] be involved in preparing families, children, and adolescents for major transitions of moving...especially during critical developmental junctures in their lives... [Have sponsors assigned to the children to] help them cope with the move... with culture shock and with the new school and location.

Jim, on the other hand, had fairly negative memories of his childhood experiences and consequently did not think that people should have children if they were in military service. He shared:

[My] father drew sea duty...about a month after I was born, and was absent from the household for extended periods of time until I reached age two. I think those two years (and other years later) had a profound negative impact. I loved him, but we never really bonded. I don't think the life of a military dependent is good for children...but people "will" have children. Those in the military need to be aware of the effects of life in the military on children and try to compensate. [I hope that Brat organizations] educate current military service members, and perhaps even their children, about the hazards of growing up as a military Brat... [because] military life can be detrimental to...family life.

CONCLUSIONS AND IMPLICATIONS

The numbers of people accessing Internet Brat organizations and chat rooms, joining Brat groups, and attending Brat conferences continue to increase. The affiliation with Brat groups is meeting the needs of many adult Brats, as the interviews and artifacts accessed in this study show. In this section, we will examine theories related to associations and how these might apply to the research findings. We will also explore implications, including recommendations for military policies and programs.

Implications: Policies and Programs

This study and the literature review supports recent research that relocation is a significant issue for military families (Ender, 2000). The families that saw moving as an adventure, recognized family members' feelings associated with moves, and involved members in the moves appeared to have adjusted the best. Problematic relocation occurred if accompanied by feelings of alienation, rejection, rootlessness, loneliness, and loss. Special treatment and attention needs to be paid to individuals and families with these experiences. Several strategies could be employed:

1. Help individuals and families know that they are not alone or the first to have problems with relocation.

2. Adopt strategies the adaptive family recognizes, including having the families recall positive experiences at previous installations such as using scrapbooks, videos, retelling stories of experiences, and encouraging communication with those friends left behind. These strategies can also be employed each time a move is anticipated.

3. Encourage families to begin gathering information on the new site and planning for the move as soon as they receive notice of an upcoming relocation. It's important for each family member, especially children, to have a role and feel part of the relocation process

4. Diminish feelings of isolation. When isolated from civilian communities (either due to geographic distance or social bias), decreasing the sense of separateness is important. Military support services must invent creative ways for families to safely relate to their environment.

5. Increase the use of the Internet. This can provide valuable information *before* a move which will help with adjustment and anticipatory socialization as well as an important vehicle *after* the move for maintaining relationships.

It is important to realize that relocation, for many, includes the ultimate relocation: leaving military service or returning to the United States after prolonged experiences overseas. Data from this study and others show that Brats accumulate their identity from the cultures where they spent their youth, and acknowledging all parts of that identity is important. School personnel should be aware of transition issues for Brats and encourage Brats to share their life experiences with their classmates while they learn about experiences of their nonmilitary classmates. Designated military family support personnel should increase the awareness of teachers who are confronted with special issues associated with relocation and extended parental absences. Connecting incoming Brats with those already established is a worthwhile strategy. Creating transition services to help personnel who are preparing to leave the military to reenter civilian life is essential.

It would seem to follow that the military should pay attention to the experiences of children and families, listen to what they say about their responses to the crises and challenges in their lives, and support associations created for former Brats. By supporting Brat organizations and making people leaving the military aware of them, the military could ensure that the needs of Brats are being considered, even after the family has left the military.

Many families who would benefit from family and individual support services are not accessing them for fear of being stigmatized or having them impact negatively on their careers. *All families* can benefit from knowing the stages of child and family development, ways to cope with the normative crises all families face, and when to get additional help. Future intervention programs for the military family should help immunize the family against stress by strengthening cohesiveness and ensuring adaptation to new environments. The military should contract with Certified Family Life Educators (CFLE) who are knowledgeable in life span and family development. Family systems professionals use tools to provide them with a picture of how a family is functioning and ways to best help them. These tools include the Moos' Family Environmental Scale (1974), Family Inventory of Life Events and Changes (McCubbin, Patterson, & Wilson, 1981), Military Environmental Inventory (Wegner, 1991), and the Double ABCX Crisis Model (McCubbin & Patterson, 1983).

Voluntary Group Association

Again, research on the topic of those who search out organizations and their reasons for group affiliation is important in understanding why adult children of military families become members of Brat organizations. Blau (1977) contended that people associate with those who share similar social characteristics. He called this the "homophily principle," and it seems clear from this study that the homophily principle holds for people who join Internet Brat organizations. Physical proximity was less important than what Blau called the distance from one another in "social space." This concept is supported by the work of Popielarz and McPherson (1995), who suggested that organizations recruit from a specific area of social space or organizational niche and that those in this niche are at the highest risk of being recruited because they are most like the present members. Those who leave or never join a particular organization are those who are at the "edge" of the niche or are being recruited by multiple organizations (the niche overlap hypothesis). Consequently, military Brats groups, like voluntary organizations, remain overwhelmingly homogeneous (Ender, 2000; McPherson & Smith-Lovin, 1986, 1987; Popielarz, 1990, 1992). Participants in this study share a focus with strong similarities and identifiable and shared experiences.

I noted above that Druckman (1994) found that feelings of attachment are basic to an individual's definition of self. Loyalty to group strenghtens identity and a sense of belonging. Early life involvement in groups predict later life involvement. However, what of affiliation to a group which, for many, was inherently stressful in childhood and adolescence? Clearly the literature showed that children who were military dependents experienced unique stressors. It may be that belonging to military Brats organization in adulthood actually decreases stress and helps provide coping mechanisms. Reitschlin (1988) found that voluntary group membership resulted in a reduction of depressive symptoms in men and women from 22 to 89 years of age and even had stress buffering effects. Prestby, Wandersman, Florin, Rich, and Chavis (1990) took this even further and found that participation in "neighborhood associations" can meet members' social needs by reducing chronic stress or providing coping mechanisms. Although Prestby et al. (1990) focused on voluntary memberships in local (face-to-face) community organizations, Brats clearly identified other Brats as being their community, filling a need in their lives that their civilian settings and experiences did not, through a device called the Internet and by establishing a virtual community.

NOTE

[1] Overseas Brats Web site, http://www.overseasbrats.com/index.asp.

REFERENCES

Ainsworth, M.D.S. (1989). Attachments beyond infancy. *American Psychologist, 44,* 709–716.

Albano, S. (1994, Winter). Military recognition of family concerns: Revolutionary war to 1993. *Armed Forces and Society, 20,* 283–302.

Armitage, D.T. (1984). Legal issues encountered in treating the military family. In A.S. Gurman (Series Ed.) and F.W. Kaslow & R.I. Ridenour (Vol. Eds.), *The military family: Dynamics and treatment* (pp. 18–45). New York: Guilford Press.

Bandura, A. (1977). *Social learning theory.* Upper Saddle River, NJ: Prentice Hall.

Blau, P.M. (1977). *Inequality and heterogeneity: A primitive theory of social structure.* New York: Free Press.

Bloom, R.W. (1993). A reason to believe: The sustenance of military families. In F.W. Kaslow (Ed.), *The military family in peace and war* (pp. 98-120). New York: Springer.

Bogdan, R.C., & Biklen, S.K. (1998). *Qualitative research for education: An introduction to theory and methods.* (3rd ed.). Boston: Allyn & Bacon, Inc.

Bowen, G.L. (1989). Satisfaction with family life in the military. *Armed Forces and Society, 15,* 571–592.

Bowlby, J. (1988). *A secure base: Parent child attachment and healthy human development.* New York: Basic Books.

Cantwell, D.P. (1974). Prevalence of psychiatric disorder in a pediatric clinic for military dependent children. *Behavioral Pediatrics, 85,* 711–714.

Chess, S., & Thomas, A. (1984). *Origins and evolution of behavior disorders: From infancy to early adult life.* New York: Brunner/Mazel.

Churchill, J.E. (1984). Treating military families overseas:

Focusing on conjoint and multiple impact therapy. In A.S. Gurman (Series Ed.) & F.W. Kaslow & R.I. Ridenour (Volume Eds.), *The military family: Dynamics and treatment* (pp. 197-216). New York: Guilford Press.

Denzin, N.K., & Lincoln, Y.S. (1994). Introduction: Entering the field of qualitative research. In N.K. Denzin & Y.S. Lincoln (Eds.), *Handbook of qualitative research* (pp. 1-22). Thousand Oaks, CA: Sage Publications.

Druckman, D. (1994). Nationalism, patriotism, and group loyalty: A social psychological perspective. *Mershon International Studies Review, 38,* 43–68.

Dunivin, K.O. (1994). Military culture: Changes and continuity. *Armed Forces and Society, 20,* 531–547.

Eastman, E., Archer, R.P., & Ball, J.D. (1990). Psychosocial and life stress characteristics of navy families: Family environmental rating scale and life experiences scale findings. *Military Psychology, 2,* 113–127.

Ender, M.G. (1996). Growing up in the military. In C. Smith (Ed.), *Strangers at home: Essays on the effects of living overseas and coming "home" to a strange land* (pp. 125-150). Bayside, NY: Aletheia Publications.

Ender, M.G. (2000). Beyond adolescence: The experiences of adult children of military families. In J.A Martin, L.N. Rosen, & L.R. Sparacino (Eds.), *The military family: A practice guide for human service providers.* (pp. 241-255). Westport, CT: Praeger.

Erikson, E.H. (1963). *Childhood and society* (2nd ed.). New York: Norton.

Erikson, E.H. (1968). *Identity: Youth and crisis.* New York: Norton.

Freud, S. (1961). An outline of psycho-analysis. In J. Strachey (Ed. and Trans.), *The standard edition of the complete psychological works of Sigmund Freud* (Vol. 19) (pp. 149-153). New York: Norton. (Original work published in 1924).

Hillenbrand, E.D. (1976). Father absence in military families. *The Family Coordinator,* 451–458.

Hunter, E.J., & Nice, D.S. (Eds.). (1978). *Children of military fami-*

lies: A part and yet apart. Washington, DC: U.S. Government Printing Office.

Jensen, P.S., Lewis, R.L., & Xenakis, S.N. (1986). The military family in review: Context, risk, prevention. *Journal of the American Academy of Child Psychiatry, 25,* 225–234.

Kenny, J.A. (1967). The child in the military community. *Journal of the American Academy of Child Psychiatry, 6,* 51–63.

LaGrone, D.M. (1978). The military family syndrome. *American Journal of Psychiatry, 135,* 1040–1043.

Lincoln, Y.S., & Guba, E.G. (1985). *Naturalistic inquiry.* Newbury Park, CA: Sage Publications.

Long, P. (1986, December). Growing up military. *Psychology Today, 20,* 31–37.

Mariglia, L.M.L. (1997). *The emergence of associations for adults who were children in military families.* Unpublished master's thesis, University of Wyoming, Laramie, WY.

McCubbin, H.I., & Patterson, J.M. (1983). *One thousand Army families: Strengths, coping and supports.* St Paul: University of Minnesota Press.

McCubbin, H.I., Patterson, J.M., & Wilson, L. (1981). *Family inventory of life events and changes.* St. Paul: Family Social Science, University of Minnesota.

McIntyre, W.G., & Drummond, R.J. (1978). Familial and social role perceptions of children raised in military families. In E.J. Hunter & D.S. Nice (Eds.), *Children of military families: A part and yet apart* (pp. 15-24). Washington, DC: U.S. Government Printing Office.

McPherson, J.M., & Smith-Lovin, L. (1986). Sex segregation in voluntary associations. *American Sociological Review, 51,* 61–79.

McPherson, J.M., & Smith-Lovin, L. (1987). Homophily in voluntary organizations: Status distance and the composition of face to face groups. *American Sociological Review, 52,* 370–379.

Moos, R.H. (1974). *Family environmental rating scales and preliminary manual.* Palo Alto, CA: Consulting Psychologist Press.

Morrison, J. (1981). Rethinking the military family syndrome. *American Journal of Psychiatry, 138,* 354–357.

O'Keefe, R.A., Eyre, M.C., & Smith, D.L. (1984). Military family service centers. In A.S. Gurman (Series Ed.) & F.W. Kaslow & R.I. Ridenour (Volume Eds.), *The military family: Dynamics and treatment* (pp. 254-268). New York: Guilford Press.

Paden, L.B., & Pezor, L.J. (1993). Uniforms and youth: The military child and his or her family. In F.W. Kaslow (Ed.), *The military family in peace and war* (pp. 3–24). New York: Springer.

Paulus, P.B., Nagar, D., Larey, T.S., & Camacho, L.M. (1996). Environmental, lifestyle, and psychological factors in the health and well-being of military families. *Journal of Applied Social Psychology, 26,* 2053–2075.

Peck, B.B., & Schroeder, D. (1976). Psychotherapy with the father-absent family. *Journal of Marriage and Family Counseling, 2,* 23–30.

Piaget, J. (1977). *The development of thought: Equilibration of cognitive structures.* New York: Viking Press.

Popielarz, P.A. (1990). *On the edge: Niche position and membership duration in voluntary associations.* Unpublished master's thesis, Cornell University, Ithaca, NY.

Popielarz, P.A. (1992). *Connection and competition: A structural theory of sex segregation in voluntary associations.* Unpublished doctoral dissertation, Cornell University, Ithaca, NY.

Popielarz, P.A., & McPherson, J.M. (1995). On the edge or in between: Niche position, niche overlap, and the duration of voluntary association memberships. *American Journal of Sociology, 101,* 698–720.

Prestby, J.E., Wandersman, A., Florin, P., Rich, R., & Chavis, D.M. (1990). Benefits, costs, incentive management and participation in voluntary associations: A means to understanding and promoting empowerment. *American Journal of Community Psychology, 18,* 117–150.

Reitschlin, J. (1988). Voluntary association membership and psychological distress. *Journal of Health and Social Behavior, 39,* 348–355.

Rodriguez, A.R. (1984). Special treatment needs of children of military families. In A.S. Gurman (Series Ed.) & F.W. Kaslow & R.I.

Ridenour (Vol. Ed.), *The military family: Dynamics and treatment* (pp. 46-72). New York: Guilford Press.

Shaw, J.A. (1987). Military psychiatry: Children in the military. *Psychiatric Annals, 17,* 539–544.

Srabstein, J. (1983). Geographic distribution of military dependent children: Mental health resources needed. *Military Medicine, 148,* 127–132.

Truscott, M.R. (1990). *Brats: Children of the military speak out.* New York: E.P. Dutton.

Ursano, R.J., Holloway, H.C., Jones, D.R., Rodriguez, A.R., & Belenky, G. L. (1989). Psychiatric care in the military community: Family and military stressors. *Hospital and Community Psychiatry, 40,* 1284–1289.

Useem, J., Useem, R., & Donoghue, J. (1963). Men in the middle of the third culture: The roles of Americans and non-western people in cross-cultural administration. *Human Organization, 22,* 169–179.

Vygotsky, L.S. (1962). *Thought and language.* New York: Wiley.

Wegner, K.W. (1991). Military Environment Inventory. In D.J. Keyser & R.C. Sweetland (Eds.), *Test Critiques* (pp. 436-442). Austin, TX: ProEd.

Werkman, S. (1979). The child raised overseas. In J.D. Noshpitz (Ed.), *Basic handbook of child psychiatry: Vol. 1. Development* (pp. 316-320). New York: Basic Books.

Wertsch, M.E. (1991). *Military brats: Legacies of childhood inside the Fortress.* New York: Harmony Books.

6

BEYOND ADOLESCENCE: THE EXPERIENCES OF ADULT CHILDREN OF MILITARY PARENTS*

MORTEN G. ENDER

INTRODUCTION

Many Americans have grown up in and around the military and other agencies such as the Foreign Service, missionary groups, and the international business community. They spent some or all of their childhood and/or adolescence sharing their organizational parents' career, including a lifestyle marked by mobility and foreign residence. This lifestyle sets them apart from their civilian peers. Their socialization in a family that was occupationally committed to a service organization has a long-term impact that is not yet fully understood. This chapter provides results from an ongoing study of this unique population and offers human service providers insight into the background and current characteristics of these men and women.

A small social movement has emerged among adult children from military and other kinds of organization-affiliated families, such as the State Department, international business, and missionaries. Among a number of similarities is a shared experience living abroad. The movement encompasses a loose network of ties among adult children from organization families, with the largest group from military families. "Military Brat" and "PK" (Preacher Kid) are some of the popular labels used by children, adolescents, youths, and adults from military and missionary families to identify themselves and by others to identify them.

Popular portrayals of growing up in a military or foreign service family are offered in such books as *Growing Up in Khaki: Life as a Service Brat* (Allingham, 1998); *Hidden Immigrants: Legacies of Growing Up Abroad* (Bell, 1997); *APO San Francisco 96525: Growing Up in the Military* (Grubbs, 1987); *Notes from a Traveling Childhood: Readings for Internationally Mobile Parents and Children* (McCluskey, 1994); *Army Brat: A Memoir* (Smith, 1980); *Strangers at Home: Essays on the Effects of Living Overseas and Coming "Home" to a Strange Land* (Smith, 1996); *The Absentee American: Expatriates' Perspective on America* (Smith, 1994); *Brats: Children of the Military Speak Out* (Truscott, 1989); *Army Brats: A Legacy of Military Family Life Inside the Fortress* (Wertsch, 1991); a popular magazine, *Nomad: The Brat Journal* (Ang, 1996); magazine articles (Long, 1986); comic strips (Army Times Publishing, 1997); and books made into films such as *The Great Santini* (Conroy, 1976). The label has also appeared in the names of associations such as Overseas Brats, Military Brats of America, Inc., Operation Footlocker, the American Overseas Schools Historical Society, and Military Brats, Inc. Adults from Foreign Service and missionary families have similar books and organizations (e.g., Global Nomads International).

The labels, popular media, and organizations denote the development of a social movement. In this sense, adult children from organization families share a collective form of behavior in which large numbers have organized to support and bring about awareness of their shared experience. The movement began with a few high school reunions, a recognition of a collective identity, the confirmation of a shared ethos that remain fairly constant across and within generations, and the establishment of formalized not-for-profit and for-profit associations. Information technologies, including the Internet, e-mail, and other electronic forums, continue to propel the movement. Electronic resources provide a virtual community for people who do not have a common geographic space. Instant worldwide communication provides access to a collective space for members of this "community" who are scattered throughout the world.

Appendix 6.1 provides a list of some online organizations and individual homepages, alumni associations, and school homepages, USENET groups, LISTSERVs and electronic discussion lists, for-profit companies online, and other not-for-profit electronic sites related to growing up in an organization family, especially growing up overseas. Homepages from such groups are being added to the Internet at a rate of approximately one to three per week.

The number of people who have experienced the organization lifestyle is impressive. For example, in 1990, when the downsizing effect of the U.S. military had not yet been substantial, the 2 million active-duty military personnel had some 1,625,111 children under 21 years of age. One-fourth of these service members lived outside the United States. By the end of the Cold War in 1990, more than 5 million men and women were either on active duty, retired from, or in a reserve component of the U.S. armed forces (*Defense Almanac*, 1990).

This chapter highlights information from a study of adult children from primarily military families but includes others whose parent(s) worked overseas for a period during their childhood and/or adolescence. While similar studies with large samples are available (Cottrell & Useem, 1994; Gerner, Perry, Moselle, & Archbold, 1992; Salmon, 1988), the present study provides the largest single sampling of adult children from military families. Human service providers will benefit from the research on this community of people scattered around the world. Foremost, they will gain an appreciation for the diversity of experience that exists in military and other organization families.

RESEARCH DESIGN

Sample

The participants in this study (a sample of 607 men and women) were surveyed between 1991 and 1997 from a variety of sources using a snowball sampling approach (one contact was used to locate another). Potential participants were solicited through (1) under-graduate sociology courses at two eastern U.S. universities, (2) two Department of Defense Dependents Schools (DODDS) high school reunions in the Washington, D.C., area in 1992 and 1993, (3) an electronic chain referral sampling method via the Internet, NEWS-GROUPS, LISTSERV, electronic bulletin boards, and electronic mail distribution lists, (4) print advertisements in the *Overseas Brats* magazine, which caters to adults who attended DODDS outside of the United States, and (5) two regional newspapers in the U.S. upper Midwest.

Some respondents volunteered to serve as "electronic" research assistants. Many respondents requested multiple questionnaires to distribute to others considered eligible to participate. These individ-uals provided questionnaires to family members, friends, and/or their alumni. Others provided additional participant contacts through siblings, friends, and acquaintances. Many of the sources were eventually cross listed. For example, electronic bulletin board messages were downloaded and published in print media newspa-pers and newsletters.

Measures

The original questionnaire used for the larger study is 11 pages in length and includes both forced response and open-ended ques-tions. Forced response items include (1) organization family history, (2) social history and demographics, and (3) present lifestyle. Two specific forced response scale items are an organizational lifestyle stress inventory based on the demands of the military lifestyle and a life satisfaction scale. Open-ended questions provide an opportunity for respondents to elaborate on their experiences.

Procedure

After reading or hearing of the call for participants, potential respondents contacted me via regular mail, telephone, or electronic

mail and volunteered to participate or requested additional information about participating in the study. Eligible respondents provided a
regular mailing address. Each eligible participant received one or
more copy(ies) of the 11-page questionnaire with instructions on
how to complete and return it in the self-addressed stamped envelope. The survey was administered between 1991 and 1997. Potential respondents totaled 1,160 with 607 completing (response rate of
52%).

Family History

The data in Table 6.1 show the frequency and percentage distribution of the respondents' parents' organizational affiliation service
branch. Just over three-fourths of the sample (78.5%) came from
military families (Army 34.4%; Air Force 36.4%, Navy 6.6%,
Marine Corps 0.8%; or Coast Guard 0.2%). Of the military family
respondents, parents were reported as either officer (60.7%) or
enlisted (39.3%) service members. The remaining 21.5% of the
respondents came from foreign service (3.9%), international business
(1.5%), missionary (1.7%), civilian government employee (11.5%),
or "other" (2.9%) agencies. Other occupations include international
school educators, visiting professors, Red Cross workers, or other
non-governmental workers (NGOs) such as medical doctors.

Of those responding ($n = 590$), most had siblings (95%). The
average was two, with a range from none to seven or more. Almost
three-quarters (73.3%) of the respondents reported that their parent
had served in a major war during the 20th century. Most had served
in Vietnam (33.3%) or World War II (23.6%). A small, but notable,
number served in World War II, Korea, *and* Vietnam (13.4%).

Most of the parents of respondents had retired from service by
the time they participated in the survey (90.5%). The respondents
at the time of the parents' retirement ranged in age from 1 to 49
(their average age was about 21). Almost all of those responding
reported that their parents had retired in North America (96.1%).
Of those providing valid responses, the five popular retirement
states are, in order of popularity, Texas, California, Florida,

Virginia, and Maryland. All other states and the District of
Columbia are represented except Arkansas. These results parallel
where former U.S. military service members generally retire (*Defense
Almanac*, 1990).

Table 6.1. Frequency and Percentage of Adult Children by Parents' Service Branch.

Branch of Service	frequency	%
Army	203	34.4
Air Force	215	36.4
Navy	39	6.6
Marines	5	.8
Coast Guard	1	.2
Foreign Service	28	3.9
International Business	9	1.5
Missionaries	10	1.7
US Government Civilian	68	11.5
Other	17	2.9
Total	590*	100%

*Seventeen cases did not provide valid responses.

DEMOGRAPHICS AND SOCIAL HISTORY

At the time of the survey, the respondents ranged in age from 15
to 46. The average age was approximately 39 years. More women
than men responded to the survey (58.4%). The vast majority lived
in North America (96.6%), and more than half reported living in
large urban areas and suburbs near large cities (55.8%). Similar to
where organization parents retire, most respondents report living in
Virginia (14.8%), Texas (9.7%), California (9.3%), Maryland (9%),
and Florida (5.1%) at the time of the survey. All states and the
District of Columbia are represented with the exception of Rhode
Island.

Of those responding, whites are overrepresented (90.5%).
African (2.5%), Hispanic (1.5%), Asian (1.0%), mixed (1.7%), and
other Americans (2.8%) are underrepresented. African Americans
are generally overrepresented in the U.S. military, especially in the

lower and enlisted ranks, in contrast to their proportional representation in the larger U.S. society.

Most respondents reported being married at the time of the survey (61.9%), and the number of their children ranged from none to five or more. The average number of children was one, and most reported having no children (43.4%). Twenty-one percent of the married and divorced respondents met their spouse while they were overseas with their families.

The respondents reported significant educational achievement. Slightly more than 95% indicated at least some college and 29.1% possessed an advanced degree beyond baccalaureate. Occupationally, of those responding, most were either professionals (29.5%), in business management (16.2%), students (11.2%), or spread across other categories including clerical work, skilled and unskilled labor, military, government employed, homemaker, unemployed, or other work situations at the time of the survey.

A small number of respondents reported to be currently serving in the military (5.7%) at the time of the survey, and a large proportion had prior military service (21.8%). Of those with military experience, most were in the enlisted ranks (57.4%). The majority served in the Army (45.7%), followed by the Air Force (34%), Navy (16%), and the Marine Corps (4.3%). Of those responding, most reported having served six years or less (61.3%). Among current servers, most were officers (63.3%) and serving in the Air Force (52.4%).

Among those reporting never serving in the military, slightly more than half said they generally had no interest in serving (53.3%). The next largest coded category attributed not serving as a consequence of their gender, in particular being female (16.9%). Others said they did not like the regimented orientation or the lifestyle of the military. A handful reported to be pacifist. Political orientations were reported and were equally distributed on a five-point scale ranging from very conservative (7.9%) to very liberal (11.7%), with most reporting to be middle of the road.

Today, many adult children from organization-families report traveling outside of the United States. About half (44.3%) travel outside the United States once a year or more for leisure and fewer for business (13.2%).

The information in Table 6.2 shows the frequency and percentage of total moves in two move intervals between birth and their first relocation after completing high school. The average number of moves is eight. Adult children from Army families reported the most moves at nine, followed by the at Navy eight; Air Force, eight; foreign service, eight; the Marine Corps, eight; missionary and others, seven; international business, seven; the Coast Guard, six; and civilian government workers six.

Geographic mobility and foreign residence permeate the experience of the sample. While growing up in their organization families, virtually all respondents reported having spent time overseas between birth and completing high school. The range of time was from 1 to 20-plus years. The average number of years overseas was seven. The most frequent number of years spent overseas was four. For most, this meant spending at least one "tour" with their parents overseas. As a group, eight years was the average number of years spent overseas over the course of their lifetime. Some reported having returned overseas as adults to live and work.

Table 6.2. Frequency and Percentage of Adult Children from Military and Other Organization Families by Number of Moves.

Number of Moves	frequency	%
1 to 2 moves	24	4.0
3 to 4 moves	50	8.3
5 to 6 moves	122	20.3
7 to 8 moves	174	29.0
9 to 10 moves	136	22.7
11 to 12 moves	66	11.0
13 or more moves	28	4.7
Total	600*	100%

*Seven cases did not provide valid responses.

Respondents were asked to identify one to three countries where they had lived while growing up. The vast majority listed residence in at least one foreign country (97%), fewer listed a second (63%), and still fewer listed a third (31%). Seventy countries were represented in the sample, including the more obvious but notable places such as Germany, Britain, Italy, Thailand, and Japan, and the less notable such as Senegal, Bahrain, Cuba, and Honduras.

More in-depth, respondents were asked to rank the degree to which they had mingled with the local populations in their host country. Almost two-thirds (65%) of the respondents reported that they had mingled between "often" and "totally" with people in their host country.

Finally, respondents were asked about second-language acquisition while growing up. Twenty-five languages were reported, including an "other" category. A stunning 80.9% reported to have spoken one additional language other than English while growing up, 37.9% spoke two additional languages, and 14.3% reported speaking at least three. Among the one additional language group, about 57% reported their proficiency level to be moderate or proficient. The five most popular languages spoken were German, Spanish, French, Japanese, and Italian. Less frequently occurring languages include Farsi, Vietnamese, and Swahili.

ATTITUDES AND OPINIONS

The information in Table 6.3 shows the average for levels of stress for each of nine organization lifestyle demands by the respondents' parents' branch of service affiliation. Two "Other" categories also are reported. Respondents were allowed to write in one or two stressful demands that they thought warranted reporting. The latter three columns in the table have parents' service affiliations aggregated. This is done because some respondent subgroups are fairly small. The scores on the item measure are 1 = "Not at all," 2 = "Slightly," 3 = "A little bit," 4 = "Moderately," 5 = "Quite a bit," and 6 = "Extremely."

In comparing the subgroups of respondents, adult children of civilian government workers had the most variability in their answers. They experienced less stress with normative constraints of their organization, parental separation, and transition to civilian status, and slightly more stress with antimilitarism and residence in foreign countries than any other group. Adults from international business, foreign service, missionary, and other types of families varied somewhat as well. They reported less stress with organization-sanctioned machismo, personal antimilitarism, and risk of parental death or injury.

Table 6.3. Means* for Organization Lifestyle Demand Stresses by Parents' Service Affiliation (N = 582).**

Organization Lifestyle Demands	Total Sample (N = 582)	Army (n = 200)	Air Force (n = 214)	Navy, Marines, & Coast Guard (n = 42)	International Business, Foreign Service, Missionaries, & Others (n = 58)	Government Civilians (n = 68)
Geographic Mobility	3.19	3.20	3.07	3.52	3.39	3.20
Normative Constraints	2.84	2.98	2.89	3.04	2.42	2.51
Family Separation	2.64	2.75	2.71	2.81	2.52	2.13
Transition to Civilian Life	2.45	2.62	2.73	2.12	1.57	1.91
Parental Risk of Death/Injury	2.07	2.35	2.14	1.95	1.49	1.55
Foreign Residence	2.04	2.12	1.83	2.24	2.12	2.29
Parental Shiftwork	1.78	1.77	1.85	1.57	2.02	1.55
Masculine-Dominated Subculture	1.53	1.64	1.52	1.59	1.15	1.52
Personally Anti-Military	1.39	1.3	1.37	1.54	1.23	1.62
Other 1*** (n = 160)	4.89	4.77	5.09	4.91	4.74	4.76
Other 2 (n = 72)	4.96	4.88	5.22	4.00	4.89	5.25

*Scaled responses range from 1 (not at all) to 5 (extremely stressful).
**Twenty-five respondents did not provide valid responses.
***Both Other items are added to the scale on the questionnaire to allow the respondent to write in any untapped demands of organization life and report the level of stress.

Overall, the highest averages for all groups between the lifestyle demands are geographic mobility, normative constraints imposed by the organization, and parental separation. The overall least stressful demands are antimilitarism, living in a masculine-dominated culture, and potential shiftwork.

Life-satisfaction-type questions were asked of these respondents. Life-satisfaction questions are standard questions asked of a random sample of Americans on the General Social Survey. Items query respondents about levels of satisfaction with life areas from "A very great deal" to "No" satisfaction in six areas of their life—family, friends, job, nonwork activities, health, and the place they live. Since 1972, Americans in general have been fairly consistent in their responses to the scale. Family, friends, and health are reported to be the most satisfying, with work, nonwork activities, and place of residence still high in satisfaction, but less than the first three. In the present study, the top three areas of satisfaction (in order from highest to lowest satisfaction) are almost identical to the general U.S. population—family, friends, and nonwork activities, followed by job, health, and place of residence.

DISCUSSION

Growing up in a military or other type of organization family, such as Foreign Service or missionary, nestled in a work environment during the Cold War set people geographically and culturally apart from their "civilian" peers. Characteristics of their lifestyle growing up include significant geographic mobility, risk of parental death or injury, family separation, parent's shiftwork, constraints imposed by the organization and the host country, masculine-dominated employment subcultures, counterculture leanings, foreign residence, and transitions to civilian life. These occupational demands impinge on families. Many of these demands are found individually in the civilian society; however, these demands are unique to military and other organization life.

While the present study is not the largest sample of such a population to be collected (Cottrell & Useem, 1994), it is the largest sample of adult children from military families collected to date. It should be noted that the present sample is by no means representative of the entire population of adult children from military or other organization families. Indeed, once I advertised for and located people to participate in this study, they inevitably self-selected themselves to participate.

Nonetheless, until a random sample or significantly larger sample is collected, the present study provides a profile of the typical adult child from military or other organization families who came of age during the Cold War. This being duly noted, the typical respondent in this study can be described.

Today, a social movement has emerged among people from military and other organization families. A major feature of this social movement is reconnecting with people and legitimizing one's experience growing up mobile and abroad. This group is culturally rooted in a society that values individuality, family, community, and nationality. They have transported these values from new home to new home and even abroad. Today, these adults find themselves relatively settled and seeking to anchor their experiences of family separation from parents and extended kin, organization rules and regulations, geographic mobility, and living abroad. Information technologies are assisting them in their efforts and providing them with a collective consciousness in the form of virtual community. While rooted in the universal values of American culture, they have acquired shared experiences through organization life that set them apart from their civilian peers.

Adult children from organization families appear diverse. Foremost, the social structure demands of the various organizations can vary. For example, missionary life requires extended tours in a particular country, generally isolated from other Americans. Military family life abroad almost always involves transferring American accoutrements such as movies, commissaries, and schools abroad. Second, their numbers vary. Adult children from military families make up the largest proportion within this population. Their numbers are followed by Foreign Service and missionary people. International business, civilian government workers, educators, and NGO workers comprise smaller numbers of the remaining groups. Third, some parents might work for more than one organization while their children are still living at home. For example, an Army officer might retire from military service and begin work for a U.S. embassy abroad.

The typical respondent in the present study is different from his or her civilian peers and somewhat different from adult children of military families in general. He or she comes from an officer's family where the father is a war veteran. This number is somewhat skewed as most service members come from the enlisted service member ranks, where enlisted service members outnumber officers 70 to 1 (with the caveat that most of the enlisted soldiers are young, between 18 and 24 years of age, and in their first term of service). In the larger population, adult children from military and other organization families are found in all age categories, including when their parents retire. In the present study, 21 years is the average age. Further, the typical respondent probably lives near his or her retired parents in an urban or semi-urban area—perhaps near a military installation with support services such as medical care, commissary, and post exchange privileges. Yet, they may live anywhere in the United States or abroad. The respondents also is likely to travel abroad for work and play.

The typical respondent in this study probably grew up in a traditional household with the father as a service member. However, the military is increasingly reflecting the changes in the larger U.S. society where a postmodern family is becoming normative. Military families are increasingly nontraditional—single mother or father, reconstituted families, dual-career families, and extended kinship families beyond the nuclear family (Segal, 1989). There is no reason to suspect other U.S. agencies are not being influenced by social trends in American families in the larger society and reflecting these trends as well.

In the present study, the typical respondent was 39 years of age, married, a professional with some military training, was politically moderate, and travels. Yet, the ages of the respondents will continue to vary as U.S. military service members continue a trend of marrying and having children earlier than their civilian peers. The typical study respondent was highly educated. Many were working on an advanced degree beyond their undergraduate degree. This level of education reflected two attributes—a high value placed on education among service families and occupations of parents where credentialing played a significant role in career advancement. In addition, the highly educated may have played a role in skewing the sample for the present study. While the access to computers and the Internet are becoming more and more popular throughout American society, at the time of data collection for the present study, the more educated in society had greater access to information technologies and may have been more receptive to my electronic call for participants.

The data on geographic mobility and overseas tours reflect mobility in service organization families. In the present study, the typical adult child from an organization family member moved about eight times before graduating from high school. He or she lived overseas, mostly in Germany, for at least four years. In contrast to popular perceptions of isolated American military communities in Germany and elsewhere, adult children reported to have inter-acted with people from their host countries, learned the language to varying degrees, and made friends. This finding supports earlier research in the 1970s and 1980s on military family adolescents over-seas focused on second-language acquisition (Rainey, 1978) and interactions with the local populations (Tyler, 1990).

Geographic mobility, normative constraints, and family separa-tion are reported as the most stressful lifestyle demands from experi-ences from adults growing up in an organization family. The stresses of mobility reported here by adults are consistent with research findings from the 1960s through the 1990s on children and espe-cially adolescents (Hunter, 1982; Hunter & Nice, 1978; Steinglass & Edwards, 1993). No long-term follow-up studies of these groups were conducted. The present study does support earlier findings. Moreover, those early findings couple with the preliminary results reported here, that the experiences of growing up mobile have a long-term impact on the cohort of children from the Cold War.

The stresses of normative constraints are a new finding and contribution to the research literature on military families. Norma-tive constraints are direct and indirect rules and regulations. They may diverge from civilian norms and are dictated by the host country and the organization. For example, curfews on bases might differ from locale to locale. They are directly imposed on the service members and their family members. Virtually no research has addressed normative constraints, and this area could benefit from further study. The data reported here suggest that normative constraints imposed on children and adolescents for their behavior have some stressful features, and they may be long-term.

Finally, military family separation studies are not new (Hill, 1949), nor are studies of children separated from their parents (Carlsmith, 1964). There is an increased interest in this area of research in recent years especially following experiences during the Persian Gulf War (Jensen & Shaw, 1996). These findings and others suggest some degree of long-term implication of growing up in a military or other organization, and the topic deserves continued focus on the part of social scientists and some concern among practitioners.

SUMMARY AND IMPLICATIONS

This chapter presents results from a study of adult children from military families and people whose parent(s) worked overseas for U.S. organizations for a period during their childhood, youth, and adolescence. It is one of the largest samples of data collected from adult children from military families. The chapter describes what might be the characteristics of the typical adult child from a military family while remaining grounded in the demographic, psychological, and historical research on this population.

Human service providers need to recognize the diversity of experience that exists within the population of adult children from organization families in general. This diversity is rooted in generational differences, varied household configurations, geographic residences, different organizational experiences, and, finally, a significant amount of mobility and experiences living abroad during their formative educational years. Few people have lived such a life.

This shared experience among a minority of Americans, including mobility and overseas experiences, sets them apart from their "civilian" peers. This shared sense of "otherness" has constructed an atypical socialization that they are only as adults beginning to appreciate. Increasingly, policies are being implemented to help ease the social and psychological experiences of living under the demands of organizational life, especially military family life (e.g., children of veterans, POWs, and MIAs). The paradox is that many adult children from military and other organization family situations feel their experience has provided them an unprecedented opportunity that not many people are afforded—extensive travel and living in new, different, and exciting places and cultures around the world. I believe such experiences can foster resilience, tolerance, and worldliness (Ender, 1996), characteristics essential for successful living in an increasingly diverse and global social and economic society. These experiences can also contribute to feelings of rootlessness (Cottrell & Useem, 1994). Some of the adults in this study recognize the positive and negative attributes associated with their early life experiences. The paradox is the social and psychological weight associated with geographic mobility juxtaposed with the awesome experiences gained once they have moved to and experienced a new and diverse place and culture. The approach to success appears to be reconciling the two-organization lifestyle demands of moving and living.

Geographic mobility and foreign residence are likely to increase for Americans in the future as occupations become more fluid and economies become more international. Information technology and modern transportation have bridged the distance between American and foreign cultures. At the same time, separation may become more prevalent for future generations of adult children from military and other organization families. The demands of service life will not disappear; rather the intensity of the demands will simply shift.

NOTE

*The chapter is previously published as Morten G. Ender (2000). "Beyond adolescence: The experiences of adult children of military parents." In James Martin, Leora Rosen, and Lynnette Sparacino (Ed.), *The Military Family: A Practice Guide for Human Service Providers* (pp. 241-255). Westport CT: Praeger. It is reprinted with permission.

REFERENCES

Allingham, G.E. (1998). *Growing up in khaki: Life as a service brat.* Fuquay-Varina, NC: Research Triangle Publications.

Ang, A. (1996, December 3). A magazine for nomadic military brats. *San Francisco Chronicle*, p. A9.

Army Times Publishing. (1997). Military brats. http://www. armytimes.com/bratpg.html.

Bell, L. (1997). *Hidden immigrants: Legacies of growing up abroad.* Notre Dame, IN: Cross Cultural Publications.

Carlsmith, L. (1964). Effect of early father absence on scholastic aptitude. *Harvard Educational Review, 34*, 3–21.

Conroy, P (1976). *The great Santini.* Boston, MA: Houghton-Mifflin.

Cottrell, A.B., & Useem, R.H. (1994, March). ATCKs maintain global dimensions throughout their lives. *Newslinks: The Newspaper of International Schools Services*, pp. 1, 14, and 30.

Defense Almanac. (1990). Defense 90. Alexandria, VA: Armed Forces Information Services.

Ender, M.G. (1996). Recognizing healthy conflict: The postmodern self. *Global Nomad Perspectives Newsletter, 4*(1), 13–14.

Gerner, M., Perry, F., Moselle, M.A., & Archbold, M. (1992). Characteristics of internationally mobile adolescents. *Journal of School Psychology, 30*, 197–214.

Grubbs, J. (1987). *APO San Francisco 96525: Growing up in the military.* Springfield, IL: Independent Publishing.

Hill, R. (1949). *Families under stress: Adjustment to the crises of war separation and reunion.* New York: Harper & Row (reprinted by Greenwood Press, Westport, CT, 1971).

Hunter, E.J. (1982). *Families under the flag: A review of military family literature.* New York: Praeger.

Hunter, E.J., & Nice, D.S. (Eds.). (1978). *Children of military families: A part yet apart.* Washington, DC: Superintendent of Documents, U.S. Government Printing Office.

Jensen, P.S., & Shaw, J.A. (1996). The effects of war and parental deployment upon children and adolescents. In R.J. Ursano & A.E. Norwood (Eds.), *Emotional aftermath of the Persian Gulf War:*

Veterans, families, communities, and nations (pp. 83–109). Washington, DC: American Psychiatric Press, Inc.

Long, P. (1986, December). Growing up military. *Psychology Today*, 31–37.

McCluskey, K.C. (Ed.). (1994). *Notes from a traveling childhood: Readings for internationally mobile parents and children*. Washington, DC: Foreign Service Youth Foundation Publication.

Rainey, M.C. (1978). Language learnings of internationally mobile military youth: Some third culture comparisons. In E.J. Hunter & D.S. Nice (Eds.), *Children of military families: A part yet apart* (pp. 83–100). Washington, DC: Superintendent of Documents, U.S. Government Printing Office.

Salmon, J.L. (1988). *The relationship of stress and mobility to the psychosocial development and well-being of third-culture-reared early adults*. Unpublished doctoral dissertation, University of Florida, Tallahassee, FL.

Segal, M.W. (1989). The nature of work and family linkages: A theoretical perspective. In G.L. Bowen & D.K. Orthner (Eds.), *The organization family: Work and family in the U.S. military* (pp. 3–36). New York: Praeger.

Smith, C.D. (1994). *The absentee American: Repatriates' perspectives on America and its place in the contemporary world*. Bayside, NY: Aletheia Publications.

Smith, C.D. (Ed.). (1996). *Strangers at home: Essays on the effects of living overseas and coming "home" to a strange land*. Bayside, NY: Aletheia Publications.

Smith, W.J. (1980). *Army brat: A memoir*. New York: Persea Books.

Steinglass, P., & Edwards, M.E. (1993). *Family relocation study, final report*. A report by the Ackerman Institute for Family Therapy for the Family Liaison Office. New York: United States Department of State.

Truscott, M.R. (1989). *Brats: Children of the military speak out*. New York: E.P. Dutton.

Tyler, M.P. (1990). American teenagers abroad: A view from one military community. *SOWI Socialwissenschaftliches Institute der Bundeswehr* Forum, IX, 13–17.

Wertsch, M.E. (1991). *Military brats: Legacies of childhood inside the fortress*. New York: Harmony Books.

Appendix 6.1
Available Resources (Web sites and e-mail addresses are accurate as of 1999)

Online Organizations:

THE AMERICAN OVERSEAS SCHOOLS HISTORICAL SOCIETY Homepage
Web site: http://www.cpcug.org/user/cwoodell/aosa.html
Contact: Thomas T. Drysdale, Ed.D., President (overseass-chools@juno.com)
AMERICAN WORLD WAR II ORPHANS NETWORK
Contact: Annie Bennett Mix (anniemix@aol.com)
CANADIAN AIR FORCE BRATS ASSOCIATION Hompage
Web site: http://www.logicnet.com/alan.macleod/air.htm
Contact: Alan McLeod (alan.mcleod@bbs.logicnet.com)
CANADIAN FORCES BRATS Homepage
Web   site: http://fn2.freenet.edmonton.ab.ca/~cfbrat/cfbrat.html
Contact: Taunja (cfbrats@freenet.edmonton.ab.ca)
THE CANADIAN MILITARY BRAT LIST Homepage
Web site: http://www.milbrats.net/
Contact: Susan Minaker (minaker@zoology.ubc.ca)
EXPAT FORUM Homepage
Web site: http://www.expatforum.com
Contact: (webwiz@expatforum.com)
GLOBAL NOMADS INTERNATIONAL Homepage
Web site: http://globalnomads.association.com
Contact: (info@gni.org)
MILITARY BRATS Online
Homepage: http://www.lynxu.com/brats/index.html#top
Contact and Page Owner: Vann Baker (vannb@aol.com)
MILITARY BRATS Registry Homepage
Web site: http://www.military-brats.com/
Contact: Mike B. Curtis (usbrats@aol.com)

OPERATION FOOTLOCKER Homepage
Web site: http://www.tckworld.com/opfoot/index.html
Contact: Gene Moser (opfoot@tckworld.com)
UNIVERSITY OF MARYLAND MUNICH GERMANY ALUMNI
Homepage
Web site: http://cpcug.org:80/user/cwoodell/)
Contact: Carlton Woodell (cwoodell@cpcug.org)

USENET NEWS GROUPS

alt.culture.military-brats
can.military-brats

ELECTRONIC DISCUSSION LISTS

MILITARY BRATS DISCUSSION LIST: M-BRATS@LIST-
SERV.IUPUI.EDU
Contact: Ann Holcombe (aholcomb@indyunix.iupui.edu)

PART 2: GROWING UP ABROAD IN ORGANIZATION FAMILIES

7

ATTACHMENT THEORY: A VIEW INTO THE GLOBAL NOMAD EXPERIENCE

BARBARA F. SCHAETTI

INTRODUCTION: UNDERSTANDING ATTACHMENT THEORY

From the moment of birth, an infant and the people in his or her immediate environment instinctively begin to develop mutually interdependent social bonds. In their vast array, these bonds are designed to ensure that humans meet one another's physiological, psychological, and sociocultural needs. Attachment theory delimits one such social bond. It pertains specifically to the bond between two people that reduces anxiety and thereby regulates security; as such, it is the bond that is most immediately implicated in species' survival (Bretherton, 1980).

Attachment theory was originally and is still typically conceived of as a relationship between an infant and his or her primary caregiver. It is distinct from affection per se: while an attachment relationship typically includes bonds of affection, not all bonds of affection indicate an attachment relationship (Ainsworth, 1991; McRoy, 1994).

At the heart of attachment theory is the supposition that humans are motivated to maintain a dynamic balance between, on the one hand, exploring the world in order to learn and, on the other, staying in close proximity to safety as embodied for an infant by his or her primary caregiver (Bretherton, 1992). In its broad sense, attachment theory articulates the systemic relationship between two (or more) individuals that enables each to find and maintain this balance.

Attachment Relationships

Attachment relationships begin to develop through the dynamic interplay of behavior/response/behavior. For example, a newborn infant cries when aroused by any one of numerous stimuli such as hunger or pain. A caregiver responds. Over time, as a caregiver both elicits and responds to the infant's increasingly broad range of behaviors, the behaviors become imbued with meaning and the infant, and the caregiver form a dyadic attachment relationship (Sroufe & Fleeson, 1986).

The quality of this relationship correlates directly to the ways in which the caregiver responds to the infant's signals (Ainsworth, Bell, & Stayton, 1971; Bowlby, 1973; Bretherton, 1980; Main, Kaplan, & Cassidy, 1985; Sroufe, 1979). When the caregiver responds consistently with warmth and sensitivity, a "secure" attachment relationship is said to develop; the infant learns that care is available when needed and that she or he is worthy of such care. When the caregiver response is inconsistent and/or inappropriate, an "insecure" attachment relationship develops.

Continuity is central to the development of secure attachment, in particular continuity of the attachment figure, of the quality of care she or he provides, and of the broader home environment. The attachment literature asserts discontinuity as potentially problematic for the development of a secure attachment style (Bowlby, 1973; Bretherton, 1992; Marris, 1991). It suggests that a "good" society is one that seeks to minimize disruptive events, thus protecting from harm each child's developing experience of attachment (Marris, 1991).

Ultimately, an individual's attachment system may be directed to a variety of people. Different attachment patterns may arrange themselves within a given individual as an "internal hierarchy" of attachment relationships, with the pattern associated with the primary caregiver being the most basic (Rachel & Manire, 1994).

Attachment relationships as per Bowlby and Ainsworth are limited to human relationships; individuals, however, are also impacted in their psychological development by their attachment to places, pets, and possessions (Altman & Low, 1992; Bowlby, 1973). These serve to remind us of where we come from, who we are, and of our relationship to the broader environment. They provide a sense of stability in our lives and both confirm and affirm our attachments to other people. Nonhuman attachments may serve as transitional objects (Winnicott, 1971), bridges dependence on an attachment figure for anxiety-reduction and their own ability to internalize that function directly (S. Manire, personal communication, September 29, 1999).

Attachment Systems: Internal Working Models

As the infant matures into adolescence and ultimately into adulthood, his or her attachment system becomes less organized around specific caregiving figures and more particularly around his or her own emergent self. What was dyadic regulation becomes self-regulation (Sroufe & Fleeson, 1986); what was first a behavioral organization referenced to the caregiver becomes over time an internal organization. Attachment theorists term this internal organization the attachment system, the representational system, or the individual's "internal working model" of relationship.

The notion of internal working models has significant implications. One of the most important may be that the relational and behavioral patterns that an individual first learns through dyadic regulation with the caregiver become patterns incorporated into self-regulation and, therefrom, become patterns that influence all of his or her subsequent relationships (Karen, 1990). Internal working models serve as "interpretive filters" through which meaning is made of each new experience. They influence an individual's ability to relate interpersonally and to develop competence in the instrumental environment (Rachel & Manire, 1994).

An individual who has formed an early secure attachment relationship will have internalized a working model of self-in-relationship, which assumes the self as worthy of love and of care as being readily available. Each new experience will be engaged through the influential filter of this foundational understanding. Conversely, an individual who has formed an early insecure attachment relationship will have internalized a working model in which worthiness and access to care are always in doubt. Research suggests that infant attachment patterns are thereby predictive of social competence and self-reliance among preschoolers (Karen, 1990), of healthy functioning in adolescence (Sroufe, in Karen, 1990), of success within the foster care and adoption systems (McRoy, 1994), of psychological adjustment in adulthood (Main et al., 1985), and of the kinds of preparation and support that will be most effective for individual international sojourners (Rachel & Manire, 1994).

Attachment Behaviors

Internal working models are identifiable through the patterning of an individual's attachment behaviors over time and in particular contexts (Sroufe & Fleeson, 1986; Sroufe & Waters, 1977). Attachment behaviors refer to any of many different behaviors in which a child may commonly engage so as to attain and/or maintain a desired proximity to the caregiver (Bowlby, 1982).

Theorists emphasize that most behaviors serve more than one behavioral system (Bretherton, 1980; Rachel & Manire, 1994; Sroufe & Waters, 1977). The same behavior can variously express the desire to explore, to interact, to be cautious, to be comforted, and so on. A child who runs over to his or her attachment figure and reaches out to be picked up may, for example, be seeking to reduce his or her anxiety but may as easily be looking for someone with whom to play. The behavior itself is essentially meaningless unless the broader context is also considered: were the child and attachment figure recently separated; did the child perceive a threat that

caused anxiety? Behaviors that in one context are designed to activate attachment relationships, that is, to activate the dyadic proxim-
ity- and security-regulating system, in another context may be
designed with something quite different in mind.

Attachment behaviors can also be enacted by attachment
figures. When they perceive a risk to the child that the child does
not, or which the child chooses to ignore in the face of a more
compelling stimulus for exploration, attachment figures may be the
ones to activate proximity-seeking behaviors (Bretherton, 1987;
Main et al., 1985).

Infant/Child Attachment Patterns

Mary Ainsworth identified three patterns of infant/child attachment summarized in Table 7.1: (1) secure attachment, (2) insecure
avoidant attachment, and (3) insecure ambivalent (anxious) attachment (Ainsworth et al., 1971). Mary Main later identified a fourth
(4) disorganized (disoriented) attachment (Main, 1990). Differences
among the four patterns can be understood by correlating each with
(1) the quality of caregiving received, (2) the degree to which an
infant attends preferentially to interpersonal relationships and/or to
the non-relational world, and (3) the child's emerging view of self
and other.

The four infant attachment patterns are types, and, except for
the last, are not pathologies (Butler, 1997). Research suggests that
secure attachment patterns provide the most flexibility and resilience
(Rachel & Manire, 1994). They correlate with an ability to build
relationships, demonstrate empathy, persist in the face of difficulty,
and solve problems competently.

While providing less flexibility and resilience, avoidant and
ambivalent patterns nevertheless represent children's strategic
attempts to fit into their environments; they are adaptations and
presumably the best ones possible under the prevailing circumstances (Sroufe, 1988). At the same time, however, avoidant and
ambivalent patterns are considered maladaptations. They compro-
mise the person's capacity for dealing with future developmental

issues, especially those involving intimate social relationships and parenting (Sroufe, 1988).

Table 7.1. Summary Table of Infant Attachment Patterns.

Infant Attachment Patterns	Preferential Focus of Attachment Patterns	View of Self and Other
1. Secure Also "Group B": Secure	Interpersonal relationships *and* nonrelational world	I'm Ok, you're Ok
2. Insecure Avoidant Also "Group A": Anxious avoidant	Nonrelational world	I'm Ok, you're not
3. Insecure Ambivalent Also "Group C": Anxious resistant	Interpersonal relationships	I'm not, you're Ok
4. Disorganized Also "Group D": Disoriented	Anxiety throughout	I'm not, you're not

1. Secure children have an attachment figure who is sensitive, accessible, and responsive; children learn to view others as trustworthy and dependable (Butler, 1997). They alternate easily between a focus on interpersonal relationships and on developing autonomy and independence (Rachel & Manire, 1994). Their emerging view of self and other can be summarized as "I'm OK and you're OK" (Bartholomew & Horowitz, 1991).

2. Insecure avoidant children have an attachment figure who is generally unavailable; children learn to attend only to themselves and to depend on no one else (Butler, 1997). They focus preferentially on the nonrelational world, seeking to develop autonomy and independence while ignoring interpersonal relationships (Rachel & Manire, 1994). Their emerging view of self and other is "I'm OK, you're not" (Bartholomew & Horowitz, 1991).

3. Insecure ambivalent (anxious) children have an attach-

ment figure who is inconsistent in his or her response; children learn to be more and more insistent as they search for the kind of parenting that is only sometimes available (Butler, 1997). These children focus on staying in close proximity to the caregiver while ignoring the nonrelational world and the opportunities it offers to develop autonomy and independence (Rachel & Manire, 1994). Their emerging view of self and others is "I'm not OK, you are" (Bartholomew & Horowitz, 1991).

4. Disorganized (disoriented) children have an attachment figure who is both unpredictable and who engenders fear (Butler, 1997). These children demonstrate anxiety both in relation to the caregiver and in relation to the broader environment, focusing successfully on neither. Unlike the avoidant or ambivalent children who demonstrate a coherent strategy in their attempts to invoke caregiving, disorganized children appear to lack strategy altogether (Karen, 1990). Perhaps, not surprisingly, their emerging view of self and others is "I'm not Ok and neither are you" (Bartholomew & Horowitz, 1991).

Attachment Across Cultures

From the very beginning, attachment researchers have stressed the universal, biologically driven nature of attachment (Ainsworth, 1991; Bowlby, 1973). They have also stressed that attachment is contextualized by culture (Bowlby, 1973; Main, 1990). "Attachment...affects individuals, it affects culture, and it affects the experience of an individual within a specific culture" (Rachel & Manire, 1994, p. 16).

In their review of the cross-cultural attachment literature, Rachel and Manire (1994) note that secure patterns of infant attachment are the norm worldwide. At the same time, however, they note that some cultures have a greater prevalence of avoidant attachment styles and others a greater prevalence of ambivalent attachment styles. Depending on the cultural context in which they are raised, securely attached individuals will tend to have a more avoidant or a more ambivalent secondary attachment preference. Rachel and Manire (1994) offer as an example the likelihood that securely attached individuals raised in a country such as The Netherlands would positively emphasize independent achievement and autonomy, while securely attached individuals raised in a country such as Japan would positively emphasize interpersonal relationships and interdependency.

Moreover, what appears in one culture as avoidant behavior may in another cultural system demonstrate secure attachment behavior. Similarly, two different cultures may reward the same attachment behavior but may do so for two very different reasons.

Section Summary

Attachment is universal and biologically driven. It begins in infancy in the context of a dyadic relationship with the primary caregiver and becomes increasingly self-regulating through the unconscious development of internal working models of self, others, and relationships. Attachment behaviors, viewed in context, identify a range of infant/child patterns. These are necessarily culturally dependent and culturally influenced, although the importance of caregiver sensitivity and competence appear to be consistent regardless of cultural context.

Attachment theory speaks directly to the global nomad experience; that is, the experience of people who lived one or more of their developmental years outside their passport country(s) because of a parent's occupation. The following section considers various facets of the global nomad experience through the lens of attachment.

IMPLICATIONS OF ATTACHMENT THEORY FOR THE GLOBAL NOMAD EXPERIENCE

Global nomads encounter many of the circumstances, or variations on the circumstances, with which attachment theory is most directly concerned. For the global nomad, these emerge in large measure through the experience of mobility and intercultural contact.

The following subsections use attachment theory as a framework through which to consider (1) global nomad mobility, (2) the attachment figure's response to mobility, (3) host national caregivers as attachment figures, (4) sequential caregivers as attachment figures, (5) global nomad attachment to family, places, and possessions, and (6) global nomad grief.

Global Nomad Mobility and Attachment

The global nomad life experience is typically fraught with change—changing places, people, pets, possessions, often in regular three-year cycles. It is possible to say that the primary source of continuity for the global nomad is, in fact, discontinuity (Pollock & McCaig, 1987; Schaetti, 1995; Schaetti, 1996b). The attachment literature would thus seem to suggest that global nomads are at significant risk when seeking to develop secure attachment relationships.

Paradoxically, the degree to which frequent change puts a child's attachment system at risk is influenced at least in part by the quality of the child's attachment system at the time change is first experienced. Research demonstrates that securely attached children have a much easier time adapting to mobility and to changing circumstances than insecure or disorganized children (Rachel & Manire, 1994; Sroufe & Fleeson, 1986). A child whose relationship history is secure, whose internal working model of relationships supports him or her in being flexible and sociable, in exploring new environments, in persistently and competently solving problems, and in functioning somewhat independently (Rachel & Manire, 1994) is likely to more successfully transition through repeated international relocations (Bridges, 1980; Bridges, 1987; Pollock & Van Reken, 1999). At the same time, the attachment literature suggests that frequent change in the external environment could, in and of itself, hinder the generalizing-out of secure attachment from the attachment figure to home, school, and the broader world (S. Manire, personal communication, September 29, 1999). Problems are most likely to occur when change places the child in a new environment that is less responsive to the child than the previous environment (McRoy, 1994).

The Attachment Figure's Response to Mobility

A child's ability to generalize-out trust to the new environment is directly related to the way his or her attachment figure engages that environment (Bowlby, 1982; Butler, 1997; Sroufe, 1979; Sroufe & Fleeson, 1986). This is especially true for infants and younger children whose attachment system is still more dyadically regulated rather than self-regulated (Sroufe & Fleeson, 1986).

Attachment figures who suddenly find themselves in environments that are unfamiliar (a new country with an unknown language and cultural context), unsafe (can't drink the water; need immunizations, malaria pills, and mosquito nets), or violent (the threat of terrorism, war, evacuation, school shootings) necessarily pass their concerns on to their children. They evoke new rules and regulations, new proscriptions for behavior. They identify danger where before they might not; they limit their children's exploration by insisting on proximity whether the child's attachment system has called for it or not.

The opposite is, of course, equally true. The attachment figure who encounters the culturally new and different as an adventure to be fully enjoyed may help inculcate such an adventuresome spirit in his or her child—especially if in the midst of his or her own sense of adventure the attachment figure remains sensitively attuned to the child's need for proximity and anxiety reduction.

It should be said that the very role of the nonsalaried spouse in an international move poses potential challenges for any attachment relationships in which she or he may be involved. The nonsalaried spouse typically has the most challenging role to play in an international relocation (Adler, 1986; Schaetti & Ramsey, 1999a). With primary responsibility for establishing the family in its new home, she or he must navigate a new country and not simply a new office or school, must do so without the benefit of a secretary or teacher as cultural informant, must typically interact with the least internationally sophisticated segment of the host national community, and, having left behind a career as so many nonsalaried expatriate spouses still do, must recraft a professional identity into something salient in the new environment. For a young infant in particular, with an attachment system still in initial formation and subject to dyadic regulation, the risks are very real when the primary caregiver is less responsive because of cultural distraction or psychological depression (Bowlby, 1982).

Host National Caregivers as Attachment Figures

It is not uncommon for expatriate infants to have host national caregivers: amahs, ayahs, nannies. In some instances, these host nationals become not simply additional caregivers but in fact take primary responsibility for the infant's or child's well-being.

Certainly, there are significant benefits to a young global nomad in constant interaction with a host national caregiver, not least the opportunity to develop fluency in the host language and literacy in the host culture. Two concerns present themselves when reviewing the attachment literature however (1) the potential for cultural dissonance with the passport country culture and (2) the inevitable loss of the attachment relationship when the child moves away. The first concern is the target of attention here; the second is addressed in the following subsection.

As discussed earlier, national cultures tend as a rule to be secure in their attachment styles and to variously emphasize characteristics of either an avoidant or ambivalent attachment (Rachel & Manire, 1994). Countries can accordingly be classified as secure-avoidant or secure-ambivalent. A global nomad from a secure-avoidant country who grows up in a secure-ambivalent country will necessarily be influenced by the emphasis there on ambivalent attachment behaviors. This will be even more the case if the global nomad has as a primary caregiver an amah or ayah who, through that dyadic attachment relationship, helps to inculcate in the infant an attachment system with ambivalent characteristics. When that infant repatriates, perhaps now an adolescent or young adult, his or her ambivalent attachment characteristics will mis-fit the "home" country's emphasis on avoidant behaviors. Despite the substantive discourse on reentry and repatriation, the intercultural implications of this level of basic personality development has been overlooked.

Sequential Caregivers as Attachment Figures

It is ultimately not the secondary attachment tendencies of host national caregivers that is of most significance but, for many global nomads, the mere fact of changing from one caregiver to another. Indeed, multimover global nomads may change caregivers several times throughout their infancy and childhood. Not surprisingly, the unfamiliar experience of building long-term relationships is a common topic of conversation among adult global nomads.

As noted earlier, global nomads have the opportunity to acculturate to frequent change. They similarly have the opportunity to learn the kinds of skills that build relationships quickly (Pollock & Van Reken, 1999) and thus, perhaps, to be better able to build new attachment relationships and affectional bonds in each new host country (Bretherton, 1980). Some, however, develop a kind of "transition fatigue" (Schaetti, 1996b). The attachment literature speaks to this experience, suggesting that what is commonly considered "fear of strangers" may be more accurately resistance to once again having to engage in the building of new relationships (Bretherton, 1980).

Attachment and Global Nomad Grief

Attachment theory has always asserted the risks to an individual's attachment system of repeated cycles of loss and grief (Bowlby, 1973; Bowlby, 1980). Such cycles are central to the global nomad experience (Bell, 1996; McCluskey, 1994; Pollock & Van Reken,

1999; Smith, 1991), yet global nomad grief is notoriously disenfranchised (Pollock & Van Reken, 1999; Schaetti, 1995).

Three characteristics identify situations in which grief is disenfranchised (1) the relationship is not recognized, (2) the loss is not recognized, and (3) the griever is not recognized (Doka, 1989). Each of these is commonly applicable to the global nomad.

Global nomads and their parents form relationships of different qualities when in a host country and culture (Pollock & McCaig, 1987; Pollock & Van Reken, 1999): what to the global nomad is home is often to the parent a foreign country; what to the global nomad is a secondary or perhaps even primary caregiver is to the parent a servant; what to the global nomad is a "sacred object," emblematic of roots and of belonging, may be to the parent simply a pretty picture on the wall. The intensity of global nomad relationships with places, people, and possessions may be unfathomable to parents whose own, less formative experience of change, starts late in life. Ainsworth (1991) notes that affectional bonds, and perhaps even attachment relationships of a kind, are known to form when two individuals support one another during dangerous or fearful conditions. Global nomad friendships typically form under just such intrapsychic conditions: While a global nomad's physical safety may not be at risk upon arriving in a new host country, his or her sense of emotional security is indeed in jeopardy and remains so until a friendship is formed (Schaetti, 1995). Necessarily, and for the adolescent global nomad especially, such relationships assume attachment proportions that may nevertheless remain invisible to anyone else.

When parents and other adult caregivers do not recognize the intensity of a global nomad's relationships, then neither can the loss be appropriately recognized. When loss is not recognized, then expressions of grief are not validated as legitimate (Doka, 1989).

When global nomad grief is thus disenfranchised, the mourning of loss almost inevitably becomes "complicated." Mourning is also complicated when many losses are experienced simultaneously, when the loss involves a conflicted relationship, when the loss is sudden or violent or unexpected, and/or when there is little or no support for expressing the loss (Rando, 1993). While other factors also contribute to complicated mourning, those listed here are ones that typically relate to the global nomad experience (Pollock & McCaig, 1987; Pollock & Van Reken, 1999).

Section Summary

Considering the global nomad experience through the attachment literature calls forth many implications and concerns. These include the discontinuity in people, place, pets, and possessions wrought by global nomad mobility; the increased stress imposed upon attachment figures at the time of a move; the risks (as well as rewards) of host nationals taking on the role of primary caregiver; the potentially sequential nature of primary attachment relationships; and the disenfranchisement of global nomad grief.

ATTACHMENT-CORRELATED STRATEGIES IN SUPPORT OF GLOBAL NOMADS

The attachment literature offers suggestions for maximizing global nomad development of secure attachment. Interestingly, without any existing literature correlating attachment theory to the global nomad experience, many of the suggestions presented below are nonetheless commonly recommended by experienced relocation practitioners. Perhaps that is at least in part because attachment is about anxiety reduction, and anxiety is a key characteristic of living and moving among cultures.

Customizing Expatriate Family Services

Rachel and Manire, the first attachment scholars to apply attachment research specifically to the expatriate arena, emphasize the ways in which an understanding of attachment can substantially increase the effectiveness of employer-sponsored expatriate family services (Rachel & Manire, 1994). They can, in brief, be designed to maximally engage not only secure but also avoidant and ambivalent children. This might mean, for example, designing each learning component of a predeparture program so that it includes opportunities for independent mastery (for avoidant children) as well as for social interaction (for ambivalent children).

While avoidant children may prefer to surf the web for information about the country to which they are moving, ambivalent children may prefer to speak with somebody who currently lives there. Avoidant children may be less inclined to engage in the emotional work of leave-taking and may need more skill-building in how to make friends in the new location. Ambivalent children, while perhaps quick to make friends in the new environment, may need help learning to channel their emotions. Secure children will likely be able to find value in all forms of support and disorganized children in few or none.

Of course, it is not just the children's attachment style, and the services offered them that must be considered. Integral to a child's experience is that of his or her parents'. Expatriate services designed with attachment styles in mind can also help ensure that adult expatriates receive the support they need and thus are better able to respond to their children with sensitivity.

Engaging the Sociological International Microculture (IMC)

Expatriate communities, termed sociological "international microcultures" (IMCs) (Fontaine, 1987), are naturally emerging attempts by expatriates to re-create for themselves a familiar environment even while in an unfamiliar location. Bowlby emphasized the role of such social networks in the development of secure attachment relationships (Bretherton, 1992).

Sociological IMCs—typically through the efforts of the local international school(s), independent practitioners, and associations staffed by nonsalaried spouses—provide newcomers with a broad range of practical support. Perhaps even more importantly, they provide global nomads and their families with a measure of continuity from one international posting to another. While each host country is different, one sociological IMC has much in common with the next; each can therefore serve to somewhat mitigate the disruptive challenges to developing attachment relationships and attachment systems that an international move inevitably presents.

As sociological IMCs become more strategic in their provision of on-site services (Schaetti, 1996b; Schaetti, 1998), they too can begin to take attachment differentials into consideration. Upon arrival in their new school, for example, avoidant children might find an informative "welcome book" most useful while ambivalent children might prefer a "buddy" or "student welcomer" program. A secure child is, again, likely to get value from both and a disorganized child from neither.

Proactively Addressing Transitions

Without a doubt, the most important ingredient for a global nomad's development of secure attachment is the availability of his or her attachment figure(s) (Bowlby, 1973; Bretherton, 1987). Whatever the family's particular circumstances, parents should make a concerted effort to be consistently available to their children. Even parents with extensive professional and social commitments outside the home can maintain high-quality connections with their children (Schaetti, 1995). Open communication and consistency in family life; regular daily routines; predictable parenting and discipline; and frequent shared family activities are all particularly important (e.g., Bowlby, 1973; Pollock & Van Reken, 1999; Schaetti, 1995).

Attachment figures, as well as providing safe havens, can use the attachment relationship to help their children proactively address transitions; they can use the existing security-regulating system to teach a child what is to be feared and what is simply different (Bretherton, 1980). Interestingly, as documented in both the immigrant (Kagitcibasi, 1987; Martinez, 1994) and expatriate literatures (Pollock & Van Reken, 1999), the same principle may operate in reverse (Ainsworth, 1991) with the attachment figure learning what is to be feared and what is harmless by watching his or her child successfully engage the host environment.

The global nomad literature has long asserted that, for all the stress imposed by discontinuity, frequent change offers the chance to build adjustment and adaptation skills (Pollock & McCaig, 1987; Pollock & Van Reken, 1999; Schaetti, 1995). The attachment literature would seem to agree: "demonstrating coherence in individual development does not rest on continuity alone. Change may be comprehended as well" (Sroufe, 1979, p. 849).

Parents can accept demands for increased proximity, recognizing that some children may respond to the sweeping changes of an international transition by regressing or temporarily freezing in their developmental progression (Kugelman, 1992; Mecklenburg, 1997). They can provide themselves and their children with a "place attachment" (Altman & Low, 1992), a "home base" such as the home of a beloved relative or a favorite vacation spot to which the family returns on a regular basis (Pollock & McCaig, 1987; Pollock & Van Reken, 1999; Schaetti, 1995). Similarly, they can use their household shipping allowance to the full, taking with them all of the family's "sacred objects," those possessions that, as with a "home base," give a sense of continuity in the midst of discontinuity.

Finally, parents can help global nomads proactively address transitions by re-enfranchising global nomad grief and by helping them to engage in conscious leave-taking (Brown & Perkins, 1992). Parents and other adults in a global nomad's life can self-educate about the process of transition (Bridges, 1980; Pollock & Van Reken, 1999; Schaetti, 1995; Schaetti, 1996b; Schaetti & Ramsey, 1999b) and about such issues as cultural identity (Pollock & Van Reken, 1999; Schaetti, 1996a; Schaetti, 2000) and the multicultural self (Seelye & Wasilewski, 1996); they can then work with both the sponsoring organization and the sociological IMC to ensure that global nomads receive support in engaging the full potential of their life experience (Schaetti, 1996b; Schaetti, 1998).

CONCLUSION

Attachment theory speaks with great insight to the developmental experience of children raised internationally because of a parent's occupation. It highlights not only areas for concern and attention, but it also suggests ways to address these concerns. It demonstrates the importance of attending to attachment styles when designing and implementing expatriate family services and undergirds strategies long espoused by practitioners in the international expatriate family arena.

Indeed, attachment theory presents a body of scholarship worthy of more concentrated exploration by members of the international relocation and orientation industry, by human resource professionals responsible for expatriating families, by international educators and service providers on-site, and by parents raising children internationally.

REFERENCES

Adler, N. (1986). A portable life: The expatriate spouse. In N. Adler (Ed.), *International dimensions of organizational behavior* (pp. 219–238). Kent, MA: South-Western Publishers.

Ainsworth, M.D.S. (1991). Attachment and other affectional bonds across the life cycle. In C.M. Parkes, J. Stevenson-Hinde, & P. Marris (Eds.), *Attachment across the life cycle* (pp. 33–51). London: Tavistock/Routledge.

Ainsworth, M.D.S., Bell, S.M., & Stayton, D.J. (1971). Individual differences in strange situation behavior of one-year-olds. In H.R. Schaffer (Ed.), *The origins of human social relations* (pp. 17–57). London: Academic Press.

Altman, I., & Low, S.M. (Eds.). (1992). *Place attachment*. New York & London: Plenum Press.

Bartholomew, K., & Horowitz, L.M. (1991). Attachment styles among young adults: A test of a four-category model. *Journal of Personality and Social Psychology, 61*, 226–244.

Bell, L. (1996). *Hidden immigrants: Legacies of growing up abroad*. Notre Dame, IN: Crosscultural Publications.

Bowlby, J. (1973). *Separation*. New York: Basic Books.

Bowlby, J. (1980). *Loss*. New York: Basic Books.

Bowlby, J. (1982). *Attachment* (2nd ed.). New York: Basic Books.

Bretherton, I. (1980). Young children in stressful situations: The supporting role of attachment figures and unfamiliar caregivers. In G.V. Coelho & P.I. Ahmed (Eds.), *Uprooting and development. Dilemmas of coping with modernization* (pp. 179–210). New York & London: Plenum Press.

Bretherton, I. (1987). New perspectives on attachment relations: security, communication, and internal working models. In J. Osofsky (Ed.), *Handbook of infant development* (2nd ed.) (pp. 1061–1100). New York: Wiley.

Bretherton, I. (1992). The origins of attachment theory: John Bowlby and Mary Ainsworth. *Developmental Psychology, 28,* 759–775.

Bridges, W. (1980). *Transitions. Making sense of life's changes.* Reading, MA: Addison-Wesley Publishing Company.

Bridges, W. (1987). *Dealing successfully with personal transition.* Mill Valley, CA: William Bridges and Associates.

Brown, B.B., & Perkins, D.D. (1992). Disruptions in place attachment. In I. Altman & S.M. Low (Eds.), *Place attachment.* New York & London: Plenum Press.

Butler, M.V. (1997). *Attachment theory.* Paper presented at The Union Institute Learner Peer Day, Minneapolis, MN, August 26.

Doka, K.J. (1989). Disenfranchised grief. In K.J. Doka (Ed.), *Disenfranchised grief. Recognizing hidden sorrow* (pp. 3–12). Lexington, MA: Lexington Books.

Fontaine, G. (1987). *Support systems for international microcultures.* Paper presented at the SIETAR International, Montreal, Quebec, Canada, May 15–21.

Kagitcibasi, C. (1987). Alienation of the outsider: The plight of migrants. *International Migration, 25,* 195–210.

Karen, R. (1990, February). Becoming attached. *The Atlantic Monthly,* 35–70.

Kugelman, P. (1992). *Parenting children on the move.* Paper presented at the Women On The Move Conference, Brussels, Belgium, March 7–9.

Main, M. (1990). Cross-cultural studies of attachment organization: Recent studies, changing methodologies, and the concept of conditional strategies. *Human Development, 33,* 48–61.

Main, M., Kaplan, N., & Cassidy, J. (1985). Security in infancy, childhood, and adulthood: A move to the level of representation. In I. Bretherton & E. Waters (Eds.), *Growing points of attachment theory and research* (Vol. 1–2, Serial #209): Monographs of the Society for Research in Child Development.

Marris, P. (1991). The social construction of uncertainty. In C.M. Parkes, J. Stevenson-Hinde, & P. Marris (Eds.), *Attachment across the life cycle* (pp. 77–90). London: Tavistock/Routledge.

Martinez, I.Z. (1994). Quién Soy? Who am I? Identity issues for Puerto Rican adolescents. In E.P. Salett & D.R. Koslow (Eds.), *Race, ethnicity, and self* (pp. 89–116). Washington D.C.: National MultiCultural Institute.

McCluskey, K.C. (Ed.). (1994). *Notes from a traveling childhood. Reading for internationally mobile parents and children.* Washington, DC: Foreign Service Youth Foundation.

McRoy, R. (1994). Attachment and racial identity: Implications for child placement decision making. *Journal of Multicultural Social Work, 3,* 59–75.

Mecklenburg, C. (1997). *Developmental guidance: Environmental influences of international students' development.* Paper presented at the European Council of International Schools, Nice, France, November 22.

Pollock, D., & McCaig, N. (1987). *The third culture kid profile.* Paper presented at the SIETAR International, Montreal, Quebec, Canada, May 14–17.

Pollock, D., & Van Reken, R. (1999). *Third culture kids: Growing up among worlds.* Yarmouth, ME: Intercultural Press.

Rachel, J., & Manire, S. (1994). *Attachment as a meta-theoretical point of entry into cultural understanding.* Paper presented at the 20th Congress of the International Society for Intercultural Education, Training, and Research, Ottawa, Canada, June 15–19.

Rando, T.A. (1993). *Treatment of complicated mourning.* Champaign, IL: Research Press.

Schaetti, B.F. (1995). Families on the move: Working together to meet the challenge. *Inter-Ed, 23,* 8–13.

Schaetti, B.F. (1996a). Phoenix rising: A question of cultural identity. In C.D. Smith (Ed.), *Strangers at home: Essays on the effects of living overseas and coming "home" to a strange land* (pp. 177–188). Bayside, NY: Aletheia Publications.

Schaetti, B.F. (1996b). Transition programming in international schools: An emergent mandate. *Inter-Ed, 24,* 12–19.

Schaetti, B.F. (1998). Transition resource teams: A good answer to an important question. *International Schools Journal, XVII,* 52–59.

Schaetti, B.F. (2000). *Global nomad identity: Hypothesizing a developmental model.* Unpublished doctoral dissertation, The Union Institute, Cincinnati, OH.

Schaetti, B.F., & Ramsey, S.J. (1999a, May). The expatriate family: Practicing personal leadership. *Mobility: Magazine of the Employee Relocation Council,* 89–94.

Schaetti, B.F., & Ramsey, S.J. (1999b). The global nomad experience: Living in liminality. *Mobility, 20,* 40–45.

Seelye, H.N., & Wasilewski, J.H. (1996). *Between cultures: Developing self-identity in a world of diversity.* Chicago, IL: NTC Publishing Group.

Smith, C.D. (1991). *The absentee American: Repatriates' perspectives on America and its place in the contemporary world.* Westport, CT: Praeger Publishers.

Sroufe, L.A. (1979). The coherence of individual development: Early care, attachment, and subsequent development issues. *American Psychologist, 34,* 834–841.

Sroufe, L.A. (1988). The role of infant-caregiver attachment in development. In J. Belsky & T. Nezworski (Eds.), *Clinical implications of attachment* (pp. 18–38). Mahwah: NJ: Erlbaum.

Sroufe, L.A., & Fleeson, J. (1986). Attachment and the construction of relationships. In W. Hartup & Z. Rubin (Eds.), *Relationships and development* (pp. 51–71). Mahwah, NJ: Erlbaum.

Sroufe, L.A., & Waters, E. (1977). Attachment as an organizational construct. *Child development,* 48, 1184–1199.

Winnicott, D.W. (1971). *Play and reality.* New York: Basic Books.

8

INTERNATIONALLY MOBILE CHILDREN IN CHILDREN'S FICTIONAL LITERATURE: LEGITIMATE REFLECTION OR REFLECTING LEGITIMATION?

ANNIKA HYLMÖ

INTRODUCTION

In recent years, children's literature is taking over the *New York Times'* best- seller list. The recent *Harry Potter* craze has meant a notable increase in children (and their parents) reading. Author J.K. Rawlins is writing from Scotland but is touching readers across the globe. Along with the *Harry Potter* books, a residual outcome is the reading of other books as well. Some of these books may include characters that lived overseas as children or adolescents. The books published about children living overseas are certainly few and far between, but every so often they appear to whisk the reader to some faraway place in the imagination. These books and the stories that they present are the focus of the present chapter.

Every year, thousands of families move overseas from their home countries due to one of the parents' occupation, typically based in corporate, government, or military sponsorship. Children growing up overseas often have complex identities transcending cultural boundaries (Langford, 1999; Useem & Downing, 1976). For the purpose of this chapter, these individuals will be described as expatriate children or adolescents. Expatriate in this context will be taken to mean those individuals who voluntarily live and work outside their country of passport during a given period of time. The expatriate child or adolescent refers to those children and adolescents who follow their working parents and live outside their country of passport for that same period of time (though many children, admittedly, may or may not actually have been allowed the choice to do so).

Expatriate children grow up in a reality that is significantly different from that of their domestic peers. Their environment is one that is embedded in international politics, economics, and sociocultural relations. This environment impacts the lives of these children on a deep level. For many of the expatriate children, the reality of the international environment, along with the relationship between their home country's policies toward the host country and the host country's subsequent response, plays an important role in shaping who the children are and who they become as adults. For example, U.S. children living in Colombia may be affected more directly by policies that the United States will implement toward Colombia's drug traffic than will U.S. children living in Alabama. The U.S. children living in Colombia may be asked more directly to make sense of both the U.S. policy and the Colombian response as they talk to their friends and their families living both in Colombia and in the United States. Many expatriate children are likely to experience complex international relationships such as these during and following their sojourn abroad. Such complex international relationships are also portrayed in children's literature about expatriate children.

While the daily reality of expatriate children may be quite different from that of domestic children, those who only observe expatriate experiences from a distance may not acknowledge that difference. Misconceptions of the reality behind expatriate living are perpetuated by a variety of factors, not the least of which is the portrayal of the expatriate experience in the media as something that is often more glamorous and exotic than real. In many ways, this image may also be perpetuated in children's literature that thereby serves as a rhetorical device for a particular ideology, or preferred way of thinking. Children's literature is often discussed and critiqued in terms of the domestic images of diversity that are portrayed in the texts (Clark & Kulkin, 1996; Taxel, 1997). Looking at children's literature about expatriate children allows us to extend the discussion about multicultural children's literature as rhetorical devices for a particular set of ideologies to an international environment.

This chapter begins with a discussion of children's literature as rhetorical constructions that serve to legitimate particular ideologies to specific audiences. In other words, I will examine how children's literature has not only been written with a particular audience in mind, but also how specific ways of thinking and viewing the expatriate experience are presented to that audience. Specifically, I focus on children's literature as a socializing agent that may reify, or reinforce, what we already take for granted, given conditions of experience. I explore four different books written for children about the experience of living abroad (see Table 8.1). I discuss how these books in some cases serve to give voice to internationally mobile children by reflecting the complex reality of an expatriate childhood and the relationship of the expatriate child to the host community as well as to the parent's occupation. I discuss how, in other cases, these books serve to silence the overseas childhood experience by romanticizing the experience and by ignoring the often contradictory reality that the expatriate child is left to make sense of.

Table 8.1. Children's Literature about Expatriate Children and Adolescents.

Author, Year, Title, Publisher	Pages	Age Group	Available
Kessler, C. 2000. *No condition is permanent.* NY: Philomel Books	188	Adolescent/ Young adult	Book stores: $17.99 hardcover ISBN: 0399234861
Neville, E. C. 1991. *The China year.* NY: HarperCollins Children's Books	256	Adolescent	Library ISBN: 0064404072
Pevsner, S. 1983. *Lindsay, Lindsay, fly away home.* NY: Clarion Books	192	Adolescent/ Young adult	Library ISBN: 089919186X
Williams, K. L. 1991. *When Africa was home.* NY: Orchard Books	32	Juvenile	Book stores: $5.95 hardcover ISBN: 0531070433

Finally, I give special attention to the relationship between the expatriate childhood experience as portrayed in children's literature and the larger sociopolitical and economic situations that are reflected (or not) in those portrayals as part of an ideological context. By focusing particular attention on the ideological context, I explore this genre of children's literature as a form of legitimating experience and power in international relations from a child's perspective. Examining children's literature as legitimating international relationships also means examining the impact this may have on the perceptions of children (expatriate and domestic) on their role and relationships in the global arena.

EXPATRIATE CHILDREN AND ADOLESCENTS IN LITERATURE

One medium where portrayals of expatriate children can be found with some frequency is in the fictionalized accounts found in children's literature. In the U.S. , children's literature has undergone substantial metamorphoses during the past few decades as the existing body of literature has been criticized for its monocultural perspective (Taxel, 1992). Rather than being a body of literature written for and about white children, the debate has led to an increased recognition of the need to expand the existing body to also include accounts written by, for, and about other ethnic groups (Bishop, 1992). Along with this debate has come an increased recognition about the inherently political nature of children's literature through the values expressed and repressed in the text and the ideology (or ideologies) presented to young readers (Taxel, 1992).

The examination of literature about expatriate children may begin with the vantage point of three different audiences that are simultaneously present but who may not be simultaneously heard. As Wander (1984) argues, the first and most obvious audience is the audience that is the primary target audience and who is reached directly. This would typically be the young reader who, given the location of publication of many of these books, may or may not be a reader who has experienced international mobility firsthand. These readers may well be found around the world, just as Scottish

author J.K. Rawlin's *Harry Potter* series have reached readers globally. This audience would also include those adults who choose the
reading materials for their children. Adults often choose the reading
material for children who, early on, are read to and have the readings interpreted by their parents as stories of socialization (May,
1997).

The next group of readers is an audience that is reached inadvertently. This audience may include parents and other adults who
read the books for their own enjoyment (Murphy, 1985). They may
not have been intended as the primary audience but have become
part of the audience for the text. This group may also include
former Third Culture Kids (TCKs) and others who are interested in
learning more about the TCK context through the experience of
fiction. Lastly, Wander (1984) argues that we need to consider the
third persona, or the audiences who are not present, but who are
either rejected by the text or whose presence is negated. By rejecting
or silencing certain individuals or groups to the point of objectifica-
tion, Wander's third persona recognizes that a text "not only
persuades and constructs reality but also structures power relations
and situates some people and groups as marginal" (Mumby, 1997, p.
12). In other words, when reading expatriate children's books, it is
important to consider not only the experiences of the expatriate
children portrayed in the text but also those experiences that are not
spoken of or that are negated a voice in the story. By examining the
voices that are heard as well as those that are not, it becomes
possible to probe the reflection of legitimacy and legitimation, or
justification of legitimacy, of expatriate children's experiences as
portrayed in children's literature. Legitimacy will be the focus of the
next section, followed by legitimation.

Legitimacy, Experience, and Ideology

Legitimacy of experience is grounded in the existing social order
driven by the power of ideology. Althusser (1971) argues that to
examine power we need to examine two forms of state apparatuses:
ideological state apparatuses or ISAs such as family, communication,

cultural, educational, political, legal, religious institutions, and repressive state apparatuses or RSAs such as police or military, that function via threats or violence. For the present purposes, the ISAs in particular warrant attention.

Expatriate Living and the Reproduction of Social Privilege

The expatriate community draws on reified social privileges that its members actively participate in reproducing (Ahmed, 1999). Expatriate living and subsequent domination have always been made possible by ISAs that function by ideology to allow a dominant group to maintain social power through processes of control. For example, many expatriate communities establish their own schools that follow the curricula of their home countries. The curricula that are taught follow a particular ideology, typically that of the home country. This allows a certain level of control of the ways that the students are taught to think and process the material. In many cases, these schools are also favored as educational institutions over the local schools by parents in the local community. This means that in those cases, the expatriate school is also able to shape the way that, typically, the elite of the local community learns to think. In this way, one of the ISAs that is part of the expatriate group serves to dominate not only their own, but also others' way of thinking.

Althusser (1971) argues that by producing and reproducing cultural artifacts expressing the dominant point of view, the ideology of the dominant group is reinforced through illusions of reality and leads the individual to act according to her or his beliefs. What he means by this is that we think that we know what reality and truth are, even though the way that we may think about reality and truth may be different from the way that other people think about reality and truth. We learn that reality, in part, through cultural artifacts such as books and movies that other members of our culture produce. These cultural artifacts are tangible objects with a material existence. Because the cultural artifacts present

different ideas to us that we think are important, they also represent
our ideology (Garner, 1999).

By engaging in everyday practices such as reading, the reader is
participating in the reproduction of ideology. Ideology interpellates,
or "hails," the individual subject through these practices so that the
subjects begin to recognize themselves within the ideological call
(Althusser, 1971). By reading the readers recognize themselves as
having a place in and identifying themselves with that part of the
reality constructed by the text. The reality that is constructed by the
text is performed for the reader by the acts of the hero or heroine as
role model. As individuals are interpellated by ideology through the
practice of reading, they become subject to participation in the
reproduction of existing relationships of power.

Children's literature is part of the material existence that presents
ideology. Most children's literature reflects the ontology or worldview
of the dominant group and, in addition to providing pleasure and
delight, provides statements about important critical social and political
questions: Who are we? How do we relate to each other? How do we
see each other? and so on. Various forms of class culture, such as social
or economic class, is continuously presented as common culture in most
forms of children's literature, thus reifying the present order (Taxel,
1992). This means that when we read children's books, it often seems as
though the texts represent particular views of social classes. After a
while, we begin to reify those views or take those views for granted.

Many expatriate children are part of the privileged elite due to
their membership in the expatriate community (Willis, Enloe, &
Minoura, 1994). When reading children's literature depicting their
experience, then, it becomes important to question which class
culture the text represents and legitimates. Furthermore, as Bishop
(1992) argues, when we examine children's literature, we need to
question the cultural authenticity of the environment that it
portrays. In other words, we must examine the ability of the text to
reflect the experiences of the characters in terms of their cultural
context. In terms of expatriate children's literature in particular, this
means that the text needs to reflect not only the cultural context of

the situated story and plot but also the overlay of simultaneously coexisting multiple cultural experiences as well.

Legitimacy and the Hidden Curriculum

By reading we learn not only about a particular story and the events that the characters must go through, we also learn about values and morals, what is expected of us in particular contexts and situations. This is what the socialization literature has termed "the hidden curriculum" (Benson, 1999; Orenstein, 1994; Oseroff-Varnell, 1998). The hidden curriculum may be expressed through children's literature and serves to socialize the reader into the cultural norms and values that the text depicts. For example, children's literature depicting the cultural norms and values of the United States may emphasize individual achievement as opposed to Japanese children's literature that may emphasize achievements made by a group.

Socialization provides the reader with knowledge and adoption of culturally appropriate assumptions about attitudes, values, beliefs, and behaviors. As we read about other expatriate children and adolescents, we learn about their actions and relationship to both the characters' home culture and their host culture. Through the process of socialization, we come to identify with and accept the attitudes and behaviors that are depicted by our role models in the books (Garner, 1999). Once the reader accepts the depicted norms and values, those norms and values are granted legitimacy and become reified, or taken for granted, by the reader.

Two dimensions of socialization communication may be identified (1) Explicit messages that concern content and policies and (2) implicit messages that concern relationships and role expectations. The implicit messages form the core of the "hidden curriculum" that allows an individual to develop a sense of self in relation to the larger group (Johnson, Staton, & Jorgensen-Earp, 1995; Jorgensen-Earp & Staton, 1993; Oseroff-Varnell, 1998). Thus, when examining children's literature about the expatriate experience, it becomes important to explore both that which is said and that which is implied about the experience.

THE CONSTRUCTION OF LEGITIMATION AND CHILDREN'S LITERATURE

Legitimation and Cultural Values

Legitimacy is something that we often take for granted, but as Habermas (1979; 1984) argues, if we really want to understand how deeply legitimacy runs in our interpretations when we read about children's experiences while living overseas, we need to recognize that legitimacy is contestable. In other words, we need to understand that there is never any one way of seeing or interpreting a situation. Habermas argues that behind legitimacy lies the need to identify particular political orders as "worthy" of recognition. We must recognize or "see" a particular order of domination if it is to exist. For a particular political order to be recognized its claims to validity must be justified in relation to other validity claims. Each single justification is deemed a legitimation (Habermas, 1979). These justifications appear in a variety of contexts, including children's literature. As each justification appears in the text, legitimation serves as an agent of socialization into a particular culture's values.

Cultural values need to be justified just as other value claims need to be. However, as Habermas (1984) also points out, "Cultural values do not count as universal; they are, as the name indicates, located within the horizon of the lifeworld of a specific group or culture. And values can be made plausible only in the context of a particular form of life" (p. 42). The argument takes on new meaning in the context of the socialization of expatriate children. In the case of TCKs, culture transcends localization to a possible point of sharing certain sets of cultural meaning with other TCKs (Useem & Cottrell, 1996). Yet cultural meaning from within the context of TCKs may be refuted by lack of access to similar others who may serve to legitimate the intercultural overseas experience. For expatriate children without access to similar others, children's literature depicting TCKs and global nomads may serve to legitimate their experience of living overseas.

HABERMAS: THREE CLAIMS TO LEGITIMACY

Francesconi (1986) identifies three essential claims that Habermas (1979; 1984) includes in his definition of legitimacy. First, Francesconi notes that Habermas suggests that the legitimacy of political order and power needs to be explored as a rational claim. In other words, if we are going to contest legitimacy, we need to take the arguments that are presented on both sides seriously. Second, the claims that are presented should be recognized as contestable. This means that the arguments that are presented may be either accepted or rejected. Third, any claim of legitimacy will rely on a normative evaluation of its worthiness, or evaluation, based on the norms of a particular cultural group. From these three essential claims, Francesconi suggests that there are four additional key terms that need to be used to examine rhetorical texts such as children's literature: normative evaluations, contestable validity claims, discourse, and worthiness of recognition. These are the terms that I will turn to next.

Normative Evaluation

Normative evaluation refers to the idea that norms and identity coexist for any given social group (Francesconi, 1986). We create our identities by interacting with other people. Another way to describe this is to say that our identities are socially constructed. Our socially constructed identities arise out of the normative frameworks of the social groups that we interact with. For example, children and adolescents growing up abroad often experience that they are constructing their identities by interacting with several cultural groups at the same time. These cultural groups may include home and host cultures, and sometimes the additional cultures of some of their friends as well, if their friends have other home countries.

Because of those interactions, the expatriate children often develop a blended culture that includes some of the values that each of the cultural groups represent (Useem & Cottrell, 1996; Useem & Downing, 1976).

The cultural groups that allow us to develop our social identities have normative frameworks or expectations that we use to define who we are. In many cases, there will be a discrepancy between the current dominant power and the normative frameworks of the cultural group that we are using to create our identities. This discrepancy means that there is a need for legitimation or justification for why we should adopt certain norms and values and not others. The dominant power will attempt to prevent disintegration of the situation by allowing certain conditions under which we can express our social identities in such a way that our expressed identities legitimate the existing order. At a very simple level, a Saudi girl living in the United States with her parents (the dominant power) may, for example, be allowed to wear Western clothes and express her dual identity that way under certain conditions. She may not, however, be allowed to date boys the way that her U.S. friends would. In this way, her expressed identity legitimates both her parents' choice to live in the United States for a period of time and her dual identification with the cultural groups of the United States and Saudi Arabia.

Contestable Validity Claims

Next, Francesconi (1986) points to the notion that legitimacy should have some connection to truth, or contestable validity claims. In other words, validity claims can be accepted or rejected. A claim to truth is reached as consensus through the process of justification. Truth claims are created intersubjectively by communicating with other people about what we think is right and wrong. The justification that we create must have the power to reach consensus within the cultural group (Habermas, 1979). To understand the role of justification and consensus, we might use the same example of the Saudi girl living in the United States again. If we consider her cultural group to be her family, the discussions that she and her parents may have about clothes and dating are likely to include a number of arguments or truth claims about why she should be allowed to wear certain clothes and not be allowed to date. Such justification takes place through the knowledge of similar others' experiences, so both the girl and her parents need to understand each other's situations. Justifications also take place through discourse, Francesconi's third key term.

Discourse and Recognition

Discourse refers to reflective dialogue intended to reach understanding and to produce consensus (Habermas, 1973). In other words, for the Saudi girl and her parents to reach agreement, they have to talk about their expectations with the intent to understand each other. For expatriate children, the realization that their experiences are shared by similar others is also gained through discourse. Discursive reflection takes place through communicative processes that include reading. By reading, the expatriate child can reflect on her or his experiences as having a connection to truth. Reading provides an understanding and recognition of consensus that the claim that has been presented is worthy of recognition, the final key term proposed by Francesconi. Just as the Saudi girl may find her parents willing to recognize her claim that she should be able to wear Western clothes, so she has to recognize the claim that her parents have that she should not be allowed to date. By engaging in reflective discourse with similar others and by reading a text that reflects the reality of an expatriate child or adolescent, that individual may find that the claim that he or she has about the international experience is recognized and validated.

Habermas provides opportunity to examine legitimacy from a rhetorical perspective because of the focus on legitimacy as a function of addressing an audience (Francesconi, 1986), or in this case, a readership. Legitimacy is grounded in communication, that is, in the process of creating shared meaning while assuming the existence of pragmatic and ethical value of the claim that may be accepted or rejected. Acknowledging the value of the claim also provides opportunity for the perpetuation of ideology and a particular way of thinking. Next, I will look at how children's literature about expatriate children and adolescents serves to make claims about the experience and at the same time to present a particular ideology.

EXAMINING CHILDREN'S LITERATURE ABOUT THE EXPATRIATE EXPERIENCE

Children's books about the expatriate experience are not easily identified. There is no library catalog identification for "expatriate children" and for this reason the librarians or the booksellers are often unable to provide much assistance. Most commonly, the reader is directed to books about immigrants, refugees, or life as local people live it overseas. It is difficult, at best, to estimate how many fictional books have been published about the expatriate experience of children and adolescents. Most likely the annual publication of these books number in the single digits.

For the purpose of this chapter, only fictional books where the expatriate cross-cultural experience was of central concern were considered at this time. Therefore, books by, for example, Eric Campbell (*Papa Tembo*, *The Place of Lions*) were excluded because the expatriate experience was not the focus of the text. Furthermore, due to the additional ideological layers presented by the military or the missionary contexts, only books that involve expatriate living by parents who were contracted for independent organizational or corporate positions were considered. Finally, the books had to have been published during the past 20 years and accessible either through purchase or through the local library.

Four titles from the general genre of children's literature were chosen for the purpose of this examination (see Table 8.1 above): Stella Pevsner's (1983) *Lindsay, Lindsay, Fly Away Home*; Karen William's (1991), *When Africa Was Home*; Emily Cheney Neville's (1991) *The China Year;* and Christina Kessler's (2000) *No Condition Is Permanent.* All titles have heroines or heroes that hold U.S. passports. The majority (three out of the four) have females as lead characters and all have female authors, which may not be surprising given the stronger inclination of girls to be readers. Indeed, Cherland (1994) points out that reading fiction is a form of cultural reproduction that is engaged in particularly by young girls. Young boys tend to read how-to manuals, magazines, and biographies, though this may be changing with the recent *Harry Potter* phenomenon. The title that presents a boy as lead character is a picture book, *When Africa Was Home*.

Expatriate Children's Books and Legitimate Reflection

Expatriate living is, of course, situated in multiple ISAs. In each of the four books discussed here, several ISAs figure prominently. To examine legitimate reflection is illustrative to consider four ISAs as presented in the texts: the sponsoring institution, the educational institution, cultural artifacts, and customs and traditions. In addition, the books themselves form a hidden curriculum for the reader to explore the cultural values of the expatriate child. Each of the ISAs presented in the books is used to serve as an attempt to legitimately reflect local or expatriate expectations and experiences.

Sponsoring Institutions. The sponsoring institutions represented by these books tend to be professional. In two of the books, *The China Year* and *No Condition*, the sponsoring institutions are academic. In *The China Year*, eighth grader Henri (short for Henrietta) accompanies her father and mother on her father's exchange appointment at Peking University. Fourteen-year-old Jodie follows her mother, an anthropologist, who studies the role of women in village society in Sierra Leone in *No Condition Is Permanent*.

Sixteen-year-old Lindsay is experiencing a slightly different situation. Her father's occupation as an international businessman brought her to Hong Kong, Germany, France, and India, but the book, *Lindsay, Lindsay, Fly Away Home*, brings her story about her return to the United States to live with an unfamiliar aunt. In this case, the sponsoring institution figures more prominently as her relationships with her friends Jess and Ruthanne are explored and as she reflects on the people that she left behind. Jess, Ruthanne, and

Lindsay shared experiences overseas as their fathers' work crossed paths. Part of their reality while living abroad included servants whose role remained unquestioned. Even as she returns to the United States, Lindsay considers her "amah," or nanny, in terms of what her amah could do for her, not in terms of what she could do for her amah. Significantly, the servants, while always present, are largely relegated to the background of her experience rather than in terms of their influence on her cultural development. Similarly, Lindsay's Indian boyfriend is explored as a rapidly distant figure who cannot be placed at the same level as her new American friends and relatives. This is unfortunate. By failing to explore the long-term impact of host culture relationships, the text sets up a cultural divide rather than allow for the characters to serve as cultural bridges. In the process, the American culture becomes more prominent than the Indian culture, and the text serves to reinforce a sense of "other" and lower worthiness when it comes to the Indian people and Lindsay's experiences among them.

The distancing of experience is evident when Lindsay travels back to the United States from her home in India; she runs into a couple of American teenagers who have been on a trip to Europe. To them she presents her overseas experiences with her friends as somewhat of an adventure. "We've shared so many adventures, you know" (Pevsner, 1983, p. 7). This comment serves to illustrate the distance in two ways: First, she presents her life as an adventure rather than situated in a context of reality. Her friends are present, but the people whom she met and who influenced her have become the invisible third persona. Second, but at the same time, the experiences are presented as being more glamorous and adventuresome than the American teenagers could ever expect to experience and, therefore, to question.

For many expatriate children, moving to their home country presents situations that are difficult to adjust to. In *When Africa Was Home*, the young child Peter experiences the pains of moving to the United States upon the completion of his father's assignment in Africa. Unlike Lindsay, Peter is later able to return to his (as he sees it) home in Africa when his father gets another job. The sense of belonging and having a sense of "home" in the sponsoring country is common among third-culture kids in particular, who often continue to search for a sense of home where they continue to be welcome (Eakin, 1996). Political boundaries and local immigration laws may not make this feasible.

The sponsoring institution finally provides a strong force for the reification of social privilege in *The China Year*. For example, Henri observes:

> Mostly you go to a thing called the Friendship Store. The customers are almost all foreigners [...] the ordinary Chinese people can't shop there. But Daddy and all the Foreign Experts have a special card that says they can buy stuff in the Friendship [Store]. (Neville, 1991, p. 34).

Typical of many expatriate children (Useem & Cottrell, 1996), Henri continues to question the fairness of the dual system of shops for the local Chinese and shops for the foreigners and tourists, though she later reaches a point where she stops questioning and simply accepts the present.

Experiencing Educational Institutions. Living overseas does not mean that expatriate children are exempt from attending school unless they are as young as Peter, the toddler. For expatriate children, school is an important facet of the socialization process. Whether the child attends an international school, a home culture–sponsored school overseas, is home schooled, or attends a local school will significantly impact on the experiences and interpretations of those experiences (Wheeler, 1998). These differences are only partially attended to in the books discussed here.

Only in one book does the main character attend a daily school. In her life overseas, Lindsay attended the American School in India. Despite this, she has developed a somewhat surprising British accent that she spends much of the book trying to overcome. One would imagine that there would be more American students than British to interact with at the school or that she would adopt an Indian accent given that this is the country where she has spent so much time. In the cases of both Henri and Jodie, their education is provided by means of correspondence. Henri's parents recognize that the international school of Beijing is simply too far away and too expensive, and the Chinese schools not a viable possibility given the linguistic impediments. Her correspondence schoolwork is presented to the reader as a form of personal reflection on her experiences as she interweaves her thoughts into her assignments.

Unlike Henri and Lindsay, Jodie has no other option but to be home schooled. School takes a secondary role to her experiences interacting with her Sierra Leonean friend Khadi. Instead, it is Khadi's lack of opportunity at an education that is presented as Jodie teaches her friend to read and write. Educational expectations in Sierra Leone are quite different from those in the West. In Sierra Leone, education serves to reinforce the existing class structure that privileges formal schooling for males as opposed to females. By extension, women have a long road to empowerment and, in the context of this book, the ability to stop female circumcision. Jodi's friend Khadi, like most girls in the Sierra Leonean village, has not been privileged to go to school. School, reading, and writing are reserved for the males. It is therefore significant that Jodie's willingness to teach Khadi to read and write serves to give something back to the community and the friend that has taught her so much about it. This is in stark contrast to Lindsay and Henri, both of whom may interact with the local community but who tend to be more distant. Jodie's ability to teach her friend serves as an initial catalyst for change in the community as Khadi begins to question the circumcision rites and her own willingness to pass on the tradition to her own daughter in a letter to Jodie back in the United States.

Experiencing Cultural Artifacts. The third significant ISA is the cultural artifact. Two artifacts in particular warrant attention here: clothing and money. Clothing is significant as a cultural artifact because of its overt connection to cultural identity. Members of different cultures can often in part be distinguished by the clothing they wear. The further removed the cultures are from each other, the more distinct the differences in clothing. Money, on the other hand, serves as a more covert symbol of the economic privilege often surrounding expatriate families (Willis et al., 1994).

In each of the three stories, clothes in particular play a prominent role. Jodie refuses to give up her jeans when she first arrives in Sierra Leone. "I seriously regretted not taking my mom's advice that morning. She handed ma a lapa...[but]...I needed my jeans. I needed something 'normal' in my life" (Kessler, 2000, p. 46). Lindsay reacted similarly on arriving in the United States. "After we cleared customs in New York, and before I rechecked my luggage, I'd take it out. The sari. And then, just before the fasten-your-seat-belt sign came on for the Chicago landing, I'd duck into the loo and wrap myself in the outfit" (Pevsner, 1983, p. 9) while Peter feels like a statue in his snowsuit and heavy boots. It is not until he returns to Africa and gives away his red ski cap that he feels liberated. In each of these cases, the children's clothing reflects the identity that they cling to based on their individual cultural realities at the time.

The existence of dual currencies in China (typical in many countries) during Henri's stay provided Americans overseas with exceptional social power over the local people that is rarely questioned in the text. As Henri's grandmother, who is visiting as a tourist from the United States, enters a department store, she sees a leather jacket that she declines to pay the full price for. When the clerk refuses to bargain with her, she leaves the store to encounter a young girl whom she propositions for an exchange of the foreign notes for local ones, then returns to the store to purchase the jacket. Knowing the value of foreign notes to be higher than Chinese notes, Henri's grandmother remarks, "See, I have the jacket and 100 kwai in renmin-bi [local notes] left over for my 200 kwai in foreign notes" (Neville, 1991, p. 60). Henri comments to her grandmother about the possibility of the clerk's arrest because of his willingness to bargain in a government store, as well as the girl's possible arrest for her illegal exchange of notes. Still, her grandmother shrugs off Henri's remarks because she accepts the commonly reified reality and takes for granted the reality that the U.S. tour guide in China has presented to her: "Don't you worry your little head about it, baby" (p. 61). While Henri continues to question the situation in her head for a while, the situation is never clearly discussed in the context of the text. Rather, it is swiftly swept under the rug by indicating that the grandmother and the father have a relationship that is already tense, and so the grandmother's acts should not be questioned in his presence. The issue of privilege is thus circumvented allowing for the reification of present conditions rather than questioning either the rationality of the situation or the active participation of the American tourists in reinforcing existing class conditions.

Experiencing Traditions. Expatriate children and adolescents are often forced to examine the role of traditions in cultural experiences and expectations through the processes of legitimation. When these children arrive in their host country, they encounter a number of experiences and traditions that they would not in their home countries. Each of these experiences is left open to interpretation and sense making. This means that the traditional experiences and expectations have to be discussed in terms of truth claims and contestability in order to be recognized and interpreted by the expatriate children (Francesconi, 1986; Habermas, 1975; 1984). Based on those interpretations, the expatriate individuals will then create their own relationship to the culture of the host country. While accepting a multitude of traditions is fast becoming a norm for home culture nationals as well, the encounters are often not as extreme as those encounters made by, say, American children growing up in Africa or Asia. However, as in Kessler's (2000) book, *No Condition Is Permanent*, not all cultural traditions are as easy to accept.

No Condition Is Permanent portrays local traditions with great sensitivity. The story looks at Jodie's mother's work in light of circumcision and the role of women in the continuance of the tradition. As she explains:

> These things take time to change, Jodie, because the mothers and grandmothers need to be convinced to stop it. [...] Their grandmothers' grandmothers had it done. [...] It's a ritual. It's been going on for generations and could take generations

to stop. As for changing the men's minds—forget it. (Kessler, 2000: pp. 108-109)

Kessler's book attempts to address the local tradition with sensitivity even as she advocates change by legitimating the experiences of the local women by recognizing and validating the rationality behind the tradition. The difficulty of effecting change for local women in Sierra Leone is rooted in tradition and cultural beliefs and continues to be reflected throughout the story line as Jodie becomes involved in her mother's attempts to change the tradition despite her mother's warnings against it. As her mother informs her, "This isn't America, and you don't have all the answers" (Kessler, 2000, p. 80).

Legitimate Reflection and the Hidden Curriculum. The sponsoring institution, the educational institution, cultural artifacts, and traditions are all presented very explicitly in the texts. While these ISAs are presented explicitly, they also serve together as a hidden curriculum that interpellates the reader to accept certain values inherent in the situations that they present (Althusser, 1971; Orenstein, 1994). The implicit messages that the ISAs present suggest a favored sense of self in relation to a specific larger group (Johnson et al., 1995; Jorgensen-Earp & Staton, 1993; Oseroff-Varnell, 1998). Here it is important to recall the three personas suggested by Wander (1984): the intended audience, the inadvertently reached audience, and the audience that is silenced. Taken together, these four books provide a significant hidden curriculum that is presented through legitimation.

Keeping in mind that there are only a few books written about the experience of expatriate children, the hidden curriculum that is presented by the books can be summarized simply. While younger expatriate children may be permitted to feel as strong a tie (or stronger) to the host country, than the home country as in the case of Peter in *When Africa Was Home*, the expectations are different for expatriate adolescents. According to the hidden curriculum that is presented here, the adolescents can and should feel a stronger tie to the home country than the host country. This tie is expressed to the point of being willing to give up their ability to have an ongoing relationship with the host country along with the emotional ties that this would entail. This is a tall order that is presented to the reader. While this may be true in some cases, in other cases the former expatriate children and adolescents find it very important to maintain a relationship with their host country or countries (Useem & Cottrell, 1996).

The hidden curriculum may well serve the interests of most of the primary and secondary audiences, given that these audiences may be comprised of home country nationals as well as former expatriate children who need to feel legitimated in their claim to their home country. In each of these books, the home country is reified as the most powerful target for identification for the adolescents. Again, it is only in the case of Peter, the small child, that the host country is presented as the primary target. However, the hidden curriculum also presents a specific third persona in that section of the readership that belongs to the third culture (Useem, Useem, & Donoghue, 1963). By virtue of belonging to the third culture, many of these individuals may not feel a specific tie that is stronger to one culture than another. Indeed, while any one specific cultural tie may appear to be stronger than the others depending on a particular context, in reality the ties may well be equally strong to several cultures simultaneously.

The legitimation of political order as the creation of the hidden curriculum takes place is the focus of the next section.

EXPATRIATE CHILDREN'S BOOKS AS REFLECTING LEGITIMATION

According to Habermas (1979), legitimations need to be examined in terms of the worthiness of political order, normative evaluation, localization of cultural values, and contestability of the claim. These examinations taken together will serve to illuminate the hidden curriculum.

Normative Evaluation

In order to develop the argument that the home country comprises the preferred and most acceptable target for identification, these texts have to acknowledge the expatriate experience as the existing dominant power and the motivations for the expatriate expe-rience and the host culture to prevail as potential superseding targets. This means that the experience of simultaneously existing identities must be recognized. For example, when Lindsay returns to the United States, she has to experience the faster pace of life in the United States compared with India. The food at fast-food restaurants and the pace at school strike a discord compared with what she was used to. Her friend, Jess, who has spent more time in the United States than she, has experienced similar difficulties but is a pretender. Ruthanne explains to Lindsay, "He wears U.S. clothes—but with some European touch. And when kids start goofing around he doesn't actu-ally say anything but he doesn't join in either" (Pevsnder, 1983, p. 29).

Justification as Legitimation

The second factor in legitimation refers to the process of justi-fying truth. Truth has to be contestable, but it can only be made contestable through knowledge of similar others (Francesconi, 1986). There are three ways in which the main characters gain knowledge of similar others (1) through knowledge of other expa-triate children, (2) through knowledge of other home country chil-dren, and (3) through knowledge of host country children. Henri complains about the lack of other expatriate children her age in the Chinese apartment complex. She befriends a younger expatriate girl, Kate, and a Chinese boy, Minyun, of her own age who, being a former expatriate himself, has command of the English language. Both Kate and Minyun attend Chinese schools, providing Henri with contestability of her own educational options, for example, by wishing that she herself could attend a Chinese school. The contestability of educational options continues as she continues to suggest that Minyun come to the United States to attend college and to challenge his educational choices. By contesting Minyun's eduacational options, Henri's own educational options become fixed truth claims.

Similarly, Jess becomes Lindsay's guide through the maze of understanding American culture. Initially he tells her not only of the workings of the school that she is to attend but also suggests that she downplay her international experiences in the company of her new American friends even while recognizing that he himself is going through the same internal turmoil. When Lindsay questions why they are back in the United States as opposed to remaining in India, Jess responds, "I want to be here [...] and so will you after a while" (p. 52), thus justifying the truth claim of the preferred identification target of the home country. Lindsay's personal transformations unfold through Lindsay's ongoing conversations with Jess about their experiences with reentry and her dissipating relationships with India. In the end, their discourse leaves no question but a reached shared understanding of a perceived necessity of their return to the United States as American citizens.

Discourse and the Localization of Cultural Values

According to Habermas (1973; 1984), cultural values are localized through discourse that is intent on achieving shared understanding of the existence of similar experiences. In the case of Jodie, it is her mother that serves an important role as Jodie begins to question the Sierra Leonean tradition of the Secret Society that initiates young girls into womanhood. Her friend Khadi "had never questioned the Secret Society. It was something she learned from her grandmother and would pass on to her granddaughters" (Kessler, 2000, p. 102). Jodie's mother explains:

> "Khadi is of this village. This is her world. She cannot choose whether or not to be a 'woman.' If she's not circumcised, and believe me, everyone will know, she'll never be married in this place." Shaking her head in disbelief, she said, "And people won't even eat food she'll cook. She'll

become an outsider in her own village." (Kessler, 2000, pp. 106-107)

And if Jodie and Khadi are to remain friends, Jodie has to "let [Khadi] go and stay friends, or keep making her angry and never talk again" (Kessler, 2000, p. 165). The cultural values of Sierra Leone are values that are local to that community and not ones that are presented as acceptable to the expatriates. There is a clear move toward distancing between the American and the Sierra Leonean value systems. Both Jodie and her mother share the value of changing the system of circumcision, but even as they recognize the need for change, they recognize that the values that underlie the system are not the same as they themselves might adhere to. Together they reflect on the differences between the United States and Sierra Leone but even as they make strange their American environment they recognize that it is a part of themselves and their own reality. Thus, when Jodie discovers that she is working so hard she is getting blisters on her hands, she begins to question what it is that other Americans consider to be a simple life when they look at Africa. Her mother explains,

"Maybe simple refers to not having to choose which restaurant to go to, because there aren't any." "Or maybe not having to pick a movie from a list of dozens, because there isn't even one to choose from," I added. "Maybe it's supposed to be simple because you don't have any electricity bills to pay or no one can shut your water off," my mom said, laughing. "No, I know. Simple means not fighting over the remote control!" (Kessler, 2000, p. 73)

Contesting the Claim

In order for the claim that the home country should serve as the primary target for identification, the claim must be examined in terms of its worthiness of recognition and acceptance (Habermas, 1973). The claims are built throughout the texts as recognizable increasingly unquestionable to the American reader. In Lindsay's case, India begins to take on an air of lesser value. As Lindsay is given the opportunity to go to a farm, she discovers that she feels a sense of tranquility that she previously had only known when she had run away to an *ashram* in India, but India "had been kind of filthy, though. Here, everything was fresh and clean and...wholesome" (Pevsner, 1983, p. 130). At the farm she gets a summer job shucking corn, which brings her transformation more or less completely into not only an American teenager but a clearly midwestern girl at that. When Lindsay gets the choice to return to India, there is no doubt in her mind; she wants to stay in the United States. Instead, her metamorphic efforts at assimilation pay off in only a few months as one of her new friends remarks that she's not as weird anymore. In the end Lindsay and her friends laugh at her former accent as her memories of India begin to dissipate "like madras cloth left in the sun too long" (Pevsner, 1983, p. 184).

Henri and Jodie present similar claims. In Henri's case, the return to the United States is abrupt due to her mother's illness. At times she thinks about the last day that she spent with Minyun with whom she wants to continue to have a relationship, but mostly China seems unreal and distant to her. When her father had earlier brought up the possibility of an extended visit to China, she rejected it. Jodie, as well, does not want to return to Sierra Leone in the near future. Following a disrespectful run in with the preparations for Sande, or the women's initiation rite, Jodie also has to return to the United States very rapidly. Upon receiving a letter from Khadi inviting her back for a visit, she notes, "I respected [mom] and Khadi for knowing how to accept the lines that can't be crossed between cultures.... [But] I don't think I'll rush right back to Africa just yet" (Kessler, 2000, p. 179). It is only Peter who feels truly at home in Africa as he gets to wiggle his toes in the sand rather than feel like a statue in his snowsuit in the United States.

CONCLUSION

Writing about expatriate children is not an easy task. The

complexities of a multicultural childhood that crosses national boundaries and cultural expectations are difficult to comprehend for most, even those who have experienced it. Indeed, many former expatriate children report on an ongoing effort to create meaning and sense of their experiences even as adults (Useem & Cottrell, 1996). Children's literature about the expatriate childhood experience may assist former expatriate children to make sense of their own situatedness by reflecting on that of fictitional others (Garner, 1999).

However, children's literature about the expatriate experience is similar to other literature—political (Greenfield, 1985). These books include and exclude. At this point, they include the experiences of some host country nationals in addition to the expatriate children, allowing home country readers to view the other through the lens of someone at least somewhat similar to himself or herself. However, these books also exclude. There is a continued tendency to diminish the importance of the host country national's experience in relation to the home country values. There is also a tendency to diminish the value of the experience of the true Third Culture Kid who has a need for legitimation of the third culture experience. This experience requires ongoing validation and participation in multiple cultures despite geopolitical boundaries and even as adults.

Does this mean that we should reject the current books that are available? I think not. There is a lack of a range of well-written books about the experiences of expatriate children and adolescents. The books presented here are among the better books that are available. As such, they provide us with a good starting point for analysis and critique. Critiquing means recognizing what these books present to us as justifiable truth claims. The truth claims that are presented by the books provide one small part of the reflection that expatriate children's literature can provide. It is my hope that there will be other quality books that can join these that will allow us to further the discussion.

REFERENCES

Ahmed, S. (1999). Home and away: Narratives of migration and estrangement. *International Journal of Cultural Studies, 2*, 329–347.

Althusser, L. (1971). Ideology and ideological state apparatuses (notes toward an investigation). In L. Althusser (Ed.), *Lenin and philosophy and other essays* (pp. 127–186). New York: Monthly Review Press.

Benson, L. (1999). The hidden curriculum and the child's new discourse: Beverly Cleary's *Ramona goes to school. Children's Literature in Education, 30*, 9–29.

Bishop, R.S. (1992). Multicultural literature for children: Making informed choices. In V.J. Harris (Ed.), *Teaching multicultural literature in grades K-8* (pp. 37–54). Norwood, MA: Christopher-Gordon Publishers.

Cherland, M.R. (1994). *Private practices: Girls reading fiction and constructing identity.* Bristol, PA: Taylor & Francis.

Clark, R., & Kulkin, H. (1996). Toward a multicultural feminist perspective on fiction for young adults. *Youth and Society, 27*, 291–312.

Eakin, K.B. (1996). You can't go "home" again. In C. Smith (Ed.), *Strangers at home: Essays on the effects of living overseas and coming "home" to a strange land* (pp. 57–80). Bayside, NY: Aletheia.

Francesconi, R. (1986). The implications of Habermas's theory of legitimation for rhetorical criticism. *Communication Monographs, 53*, 16–35.

Garner, A.C. (1999). Negotiating our positions in culture: Popular adolescent fiction and the self-constructions of women. *Women's Studies in Communication, 22*, 85–111.

Greenfield, E. (1985). Writing for children: A joy and responsibility. In D. MacCann & G. Woodard (Eds.), *The black American in books for children: Readings in racism* (2nd ed.). Metuchen, NJ: Scarecrow Press.

Habermas, J. (1973). *Theory and practice.* Boston, MA: Beacon Press.

Habermas, J. (1975). *Legitimation crisis.* Boston, MA: Beacon Press.

Habermas, J. (1979). *Communication and the evolution of society.* Boston, MA: Beacon Press.

Habermas, J. (1984). *A theory of communicative action: Reason and the rationalization of society.* Boston, MA: Beacon Press.

Johnson, G.M., Staton, A.Q., & Jorgensen-Earp, C.R. (1995). An ecological perspective on the transition of new university freshmen. *Communication Education, 44,* 336–352.

Jorgensen-Earp, C.R., & Staton, A.Q. (1993). Student metaphors for the college freshman experience. *Communication Education, 42,* 123–141.

Kessler, C. (2000). *No condition is permanent.* New York: Philomel Books.

Langford, M.E. (1999). Observations on the mobile population of international schools. *International Schools Journal, XVIII,* 28–37.

May, J.P. (1997). Theory and textual interpretation: Children's literature and literary criticism. *Journal of the Midwest Modern Language Association, 30,* 81–96.

Mumby, D. (1997). Modernism, postmodernism, and communication studies: A rereading of an ongoing debate. *Communication Theory, 7,* 1–28.

Murphy, J.M. (1985). The literary imagination of childhood. *International Schools Journal, 10,* 75–83.

Neville, E.C. (1991). *The China year.* New York: HarperCollins Children's Books.

Orenstein, P (1994). *School girls.* New York: Doubleday.

Oseroff-Varnell, D. (1998). Communication and the socialization of dance students: An analysis of the hidden curriculum in a residential arts school. *Communication Education, 47,* 101–119.

Pevsner, S. (1983). *Lindsay, Lindsay.* Clarion Books.

Taxel, J. (1992). The politics of children's literature: Reflections on multiculturalism, political correctness, and Christopher Columbus. In V.J. Harris (Ed.), *Teaching multicultural literature in grades K-8* (pp. 1–36). Norwood, MA: Christopher-Gordon Publishers.

Taxel, J. (1997). Multicultural literature and the politics of reaction. *Teachers College Record, 98,* 417–448.

Useem, J., Useem, R., & Donoghue, J. (1963). Men in the middle of the third culture: The role of American and non-western people in cross-cultural administration. *Human Organization, 22,* 169–179.

Useem, R.H., & Cottrell, A.B. (1996). Adult third culture kids. In C. Smith (Ed.), *Strangers at home: Essays on the effects of living overseas and coming "home" to a strange land* (pp. 22–35). Bayside, NY: Aletheia.

Useem, R.H., & Downing, R.D. (1976). Third culture kids. *Today's Education, 65,* 103–105.

Wander, P. (1984). The third persona: An ideological turn in rhetorical theory. *Central States Speech Journal, 35,* 197–216.

Wheeler, K.M. (1998). *Bilingualism and bilinguality: An exploration of parental values and expectations in an American sponsored overseas school.* Unpublished doctoral dissertation, University of Minnesota, Minneapolis, MN.

Williams, K.L. (1991). *When Africa was home.* New York: Orchard Books.

Willis, D.B., Enloe, W.W., & Minoura, Y. (1994). Transculturals, transnationals: The new diaspora. *International Schools Journal, XIV,* 29–42.

9

CHILDREN'S INTERNATIONAL RELOCATION AND THE DEVELOPMENTAL PROCESS

RICHARD L.D. PEARCE

INTRODUCTION

This chapter is based upon experience and research in the International Schools. The most extensive directory of these schools (Findlay, 1997) lists 1,724 institutions in 174 countries, following at least 11 national systems and serving over one million students. The wide cultural variety between and within them raises issues that go beyond the explanatory power of theory derived from national experience. Starting from the premise that social science research and the theory that it produces reflect local culture-specific differences of outlook, it seeks a wider analysis of the relocation experience at the level of fundamental biological capacities.

"International Schools" are a self-defined group of institutions covering a philosophical spectrum from the avowedly national (such as Department of Defense Dependents' Schools) to the idealistically international (such as the United World Colleges). They accommodate a diversity of expatriate and local families, but almost all build upon one national tradition or another and offer an alternative to the host country cultural environment. Many of their administrators and teachers have come to see their activity as an idealistic advance on both the home and the host countries' school systems, to the extent that it is a model for education in a presumed globalized future. For a fuller account of their nature and diversity, Hayden and Thompson (1995) have published a series of studies.

Working as Director of Admissions in an International School, I became aware that children differed in the time they took to become enculturated as effective students. National patterns, explained by teachers from the relevant culture, were helpful but not always sufficient to guide us. It seemed more realistic to treat their adjustment as part of development and to search for universal developmental processes by deconstructing to the level of the individual cultural identity and using cross-cultural psychology. These processes are explored in this chapter, and their consequences for the practice of relocation will be discussed.

Most work on the expatriation of children has focused on the emotional impact of transition, ways of reducing perceived stress, and the effect of the experience on development at a phenomenological level. In looking at underlying process rather than evident outcomes, it is necessary to justify the novel approach.

THEORETICAL STANDPOINT

Late in her career Margaret Mead (1975) wrote: "...the forms of cultural and social anthropology developed in different countries each carry the stamp of cultural particularity" (p. 298). In the same way, I believe that the various commentators on the mobile child each approach it from their own home traditions. The differences are expressed instrumentally, each analysis being developed according to the local understanding of how the world works and hence of possible interventions.

In terms of the social psychology, which is used in the present chapter, the mainstream of thought originated in the United States, but the extent to which it can be applied universally has been questioned at various times. Amir and Sharon (1987), commenting on the source of recent experimental work, proclaimed that "...social psychology is the study of second-year American psychology students." Moghaddam, Taylor, and Wright (1993) discussed a number of European and other indigenous approaches to social psychology. Ting-Toomey (1997) phrases it: "I came to the conclusion that each of us can only write and experience through our own cultural lens" (p. 207). Arguing from first principles, Bruner (1986) observed: "To say...that a theory of development is 'culture-free' is not to make a wrong claim, but an absurd one" (p. 135). Most trenchant is the tribute by John Turner (1996) to his coworker Henri Tajfel, a leader of the "European School" of social psychology:

> Along with others he provided an intellectual justification for distinctively European work. He produced a rationale for an alternative, different psychology from the North American mainstream. His vision was pluralistic, taking for granted the proposition that social science was not and could not be value-free. (p. 8)

The aim of this chapter is to seek a level of analysis at which mainstream and other models can be recognized. In the words of the Canadian John Berry (1997): "...there was an increasing concern for local, culturally specific phenomena ('indigenous' or 'cultural' perspectives); and now increasingly there is interest in putting it all together in a pan-human psychology that is both comparative and sensitive to context..." (p. 142).

Having claimed that research is framed by the researcher's local analysis, my own relation to the mainstream must be examined. Needless to say, this speculative sketch of the cultural matrix is itself a product of a specific British cultural world view. In it, the Old World insights are largely from personal observation, while New World perspectives have been tested by reference to Edward Stewart's landmark study (Stewart & Bennett, 1991).

Margaret Mead (1975) proposed that voluntary immigration to a welcoming New World from a defective Old World implies replacement of one set of values with another. There is no space here for a thorough review of the New World and Old World outlooks. The origin may lie in migration but for present purposes the most important philosophical component is the divide between belief in cultural convergence and cultural pluralism. The main implications can be outlined.

Cultural Convergence

The core convergent belief is that all cultures are changing and will become one shared by all mankind, characterized by the universal set of virtues. It is implicit that cultural change is possible, good, and, hence, a morally obligatory personal choice; that identity, including national identity, is a matter of choice and is characterized by features that can be consciously adopted during communal life; that historical limitations can be overcome by self-improvement; and that divisions between individuals are wrong because separateness implies inequality. Concomitant with these perceptions are the beliefs that imperfections must be fixed, that cultural similarities are more significant than cultural differences, and that our time is a singularity not bound to follow historic precedent. In such a milieu, research is directed toward interventions and solutions that improve life. Abstract academics is elitist and suspect.

Cultural Pluralism

The core pluralist belief is that diverse balanced cultural groups exist, separated by deep beliefs, and have a right to do so. It is implicit that history has evolved stable systems in which socially undesirable conditions such as inequality of opportunity are normal, inevitable, and, therefore, to some extent tolerable; national identity embodies inherited loyalties learned in early life, but may be overlain with other levels of identity within or beyond national boundaries; there is a moral commitment to local virtues but there may be an ironic recognition of others, which promotes coexistence. Imperfections in society that cannot be cured must be endured, as change may endanger delicate historic equilibrium. There is an intrinsic virtue in the intellectual pursuit of knowledge and understanding of the human condition; however, in the last respect Britain lies closer to the New World in its distrust of academia.

It is not valid to divide humanity into "pluralists" and "convergers," as each individual's value system is a mosaic, but either pluralist or convergent inclinations are usually visible. Convergent views are likely to be found in voluntary immigrant societies and held by voluntary expatriates (though not by displaced aboriginals or involuntary migrants), and by children toward children and against parents. The voluntary expatriate will be inclined toward convergence, but the host society and even the trailing family may have pluralist tendencies. Pluralist views are characteristic of stable societies, especially in multilingual or economically partitioned nations, and may evolve in an immigrant society as stability grows, like an ecological succession. The current debate in the United States over the language issue, and even the publication of this volume, is a sign of an emerging pluralization that has been remarked on by, among others, Novak (1971), Ramirez and Castañeda (1974), and, more recently, Schlesinger (1998).

There is a related duality that contrasts "primordialist" self-identifications with "situationist" (or instrumentalist) (Bačová, 1999; Minoura, 1987). Primordialist identifications are those associated with inherited or essential links to homeland or kinship group and carrying the authority of the unchangeable past; situationist identifications comprise chosen qualities that are opportune in that environment but are easily substituted in different circumstances. Although questioned by Bentley (1987), and undoubtedly open to crude oversimplification, they remain meaningful terms to distinguish two mutually uncomprehending modes of evaluation, one associated with stasis, the other with change.

Both pluralist and convergent worldviews are supported by daily experience as long as pluralists adopt a social vision that operates at a level at which difference is significant and similarity trivial, while convergers categorize at a level at which equivalence is visible and difference trivial. In the same way, a deer in a forest sees trees as discontinuous, but a monkey sees their branches as continuous.

Inevitably, different constructs will be salient at these two levels, so the analysis is framed in strikingly different terms.

Only cross-cultural studies can link these perspectives. Lonner (1990) has summarized the theoretical difficulties of establishing cross-cultural validity for any supposed universal concept, but Berry, Poortinga, Segall, & Dasen (1992) have proposed three clear requirements: theoretical face validity, a body of supporting evidence from many cultures, and absence of contradictory evidence.

TERMS OF ANALYSIS

The child-in-the-family has been chosen as the unit of study. This is partly pragmatic: This is the usual unit within which children are expatriated, it is the major family unit of the Western trading nations, and it is the unit for which the sponsor of expatriation takes responsibility. The development of the child is seen as a function of social interactions and so this unit is justified as the most influential and most persistent context in which the mobile child interacts. Whether this is equally marked in all societies is open to question (Holland, 1997; Keats, Keats, Biddle, Bank, Hauge, Wan-Rafaei, & Valentin, 1983; Miller, 1988).

There are some important terms that will become better focused as they are used, but which need a brief definition for our present purposes. *Social constructivism* (Kelly, 1955) is the perception that the child develops the dimensions that uses to evaluate its world picture through interactions with the social environment. *Symbolic interactionism* (attributed to Mead, 1934) suggests that these interactions progressively build the child's world picture in terms of a set of subjective inner representations. In this, the child's active role is seen as depending upon the sense of *self*, as the person who is acting and feeling in this perceived world. This Western view of self is challenged by Miller (1988) who reviews the non-Western usage of the self is seen as inseparable from the current context rather than as distinct and autonomous. In either case, the child's self-perception constitutes his or her own *identity*. The set of socially codified meanings through which the child engages with the social world, and which the child uses for self-description of his or her identity, is seen as constituting the convention of *culture*. This analysis, then, is made in terms of the development of identity in social context through the medium of culture.

Of the many definitions of culture, I will quote three. First Hofstede (1980), whose work on cultural dimensions sprang from a cross-cultural survey of 116,000 employees of IBM and is referred to it as "the software of the mind." Second, Linton (1936), from an anthropological perspective, called it "the total social heredity of mankind." Finally, in cross-cultural psychology, it has been described (Berry et al., 1992) as "the shared way of life of a group of people." Though these each contribute useful images, it is enlightening to look beyond "culture" as a taxon and instead use D'Andrade's (1984) formulation of "cultural meaning systems," which emphasizes the subjective nature and interrelatedness of the cultural elements. Strauss (1992) valuably extends this into "culturally formed cognitive schemas."

In reality, we each converse using an individual voice. *Symbolic interactionism* proposes that we each interact with the world as we uniquely perceive it, so each human encounter starts with a tuning-in, a search for shared language. If cultures are differentiated down to the individual level, each human encounter is a cross-cultural interaction.

THEORETICAL CHALLENGE

It is supposed that all humans build their cultural identity through the successive new experiences of childhood. Professor Yasuko Minoura (1992) of Tokyo University, writing with a developmental perspective about children reared between Japan and the United States, has offered a challenging null hypothesis: "For young [Japanese] children who have not yet acquired Japanese patterns, there are no differences between Japan and the United States. For young children, almost everything is new and strange." Can the identity of growing children have the flexibility to adjust and also, the rigidity to support their individuality? We must examine the mechanism which fulfills, or fails to fulfill, this paradox.

PROPOSED MECHANISMS

Identity is seen as the perception that subjects have of their own properties, applying to themselves the value system that they have constructed by interactions within their social group. Using a biological analogy, specific culture groups can be seen as "meme pools" like "gene pools" reservoirs of available meanings that are actively shared by a group of socially interacting individuals and that establish the lexicon of possible thought. The borders of a culture are effectively the borders of that communicating group of people; the integrity of a culture is related to the consistency of communication within that group; the permeability is related, in part, to the amount (frequency and salience) of communication across the borders.

Some workers have proposed models of mechanisms for the development and incorporation of elements of cultural identity (Garza & Lipton, 1984; Minoura, 1993). Figure 9.1 outlines a map of the social environment that charts the major groups of individuals and routes through which social interaction occurs (Pearce, 1998). The social entities, referred to here as "validators," are for convenience put into groups that are relevant to expatriate situations in order to guide the design of interventions. All interaction between the participants in this matrix is seen as being expressed through the language of their cultural conventions and as providing the experience by which those conventions are developed. The process is seen as having certain fundamental biological mechanisms, which will be outlined and then explored in more detail.

In infancy, attachments are made to important people, referred to here as the validators. An interactive relationship develops with them, first through direct interaction and later through their role as referents in the child's imagination even if they are absent. Social life is composed of "social episodes." From these episodes, the child constructs scales of values, which are used to make judgments about those and other remembered events. The child evaluates the episodes, recognizing a certain range of scale values as familiar and rejecting others. This progressively builds the individual's social identity. The child is particularly sensitive to values at the margin between positive and negative identifications that divide good from bad, self from other. If new experiences fall in line with previous evaluations, the system will be reinforced, if not, they will induce changes in the internal world picture, which lead to a fresh adjustment of the internal balance. Some experiences directly affect ways of acquiring new values in the future. In this way, a system for evaluating the world is developed that equips that person to understand and operate in his or her social context, or several sets for several contexts. Although identity development continues throughout life, there is a qualitative change at adolescence when the individual takes greater responsibility for his or her existing value system and personal charge of validatory decisions in the future.

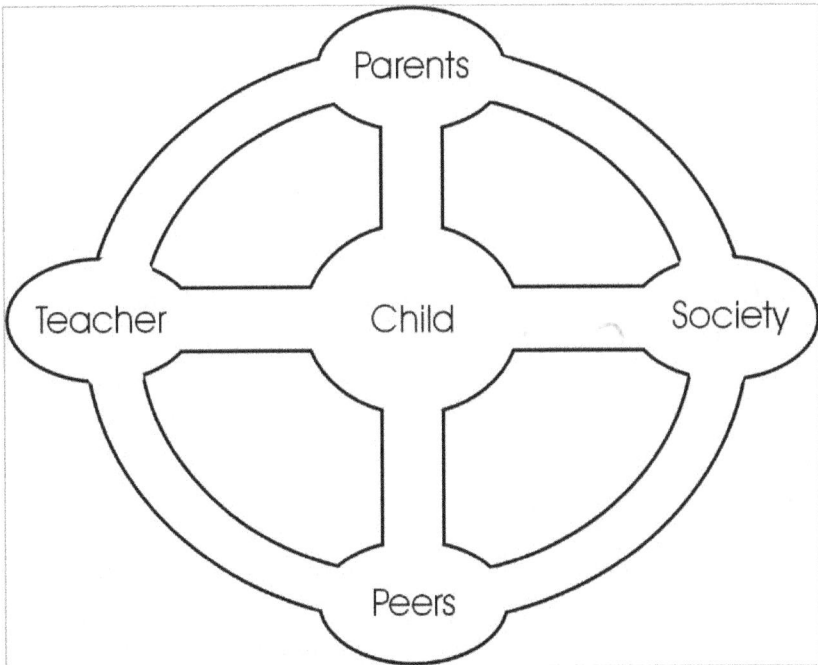

Figure 9.1 The Social Interaction Model[1]

Attachments

It is clear from the pioneer work of Bowlby (1969), as from a multitude of experiences, that strong mutual attachments are formed between children and their careers. Subsequently, lesser attachments are developed with other individuals, forming what Vygotsky (1962) called a "framework" and Bruner (1985), "scaffolding." Bruner adds (p. 32): "There is no way, none, in which a human being could possibly master that [social] world without the aid and assistance of others for, in fact, that world is others." Validators may be individuals or groups and could operate in some cases as ideal models and in others as contexts for interactive development. They have been called "significant others," "referent others," or "reference groups" (Keats et al., 1983). In mobile children, the relative strengths of the attachments may be influenced by the constancy of the parents and the ephemerality of most others. Religious, ethnic, or other primordially rooted identifications are likely to survive better than those which are valid in one situation but not another. As importantly, Barbara Schaetti (Chapter 7 of this volume) explores the affective significance of attachments in a mobile life.

Social Episodes

Harré (1974) follows Vygotsky (1962) in taking human interaction to be composed of "episodes." Social episodes give a child various kinds of recognizable experience: These may be in the form of instructions or precepts, examples of behavior, expressed evaluations of the visible world, or reactions to the child's behavior. These experiences are processed internally by the child to establish their meaning. As Thorley (1990) has written, "the word is communicated, the meaning is constructed." Both Harré (1983) and Weinreich (1983) insist upon the importance of conscious human agency in the analysis and evaluation of social episodes, but the individual's freedom to act will vary between societies in which the self is either more or less context-dependent. Western individualists may be thought of as more able to intervene in the reconfiguration of their

world view (Markus & Kitayama, 1998) and, hence, as more culturally plastic.

Some basic cultural agreement is first needed before a newly
moved child can find social episodes meaningful. In school there is
often a "silent period" in a second-language student as they tune-in
to local culture and language, which is followed in due time by
perfectly normal engagement.

Evaluation of Social Episodes

Much and Shweder (1978) proposed that "...cultural rules are
continually tested, employed, clarified, and negotiated in micro-
scopic moments of everyday life." Hollis (1977) has reviewed this
human tendency to evaluate experiences, seek general rules about
the world, and reorganize the value system so as to increase the
validity of evaluations. Each episode involves an event, a context, an
evaluation, and often validators on whose authority the existing
value is held or the new one offered; any of these may be described
as having high or low salience. Each evaluation of observed event or
of imagined or remembered possibility can be conceptualized in
several stages:

- existing values are applied to recognize and assess what is
  experienced
- the event is evaluated cognitively and emotionally as
  good or bad
- the subject identifies with a good experience or
  contraidentifies with a bad
- there is a motivation to act appropriately.

If these processes follow a familiar path, then that evaluation of
the experience is reinforced, if not, then "cognitive-affective consistency" (Weinreich, 1989) is threatened, and a readjustment is likely
to ensue.

For a mobile child, the variety of experiences is very wide.
Either a loose, tolerant system will be developed, or there will be a

200 RICHARD L.D. PEARCE

separation between the highly salient cultural repertoire, which is applied within the family, and the less significant one outside it.

Adoption and Use of Constructs

The world is evaluated by means of constructs. These standard parameters are constructed by the child as scales for comparing the cumulative understanding of the world with current experience in a single frame. Those most strongly and consistently relied upon are known as core evaluative constructs. New constructs are more likely to be adopted if they can be seen as similar to existing ones or if they are associated with validators or constructs that are already positively regarded.

Each construct has two poles, and the self is placed either at one pole or in an intermediate position from which the two poles each represent unsatisfactory extremes.

On arrival in a new location, the child will possess a set of constructs but may be disturbed to find them inadequate for evaluating the new environment. The memory can supply many instances when those constructs were adequate, but now it is clear that some element, the values, the validators, or the subject himself, is defective. Self-esteem is likely to be lowered until adjustments are made.

Identification of Self and Other

The poles of each construct are labeled with one complimentary and one pejorative descriptor, and usually the subject identifies with the positive. Conversely, those entities that find themselves at the distant "other" pole will either not recognize that construct or will label the poles in a relativistic way, which gives preference to their position. Evaluation takes place simultaneously on a number of constructs, the sum of which gives a strong or weak positive or negative identification. Weinreich, in expounding his identity structure analysis (Weinreich, 1983 Weinreich, Luk, & Bond, 1996), emphasizes that identification is of two kinds: Empathetic identification records the perceived similarity between actual self and other, and idealistic identification records the perceived similarity between the personal ideal and the other. One is normative, the other idealistic, and each plays a sometimes-conflicting part in our evaluation and motivation. Some constructs are complex. Haste (1987) has described these as "rules for making rules," and they powerfully condition the outcome of future episodes. For example, the primordialist tribal identification "I am an X" will be highly effective in influencing further evaluations, given that it is validated by the ineradicable membership of the X tribe. The converse self-definition "...therefore I am not a Y" readily occurs when the identity is under threat and triggers a mass of contra-identifications that emphasize ethnic separation.

If constructs are scales on which some measurements are "like me" and others "unlike me," the borderline between the two is important. The heightened attention to self-definition at this margin has been well explored by LeVine and Campbell (1972) in a key study of ethnic identification. Turner (1982) pronounced it to be "Tajfel's Law" that "intraclass similarities and interclass differences are enhanced as category membership becomes salient." Unexpectedly, powerful responses can be aroused if a subject's membership of a valued group is challenged, as when an expatriate finds his nation is criticized. In the course of expatriation, patriotism towards the home country and fulfillment of traditional ceremonies may become uncharacteristically salient.

Epigenetic Enculturation

As Erikson proposed (1968), development of cultural identity, enculturation, builds on earlier foundations in an epigenetic way. Elements accumulate progressively, but since early "rules for making rules" have the power to influence future development, enculturation is nonhierarchical rather than strictly sequential, directing growth in a multidimensional tree-like pattern. With such "switches" in the system, it follows that biographies cannot be predictive to any

significant extent. However, studies of identity may have great expli-
catory value (Weinreich, 1989).

Consonance and Dissonance of Experiences

Episodes that can be evaluated in terms that are already familiar
reinforce those preexisting evaluations. An unfamiliar validator with
an accepted value, or an unfamiliar value from a familiar validator,
will each gain approbation from the existing positive evaluation.
Salient validators give strong validations. Where conflict is found
with previous values, readjustment is likely. Festinger's (1957) dissonance theory predicts this would generate tensions, which must be
resolved by adjustments of the value system. Adjustments might
merely be reductions in salience or could be changes in polarity of
constructs, changes in liminal values, or adoption of new constructs.
Hinde (1997) reviews the subsequent restatements of dissonance
theory in terms of "balance theory" by Newcomb (1961) and "interpersonal congruence" by Secord and Backman (1974).

Moghaddam (1997) goes further, saying that, in his non-Western
experience, the assimilation of all social evaluations into one
coherent system was not expected. Hong (1992) has observed that in
Japan the ability to accommodate dissonance is highly regarded.
This is paralleled by the findings of Bond and others, writing as
Chinese Culture Connection (1987), that the cultural dimension of
uncertainty avoidance (Hofstede, 1980), which might be presumed a
universal aid to resolving dissonance, appeared not to be salient in
their Hong Kong subjects.

Multiple Identities

Each value system equips the subjects to evaluate their own
identity in their own social setting. Multiple identity proposals began
with William James (1890), who declared that a person "has as
many social selves as there are individuals who recognize him" (p.
294). Ervin-Tripp (1954) associated development of another cultural
identity with learning a second language, but Northover (1988) saw

this as a simplification of the position of bilinguals. Stryker (1980) and Alexander and Wiley (1981) suggested that various "situated identities" may develop, which are applicable to specific contexts, as illustrated by Hofman (1988) in Israel. In the United States, the concept of bicognitive development is supported by some psychologists working in the Hispanic American community (Ramirez & Castañeda, 1974). The expatriate child, growing up exposed to more than one culture, perhaps even within one home, has a wide repertoire of experiences from which to build an identity or identities.

Adolescence and the Adoption of Identity

At what stage does the child gain ownership of the values it is acquiring from validators? It is important to realize that values are not simply swallowed whole but constructed and assembled into an internal system. Children construct their own values from the outset but do so on the authority of validators until adolescence, when they assert prime responsibility for value judgments over the former authorities. Minoura (1992) has shown that cultural identity is "interiorized" by the child between the ages of 9 to 14. This may be thought of as giving the individual the firmness of value system requisite to become a consistent validator for the next generation, but it implies a reduction in permeability to influence from former validators, notably parents. Erikson (1968) regarded this as characteristic of adolescence, but anthropological evidence with a wider context suggests that it may not be universal. Expatriate adolescents in particular may have a choice between identifying with their parents' values, the fluctuating value system of their peers, or the clearly alien host culture, and may decide to "stay" with their parents.

The acquisition of primary cultural identity, enculturation, is commonly distinguished from the acquisition of a second cultural identity, acculturation, but from Erikson (1968) onward, culture development has been viewed as essentially lifelong. Even after adolescence each social episode will entail an evaluation, carried out by the new adult in presence of a mental jury of remembered validators.

IMPLICATIONS FOR PRACTICE

Domestic mobility is high in industrialized nations and can disturb children. The cultural rules stay the same, but the personnel of their social world changes. Many expatriate undertakings such as military bases or oil drilling facilities, which aim for self-sufficiency in politically unpredictable settings, simulate this situation as well as they can by minimizing social relations with the local people. Such an encapsulated community, however, with high expectations of uniformity reinforced by the institutional framework, and no challenge to their values, will have difficulty in imagining just how different are the norms of the host societies. The artifacts may be the same yet the system of meanings utterly different: The Westerners may drink Coca Cola to be like their friends, but the locals drink it to be different from theirs.

Any increase in involvement with the host community has deep implications, calling for both an understanding of the host community in terms of its own evaluations and constructs and for reassessment of one's familiar validators in the wider context. In particular, the recognition of "social alterity"—the inverse of identity—becomes unavoidable. This is not a problem for pluralists. Sanua (1958) noted that orthodox Jewish immigrants in New York, long accustomed to social isolation, showed little mental illness in the first generation. However, this increased dramatically among their children, who attended schools where cultural convergence was expected. Similarly, Alston (1998), working in international elementary schools in Austria, noted that relocation anxiety was less for newcomers who did not speak the ambient language. For them, what was not a part of their world was not worrying.

The earlier comparison of social scientists from the New World and Old World also applies to lay people. In a convergent society, consensus is the desired outcome of any social involvement, so conversation is kept at a depth that does not trigger disagreements of principle, while pluralist expectations of dialogue go deep enough to reveal and confront substantial divergences. Cross-cultural encounters can quite easily cause offense to both parties. Torbiörn (1982), in a pioneer study of expatriate Swedes, noted that the percentage of expatriates forming local friendship groups was closely related to the cultural proximity of the host country, as defined by the dominant religion. If the difference is extreme, it may be easier to accept alterity.

Looking more widely at the community that uses the International Schools, we can see that families approach with many national expectations. It has been suggested that in New World eyes national identity is acquirable and, hence, labile. Indeed, the concept of "global identity" is widely postulated and International Schools is suggested as one mode of entry (Lowe, in press). One Old World view, common in Europe, sees national cultural identity as essentially unalterable and merely enriched by diverse experience; another, exemplified by Japan, sees it as a lifelong project and, hence, vulnerable to any hiatus in enculturation. Enrollment at an International School may be a means of "modernization" in many less economically developed host countries or even former colonies, where the school's culture is valued above national norms (Lowe, in press). Families encourage their children to acculturate. Latin America has a multitude of foreign-system schools that are attended by local nationals. Many of these client families may have remembered roots in European countries which the schools represent, but national identity is not necessarily threatened. Small countries, particularly those economically advanced states crowded close together in Europe, have so much contact with neighbors that inhibitions about crossing borders are fewer. For instance, while many families feel an urgent need to send their children home to give them the college education which they perceive as necessary for their national adult life, Luxembourg has no universities but uses those of its neighbors to prepare its elite. It is clear that what is perceived as national identity in Luxembourg does not depend on college enculturation.

With pluralist eyes, one can see a divide between those societies whose cultural identity exists despite school influence and those whose cultural identity exists because of school influence. The U.S. - system Woodstock School in north India was founded for American missionary children whose parents work in India but also takes children of Indian Americans resident in the United States. It seems that the missionaries send their children as boarders because the American curriculum matters most, but the Indians send children because the environment matters more.

If culture shock, the syndrome resulting from relocation into an unfamiliar culture, is triggered by the mismatch between expectation and actuality, then it should be affected by experience and by cultural background. A family accustomed to alterity by either previous overseas experience or by life in a minority community should be less vulnerable. The ability of diasporic communities such as Armenians, Jews, and East African Asians to relocate and settle is a matter of common repute and admiration.

In mobile families, the child-parent attachment should be less disturbed than those with other parties. This observation has strong anecdotal support and is borne out by my (unpublished) research. However, the role of the child in the family may be altered, not least because the child, and perhaps the mother, is not necessarily a voluntary immigrant. A particularly interesting group comprises the families with parents of differing cultures, for whom one optional model of "parental identity" does not exist. Like expatriate children, this group clearly represents a significant self-reproducing community that will be disproportionately represented in the global business world.

Where an International School serves an expatriate business community, the links between family and school are important. This association may be a significant acculturating mechanism for inducting families from diverse cultures into a superficially consonant "school culture" or into the so-called "global culture" of international business. Developing curricula such as the International Baccalaureate system, which incorporate an explicit pattern of values, offer a response to this need.

Traditionally, all the major trading and colonial nations are monolingual and monocultural and may find the impact of cultural dissonance problematic. Wherever expatriates form a temporary "global" community, the International Schools are the laboratories in which new cultural systems are being developed. Whatever the new environment, the mobile child must either develop a passive tolerance of diversity or an active ability to accept alterity. The nature and mechanism of these abilities is an important topic demanding cross-cultural research.

GLOBAL NOMADS AND THIRD CULTURE KID PARADIGMS: A PLURALIST APPROACH

The dominant paradigm for the mobile child is the Third Culture Kid (TCK) or similar GN pattern, recently reviewed by Pollock and Van Reken (1999), and explored further, from different perspectives, in this volume by Barbara Schaetti and others. As a phenomenological approach, it very effectively describes the perceptions of the bulk of American expatriates and has been so successful that it forms the basis for a wide range of commonly applied interventions.

The GN and TCK paradigms were first described in the United States. I suggest that this reflects a particular sensitivity and a particular analysis of the needs, both characteristic of the New World viewpoint mentioned earlier. There are several components. First, there is a duty to seek solutions rather than tolerate discomfort, so needs must be recognized and remedial action taken. Second, if New World type national identity is characterized by recent shared experiences (rather than by inherited markers of cultural distinctiveness), it depends on just those contemporary cultural experiences that the expatriate is lacking. Third, the sense of being unlike the majority is more disturbing, since it breaches the obligation to unite into one nation. Fourth, "returning" is painful because it is easier to tolerate a lack of fit while living abroad, since "abroad" was the inadequate world from which the migrants originally came, while "home" is the land where better things are expected. Fifth, the TCK model tends to be applied in the International Schools as a single solution that meets all needs, emphasizing similarities rather than differences.

There are other aspects of the experience that are more evidently universal. For all repatriating families, the home country contains guardians of culture, such as grandparents and remembered elders, whose judgments the family regards much more seriously than opinions in the host country. And a final difficulty for children is that, while their parents made a voluntary commitment to expatriation and will strive to resolve difficulties, the children did not.

The evident success of the global nomad profile may lie in its ability to give its subjects a valid group membership. This is some recompense for failing to share the norms of "home" society, a lack which their parents will perceive particularly strongly. In fact, it is likely that life overseas will have taught the children to live as members of a minority more easily than their parents. They are "invisible immigrants" on their return if they wish to merge in the home country; if they identify as GNs, they could find satisfaction in the role of a stable minority. Other minority groups such as Hispanics (Ramirez & Castañeda, 1974), or Sikhs (Gibson, 1988) already possess this satisfactory group membership, but their visible independence is seen by some as a threat to the unity of the nation. A danger exists that if GNs were more recognizable, they too might be seen as threatening. This is the case in Japan, where national culture is very clearly prescribed and deficiencies easily perceived.

Involvement with host country communities is steadily growing, and the picture of international relocation is becoming more complicated. As studies multiply, the GN paradigm is asked to describe more cases among which there is inevitably increasing variety, as Pollock and Van Reken (1999) demonstrate. What seems to be emerging is something like a "hyphenated GN" classification. The GN concept could be developed to encompass a wider range of value systems, though Norma McCaig (Pollock & Van Reken, 1999), originator of the term, has expressed concern about the validity of extending its use without qualifying its definition. Perhaps it is time for the pendulum to make a postmodernist swing toward an analysis in pluralist terms. I have tried to offer a mechanism for such an analysis. No doubt when its usefulness is exhausted, the pendulum will swing back.

NOTE

[1] From Pearce, *International Education: Principles and Practice.* Kogan Page Publications. 1998. Reprinted with permission.

REFERENCES

Alexander, C.N. Jr., & Wiley, M.G. (1981). Situated activity and identity formation. In M. Rosenberg & R.H. Turner (Eds.), *Social psychology: Sociological perspectives* (pp. 269–289). New York: Basic Books.

Alston, E.A. (1998). *The adjustment of children aged 9-12 to international relocation.* Unpublished doctoral dissertation, Institute of Education, London, England.

Amir, Y., & Sharon, I. (1987). Are social-psychological laws cross-culturally valid? *Journal of Cross-Cultural Psychology, 18,* 383–470.

Bačová, V. (1999). *Primordial/situational identifications in Slovakia.* Paper presented at the British Psychological Society Conference, Belfast, UK, April 10.

Bentley, G. C. (1987). Ethnicity and practice. *Comparative Studies in Society and History, 29,* 24–55.

Berry, J.W. (1997). Cruising the world: A nomad in academe. In M.H. Bond (Ed.), *Working at the interface of cultures: Eighteen lives in social science* (pp. 138–153). London, UK: Routledge.

Berry, J.W., Poortinga, Y.H., Segall, M.H., & Dasen, P.R. (1992). *Cross-cultural psychology: Research and applications.* Cambridge, UK: Cambridge University Press.

Bowlby, J. (1969). *Attachment and loss: Attachment.* London, UK: Hogarth Press.

Bruner, J.S. (1985). Vygotsky: A historical and conceptual perspective. In J.V. Wertsch (Ed.), *Culture, communication and cognition:*

Vygotskyan perspectives (pp. 21–34). London, UK: Cambridge University Press.

Bruner, J.S. (1986). *Actual minds, possible worlds.* Cambridge, MA: Harvard University Press.

Chinese Culture Connection. (1987). Chinese values and the search for culture-free dimensions of culture. *Journal of Cross-Cultural Psychology, 18,* 143–164.

D'Andrade, R.G. (1984). Cultural meaning systems. In R.A. Shweder and R.A. LeVine (Eds.), *Culture theory: Essays on mind, self, and emotion* (p. 88–119). NY: Cambridge University Press.

Erikson, E.H. (1968). *Identity: Youth and crisis.* London/NY: Norton.

Ervin-Tripp, E. (1954). *Identification and bilingualism.* In E. Ervin-Tripp (Ed.) (1973), *Language acquisition and communicative choice* (pp. 1–14). Stanford, CA: Stanford University Press.

Festinger, L. (1957). *A theory of cognitive dissonance.* London, UK: Tavistock

Findlay, R. (1997). *International education handbook.* London: Kogan Page.

Garza, R.T., & Lipton, J.P. (1984). Foundations for a Chicano social psychology. In L.J. Martinez, Jr. & R.H. Mendoza, R.H. (Eds.), *Chicano psychology* (pp. 335–336). New York: Academic Press.

Gibson, M.A. (1988). *Accommodation without assimilation: Sikh immigrants in an American high school.* Ithaca, NY: Cornell University Press.

Harré, R. (1974). Some remarks on "rule" as a scientific concept. In T. Mischel (Ed.), *Understanding other persons* (pp. 143–184). Oxford, UK: Blackwell.

Harré, R. (1983). Identity projects. In G. Breakwell (Ed.), *Threatened identities* (pp. 31–51). London, UK: Wiley.

Haste, H. (1987). Growing into rules. In J. Bruner and H. Haste (Eds.), *Making sense of language: The child's construction of the world* (pp. 163–195). London, UK: Methuen.

Hayden, M.C., & Thompson, J.J. (1995) International schools and international education: A relationship reviewed. *Oxford Review of Education, 21,* 327–345.

Hinde, R. A. (1997) *Relationships: A dialectical perspective.* Hove, UK: Psychology Press.

Hofman, J. E. (1988) Social identity and intergroup conflict: An Israeli view. In W. Stroebe, A.W. Kruglanski, D. Bar-Tal, & M. Hewstone (Eds.), *The social psychology of intergroup conflict: Theory, research and applications* (pp. 89–102). Berlin, Germany: Springer-Verlag.

Hofstede, G. (1980) *Culture's consequences: International differences in work-related values.* Beverly Hills, CA: Sage.

Holland, D. (1997) Selves as cultured: As told by an anthropologist who lacks a soul. In R.D. Ashmore & L. Jussim (Eds.), *Self and identity: Fundamental issues* (pp. 160–190). New York: Oxford University Press.

Hollis, M. (1977). *Models of man: Philosophical thoughts on social action.* Cambridge, UK: Cambridge University Press.

Hong, G.Y. (1992) *Contributions of "culture-absent" psychology to mainstream psychology.* Paper presented at the Annual Meeting of Society for Cross-Cultural Research, Santa Fe, NM, (no date available, referenced in Moghadam et al., 1993).

James, W. (1890). *Principles of psychology.* New York: Holt.

Keats, J.A., Keats, D.M., Biddle, B.J., Bank, B.J., Hauge, G. & Wan-Rafaei, R., & Valantin, S. (1983). Parents, friends, siblings, and adults: Unfolding referent other importance data for adolescents. *International Journal of Psychology, 18,* 239-262.

Kelly, G. (1955). *The psychology of personal constructs.* New York: Norton.

LeVine, R., & Campbell, D. (1972). *Ethnocentrism: Theories of conflict, ethnic attitudes, and group behaviour.* New York: Wiley.

Linton, R. (1936). *The study of man.* New York: Appleton-Century-Crofts.

Lonner, W.J. (1990). An overview of cross-cultural testing and assessment. In R.W. Brislin (Ed.), *Applied cross-cultural psychology* (pp. 56–76). Newbury Park, CA: Sage.

Lowe, J. (in press). International examinations: The new credentialism and reproduction of advantage in a globalising world. *Assessment in Education, Principles, Processes and Practices.*

Markus, H.R., & Kitayama, S. (1998). The cultural psychology of personality. *Journal of Cross-Cultural Psychology 29*, 63–87.

McCaig, N.M. (1999). Foreword. In D. Pollock & R. Van Reken. *The Third Culture Kid experience: Growing up among worlds* (pp. ix–xvi). Yarmouth, ME: Intercultural Press.

Mead, G.H. (1934). Symbolic interactionism. In C.W. Morris (Ed.), *Mind, self, and society.* Chicago, IL: University of Chicago Press.

Mead, M. (1975). Ethnicity and anthropology in America. In L. Romanucci-Ross & G. DeVos (Eds.), *Ethnic identity: Creation, conflict and accommodation* (pp. 298–320). Walnut Creek, CA: AltaMira Press.

Miller, J.G. (1988). Bridging the content-structure dichotomy: Culture and the self. In M.H. Bond (Ed.), *The cross-cultural challenge to social psychology* (pp. 266–281). Newbury Park, CA: Sage.

Minoura, Y. (1987). *Culture and self-concept among adolescents growing up in a multicultural setting--a theoretical scheme and its application.* Paper presented at the IX biennial meeting of the International Society for the Study of Behavioural Development, Tokyo, Japan, July 12–16.

Minoura, Y. (1992). A sensitive period for the incorporation of cultural meaning systems. *Ethos, 20*, 304–339.

Minoura, Y. (1993). Culture and personality reconsidered: Theory building from cases of Japanese children returning from the United States. *Quarterly Newsletter of the Laboratory of Human Cognition, 15*, 63–71.

Moghaddam, F.M. (1997). The Haji Baba of Georgetown. In M.H. Bond (Ed.), *Working at the interface of cultures: Eighteen lives in social science* (pp. 191–201). London, UK: Routledge.

Moghaddam, F., Taylor, D.M., and Wright, S.C. (1993). *Social psychology in cross-cultural perspective.* New York: W.H. Freeman.

Much, N., & Shweder, R. (1978). Speaking of rules: The analysis of culture in breach. In W. Damon (Ed.), *New directions for child development: No. 2: Moral development.* San Francisco, CA: Jossey-Bass.

Newcomb, T.M. (1961). *The acquaintance process.* New York: Rhinehart Winston.

Northover, M. (1988). Bilinguals and linguistic identities. In J.N.

Jørgensen, E. Hansen, A. Holmen, & J. Gimbel (Eds.), *Bilingualism in society and school: Copenhagen studies in bilingualism, Vol. 5* (pp. 201–218). Clevedon, UK: Multilingual Matters.

Novak, M. (1971). *The rise of the unmeltable ethnics: Politics and culture in the 70s.* New York: Macmillan.

Pearce, R. (1998). Developing cultural identity in an international school environment. In M. Hayden and J. Thompson (Eds.), *International education: Principles and practice* (pp. 44–62). London, UK: Kogan Page.

Pollock, D., & Van Reken, R. (1999). *The third culture kid experience: Growing up among worlds.* Yarmouth, ME: Intercultural Press.

Ramirez, M., & Castañeda, A. (1974). *Cultural democracy, bicultural development, and education.* New York: Academic Press

Sanua, V.D. (1958). *Differences in personality adjustment among different generations of American Jews and non-Jews.* Proceedings of the International Congress of Psychology, Brussels, Belgium, 1958 and published in *Acta Psychologica, 15,* 542–543.

Schlesinger, A.M. (1998). *The disuniting of America: Reflections on a multicultural society.* New York: Norton.

Secord, P.F., & Backman, C.W. (1974). *Social psychology.* Tokyo, Japan: McGraw-Hill/Kogakusta.

Stewart, E.C., & Bennett, M.J. (1991). *American cultural patterns: A cross-cultural perspective.* (Rev. ed.). Yarmouth, MA: Intercultural Press.

Strauss, C. (1992). Models and motives. In R. D'Andrade and C. Strauss (Eds.), *Human motives and cultural models* (pp. 1–20). Cambridge, UK: Cambridge University Press.

Stryker, S. (1980). *Symbolic interactionism: A social structural version.* Menlo Park, CA: B Cummings.

Thorley, N.R. (1990). *The role of the conceptual change model in the interpretation of classroom interactions.* Unpublished doctoral dissertation, University of Wisconsin, Madison, WI.

Ting-Toomey, S. (1997). An intercultural journey: The four seasons. In M. H. Bond (Ed.), *Working at the interface of cultures: Eighteen lives in social science* (pp. 202–215). London, UK: Routledge.

Torbiörn, I. (1982). *Living abroad: Personal adjustment and personal policy in the overseas setting.* New York: Wiley.

Turner, J.C. (1982). Towards a cognitive redefinition of the social group. In H. Tajfel (Ed.), *Social identity and intergroup relations*. London: Cambridge University Press.

Turner, J.C. (1996). Henri Tajfel: An introduction. In W.P. Robinson (Ed.), *Social groups and identities: Developing the legacy of Henri Tajfel* (pp. 1–23). Oxford, UK: Butterworth-Heinemann.

Vygotsky, L. S. (1962). *Thought and language*. Cambridge, MA: MIT Press.

Weinreich, P. (1983). Emerging from threatened identities: Ethnicity and gender in redefinitions of threatened identity. In G. Breakwell (Ed.), *Threatened identities* (pp. 149–183). Chichester, UK: Wiley.

Weinreich, P. (1989). Variations in ethnic identity: Identity structure analysis. In K. Liebkind (Ed.), *New identities in Europe: Immigrant ancestry and the ethnic identity of youth* (pp. 41–76). London: Gower.

Weinreich, P., Luk, C.L., & Bond, M.H. (1996). Ethnic stereotyping and identification in a multicultural context: "Acculturation," self-esteem and identity diffusion in Hong Kong Chinese university students. *Psychology and Developing Societies, 8*, 107–169.

10

GENDER DIFFERENCES IN CULTURAL ACCEPTANCE AND CAREER ORIENTATION AMONG INTERNATIONALLY MOBILE AND NONINTERNATIONALLY MOBILE ADOLESCENTS

MICHAEL E. GERNER & FRED L. PERRY, JR.

ABSTRACT

An adolescent who spends some part of his or her developmental years in one or more countries other than his or her country of origin or citizenship due to the international work of their parents is called an Internationally Mobile (IM) adolescent or Third Culture Kid (TCK) or Global Nomad (GN) or International School Student (ISS). Research has suggested that these adolescents develop greater cultural acceptance; they have an increased openness to learning other languages; they generally are satisfied living abroad; they wish to maintain geographically mobile lives; and they are interested in future international careers. Interestingly, gender differences on these variables with internationally mobile adolescents have not appeared in the professional literature even though there is a volu-minous literature with other groups. Their reanalysis used data from the largest known study of internationally mobile adolescents on two continents with peers who have maintained residence in only one country throughout their lives $(N = 1,076)$. Findings support the impression of consistent gender differences. This analysis suggests the possibility that living abroad is a crucial experience to develop

female interest in international careers. The largest and most meaningful differences in this study are between females who have lived
abroad and both males and females who have not, and between
females and males who have never lived abroad.

INTRODUCTION

An enormous volume of literature on gender differences exists
in psychology. The investigation of gender differences in personality
characteristics, attitudes, abilities, and a host of other "psychological" variables has been long researched (see Maccoby & Jacklin,
1974) and continues to the present time (Wilgenbusch & Merrell,
1999). Interest in exploring and identifying gender differences has a
lengthy history, but gender differences have not been explored in a
large sample of internationally mobile or third culture adolescents.
"Internationally mobile children and adolescents" specifically refers
to K through 12 students who live abroad with their parents and not
"international students" at colleges who are older and who do not
live abroad with their parents during their school-age or developmental years (5 through 18). "Internationally mobile children/ado-
lescents" and "international school students" can be used
interchangeably; "third culture kids" is the original designation;
"internationally mobile" was coined in 1992 to be more descriptive
and avoid the confusion with "third world" (Gerner, Perry, Moselle.
& Archbold, 1992a).

Ruth Hill Useem (Useem & Downie, 1976) was the first to differentiate third culture kids (TCKs) from children who never leave
their country of origin (first or "home" culture). She stated that they
also differ from children in the foreign countries in which they are
temporary residents (second or "host" culture), resulting in a new,
unique culture that only other internationally mobile children share
(third culture). Research has demonstrated differences between
internationally mobile children/TCK adolescents in terms of
greater linguistic ability and openness for new language learning
(Third-culture Kids, 1988; Gerner, Perr, Moselle, & Archibold,
1992a), more flexibility than their monocultural counterparts in

interacting with different cultural groups (Gleason, 1970, 1973; Gerner et al., 1992a), greater interest in maintaining geographically mobile lives and orientation to international careers (Gerner et al., 1992a; Werkman, 1986), more emotional investment in independence and self-knowledge (Werkman, Farley, Butler, & Quayhagen, 1981), and a high level of satisfaction with living abroad (Nathanson & Marcenko, 1995), but investigation of gender differences on these variables has yet to be published in the professional literature. However, the general findings of [a] major recent study of Adult Third Culture Kids (ATCK) appeared in a trade newsletter of International Schools Services and is available on the Internet (http://www.iss.edu/pages/kids.html). Although statistical analysis, sampling procedures, and experimental methods are not yet published in the scientific literature, the preliminary findings are provocative and suggest that the differences between responses of adult women and men who have lived abroad during their developmental years reflect general gender differences more than different "living abroad" experiences (Cottrell, Useem, Useem, & Finn Jordan, 1999). For example, these authors report women showed a greater concern with interpersonal relationships and were far more likely to experience difficulty leaving childhood friends and returning to the United States. As adults, these women were more likely to believe that the experience of living abroad as a child or adolescent enhanced their community involvement and social relationships, but they also experienced more stress from competing desires for both mobility and stability. Men, on the other hand, reported a greater satisfaction with their unfolding lives in general. The authors speculate that this may be because men worry less about interpersonal relationships and their self-esteem is tied more to external achievements than relationships (see http://www.iss.edu/pages/kids.html, pp. 9-10).

Cann and Siegfried (1990) showed that females were perceived as more interpersonally oriented than males, who were perceived to be more task-oriented and domineering. This suggested possible differences between males and females in this reanalysis of variables associated with cross-cultural acceptance. Specifically, it was hypothesized that gender differences in cultural acceptance, openness to languages, and more favorable ratings of different national groups would be found, but differences would *not* be expected on variables such as travel interest and orientation to an international career.

In the original study, Gerner et al. (1992a) conducted the largest known analysis of internationally mobile adolescents on two continents with peers who have maintained residence in only one country throughout their lives (N = 1,076). Findings supported the impression that internationally mobile adolescents from the United States living abroad have greater interest in travel, learning languages, and that they rate themselves more culturally accepting and are more oriented to a international lifestyle in the future compared with their peers in the United States. This study did not look at gender differences but instead concentrated on establishing whether the characteristics claimed for internationally mobile adolescents were, in fact, true with a large and geographically diversified sample. To rectify the omission of investigating gender differences, the first two authors reanalyzed the data with gender differences as the central focus. Three groups are of primary interest: Noninternationally mobile adolescents who have always lived in the United States, internationally mobile adolescents from the United States living in Thailand or Egypt, and a group of internationally mobile adolescents from other countries.

Internationally mobile children and adolescents attend schools throughout the world that educate American, British, and children of other nationalities whose parents work abroad; they provide an excellent research setting for studying these children. The unique characteristics of these schools and the children that attend them have been described for school psychologists (Gerner, 1985, 1990, 1994) and organizations dedicated to working with internationally mobile adolescents, college students, and adults (Gerner, 1993a, 1993b; Gerner et al., 1992b). The language of instruction at American international schools is English, and the scope and sequence of the basic curriculum follows the academic program of many private and upper middle class public schools in the United States. Students from the United States may account for a sizable percentage of the school, but there can be students from 30 or more countries also attending who are multilingual or who speak English as a second language. English is frequently acquired as a second language by children from many nationalities whose parents were themselves educated at U.S. universities or who wish a U.S. college placement for their son or daughter. A significant proportion of the teaching staff may b[e] from the United States, Great Britain, or Australia in addition to ESL and bilingual educators from the host country, and school psychologists from the United States are most frequently hired at the larger international schools, although schools with only a few hundred students have reported using the services of a school psychologist (see Gerner, 1990).

Two large, independent international schools in Egypt and Thailand were selected to contrast with a noninternationally mobile sample of high school students in the United States. Both overseas schools offer a U.S. curriculum to a population of predominantly business and government agency dependents. No attempt was made to include separate military dependent schools or missionary schools because business and government-related dependents are the most numerous in many expatriate communities worldwide. The complete description of the method and procedure is detailed in the Gerner et al. (1992a) study; however, a brief summary will acquaint readers with the approach.

METHOD

Subjects

Three groups were studied. The first group was composed of adolescents who have always lived in the Unite[d] States. The second group was composed of adolescents of U.S. origin living abroad. The third group comprised adolescents from various countries other than the United States who also were living abroad or outside of their "home country," whatever that happened to be. Students at three secondary schools (grades 9 to 12) participated in the study. Two were international schools in Egypt and Thailand,

and one was a public high school in the United States. A total of 1,076 student questionnaires were used in the original analysis with failure to indicate gender occurring in 6% or 65 student questionnaires. A final sample of 1,011 was used for the gender differences investigation, which included 222 U.S. students who resided permanently within the United States from a midwestern state (Minnesota); 270 U.S. internationally mobile students living in either Thailand or Egypt; and 519 non-U.S. internationally mobile students from all other nationalities combined. The original study (Gerner et al., 1992a) did not identify pervasive differences among the various nationalities; therefore, they were merged and contrasted with U.S. international mobile adolescents as a group. Students from the United States and students of other nationalities that attend international schools have many sociological variables in common: They are predominantly from intact professional families; these families are middle to upper middle class, and education is highly valued.

The Internationally Mobile Sample. The sample included U.S. students who accounted for a higher proportion of students at the schools in Egypt and Thailand than any other single nationality. The school in Thailand had 1,770 students K to 12, 35% of whom were American students and 65% of whom were of other nationalities (International Schools Services, 1990); the school in Egypt enrolled 1,170 students K to 12, 55% of whom were American and 45% of whom were of other nationalities (International Schools Services, 1990). The internationally mobile sample combining Egypt and Thailand was composed of the following groups: 34% American, 26% Asian, 17% European, 15% Middle Eastern, and 8% from other nations of the world (e.g., countries in Africa, Latin America, and the subcontinent). The internationally mobile sample comprised students from the United States living abroad and non-U.S. students of other nationalities who were living abroad while their parents were employed as expatriate workers, managers, and professionals.

The occupation of the father was used to classify internationally mobile adolescents into group of sponsorship or the employing institution that was responsible for bringing the family overseas, such as official government (includes diplomats and foreign aid agencies), business, military, technical, missionary, and education. The occupation of the father was used because almost all of the adolescents lived abroad as a function of the father's, not mother's, employment. The sample was predominantly sponsored by business (33%) and official government agencies (24%) as expected, followed by technical (13%), military (6%), education (4%), and missionary (2%). The sponsor category of "other" accounted for 18% of the sample and was due to employment that was not easily classified (e.g., self-employed consultants, language/ translation experts, bank managers, researchers, and engineers). In the original study (Gerner et al., 1992a) there were no significant differences for family, travel, and future orientation among any of the groups, with the exception of a small sample of missionary dependents. Missionary internationally mobile adolescents rated themselves as being significantly closer to their families than the other groups. However, because of the overwhelming pattern of similarity, "sponsorship" was not used as a category in the original study or in this current reanalysis. Analysis of variance (ANOVA) also determined that there were no significant differences between the ages of the students, the educational level of the father, and the educational level of the mother.

The sample of internationally mobile adolescents had considerable international living experience: 50% had lived abroad 7 years or more, 28% lived abroad 3 to 6 years, and 22% had lived abroad 2 years or less. The number of years lived abroad was not associated with significant attitudinal differences in the Gerner et al. (1992a) study, so it was not controlled in this current investigation. There are accounts that students—within a year—begin to take on some of the characteristics reported to be associated with international mobility (Pollock, 1989). While this sample of adolescents in Egypt and Thailand did not show a marked difference in self-ratings related to years lived abroad, this might not be true with other internationally mobile groups, and there are potentially wide individual differences on this and the other variables.

The Noninternationally Mobile Sample. These students were from a rural-suburban high school in the midwestern United States. Students living in a moderate-sized midwestern town were selected as a comparison to ensure that their experience living abroad was minimal compared with the students attending the two international schools overseas. In fact, the only student in this group with international living experience was the foreign exchange student, who was not included in this study. This U.S. sample of adolescents was from a middle to upper middle class socioeconomic back-ground. In this regard, they were more comparable to those U.S. internationally mobile adolescents in Egypt and Thailand who represent a select group of students whose predominantly middle to upper middle class professional families chose to live abroad temporarily.

Instrument

The Internationally Mobile Adolescent Questionnaire. The develop-ment of the questionnaire was based upon prior exploratory research (Useem & Downie, 1976). A panel of three of the authors (Gerner et al., 1992a) suggested multiple items to measure each characteristic claimed for internationally mobile children and adolescents. This produced a 60-item questionnaire that was administered to a random sample of 40 students attending an international school in Cairo, Egypt. The students were asked to indicate which items were unclear or problematic; those were elimi-nated and several other items were reworded or added based upon the comments made by the students in the pilot study. The final questionnaire contained 57 Likert-type items. Forty-seven items consisted of statements to which students indicate their degree of agreement on a 5-point scale ranging from 1 = Strongly Disagree to 5 = Strongly Agree. Ten items ask students to rate their feelings toward 10 nationalities from 1 = Strongly Negative to 5 = Strongly Positive. The final scale consists of seven subscales: Family Rela-tionship (10 items), Peer Relationship (8 items), Cultural Accep-tance (6 items), Travel Orientation (7 items), Language Acceptance (5 items), Future Orientation (11 items), and Stereotype (10 items).

Thirteen items were added to the beginning of the scale to collect biographical data.

Procedures

Administration. Multiple copies of the questionnaire and machine-scoreable answer sheets were mailed to a designated coordinator at each of the three sites. In Egypt, the school psychologist (first author) organized the administration; at Thailand, the senior counselor organized questionnaire implementation (fourth author); and in the United States, a principal who was a close associate of the third author coordinated administration and data collection. The site coordinator bundled the questionnaires and answer sheets into class sections; these were disseminated to high school teachers to administer during a class period. The 70-item questionnaire was administered to students in the United States, Egypt, and Thailand in their high school classrooms by their teachers who followed a one-page instruction sheet. The questionnaire was administered to all students at each site at the same time and took place within a 30-day period. Every student enrolled in each high school was included.

Data Collection. Students recorded their responses on machine-scoreable answer sheets that were mailed to the first author. These were subsequently forwarded to the second author for data analysis using optical scan equipment at the American University in Cairo.

RESULTS

The analysis was organized by first evaluating the reliability of the questionnaire and each subscale is briefly characterized (see Appendix 10.1 for complete subscale content). Responses of adolescents of U.S. origin are discussed first and comparisons are made between those who have always lived in the United States and adolescents from the United States who attended school in either Egypt or Thailand with gender differences as the central concern. Then, male and female adolescents from the United Sates living abroad with their families are compared with adolescents from other countries. Finally, gender differences are evaluated in terms of effect size *(ES)*, where an *ES* of 1.00 means a difference of 15 standard score points ($M = 100$, $SD = 15$) between the average adolescent in one group compared with the average adolescent in the other group (i.e., an adolescent at the 50th percentile of one group would be at the 84th percentile of the score distribution of the other).

Reliability of Instrument

Cronbach's alpha coefficients were computed for each of the subscales (Cronbach, 1951). One subscale, Peer Relationship, was found to have a low reliability coefficient (0.46) and was deleted from the final analysis. The other subscales had items that produced moderate to high reliabilities (.61, .85, .75, .66, .85, and .71). Table 10.1 shows the alpha coefficients for each subscale with examples of their content. The number of subscale questions for analysis was 49; those that reduced the reliability of their respective subscale (8) were deleted. The final list of items comprising the questionnaire arranged by subscale is detailed in Appendix 10.1.

The Family Relationship subscale was designed to assess the degree of closeness an adolescent perceives toward his or her parents and family. The Cultural Acceptance subscale queried how accepting an adolescent was of cultural differences. Travel Orientation was designed to determine the interest of the adolescent in traveling, both in general and between countries. The Language Acceptance subscale was geared to measure receptivity to learning languages other than one's first language or in addition to languages already known. The Stereotype subscale asked adolescents to rate 10 different national/geographical groups on how favorably they viewed them. The Future Orientation subscale assessed how oriented an adolescent was toward working abroad as a career. Some items were placed as "experimental" to query a specific claim made in the exploratory literature; if they did not significantly reduce their subscale's reliability, they were retained in the analysis.

U.S. Subjects

A two-way multivariate analysis of variance (MANOVA) was conducted using the Multivariate General Linear Hypothesis (MGLH) subroutine of the SYSTAT computer program (Wilkinson, 1987). The six subscales were treated as dependent variables, while location of testing and gender were used as the independent variables.

Table 10.1. Subscale Composition, Reliabilities, and Sample Contents.

Subscale	Items	Reliability	Sample Content
FR	9	.85	I enjoy spending time with my family; I am close to my family.
PR	5	.46	I worry about losing my friends; I am reluctant to form close friendships.
CA	4	.61	I am very accepting of people's differences; Some nationalities are better than others.'
TO	6	.66	I do *not* like to travel;' The more a country is different from my home country, the more I would like to visit it.
LA	4	.75	It is important for me to speak at least one language other than my own; I like learning different languages.
SS	10	.85	Rate on a 1-5 scale (1 = Strongly Negative, 5 = Strongly Positive): Asians, Arabs, British, etc.'
FO	11	.71	I hope to pursue an international career; the idea of living and working in another country is exciting.

Note: FR = Family Relationship; PR = Peer Relationship; CA = Cultural Acceptance; TO = Travel Orientation; LA = Language Acceptance; SS = Stereotype Scale; and FO = Future Orientation
' "Negative" items were reversed for scoring purposes.
'The higher the score on the Stereotype scale, the more favorable the rating.

Main Effect for Gender. The MANOVA revealed a significant Wilks' lambda, $F(6, 481) = 12.562$, $p < .0001$. The means and standard deviations are displayed in Table 10.2. The related univariate analysis of variances (ANOVA) revealed that females were more positive than males on all subscales ($p < .0001$) except for Family Relationship, which was not significant.

Table 10.2. Descriptive Statistics for Gender by Subscales for US Subjects Only.

Scale	Male n = 246	Female n = 246
Culture		
M	3.576	4.028**
SD	0.696	0.631
Family		
M	3.054	3.129
SD	0.713	0.789
Future		
M	3.113	3.354**
SD	0.574	0.576
Language		
M	2.807	3.334**
SD	0.961	0.822
Stereotype		
M	3.294	3.537**
SD	0.599	0.630
Travel		
M	3.382	3.714*
SD	0.698	0.574

*$p < .002$
**$p < .0001$

Interaction Effect for Gender by Location. A significant Wilks' lambda was revealed for the two-way interaction, $F(18, 1,360) = 8.289$, $p < .0001$. The subsequent univariate two-way interaction for each subscale revealed that except for the Family Relationship, which was not significant, all were significant ($p < .0001$). Descriptive statistics for this interaction are displayed in Table 10.3.

Simple main effects of the interactions were analyzed by using the Tukey-Kramer pairwise comparison procedure (Kirk, 1982), which employs an unweighted solution for unequal cell sizes. Prior to this, however, Bartlett['s] chi-square analyses were conducted to examine whether there were any violations of homogeneity of variance. Only the chi-square for the Future Orientation subscale was found to be significant, $(df = 5) = 17.51$, $p < .005$.

Scale	Male n = 105	Female n = 117	Male n = 66	Female n = 48	Male n = 75	Female n = 71
Table 10.3. Descriptive Statistics for Location by Gender Interaction for US Subjects Only.						
Culture						
M	3.329	3.953	3.870	4.013	3.663	4.165
SD	0.618	0.605	0.633	0.676	0.737	0.622
Family						
M	3.005	3.128	3.131	3.029	3.055	3.222
SD	0.643	0.806	0.786	0.799	0743	0.752
Future						
M	2.873	3.128	3.269	3.506	3.314	3.601
SD	0.451	0.463	0.539	0.604	0.634	0.583
Language						
M	2.479	3.147	3.080	3.422	3.027	3.570
SD	0.886	0.852	0.902	0.674	0.987	0.817
Stereotype						
M	3.174	3.470	3.409	3.469	3.360	3.701
SD	0.622	0.660	0.529	0.602	0.602	0.578
Travel						
M	3.146	3.550	3.497	3.836	3.611	3.885
SD	0.574	0.651	0.668	0.677	0.783	0.628

Note: The Peer subscale is not discussed any further due to low reliability.

The comparison of males and females at each location provided fairly consistent results. For subscales Culture, Future, Language, and Stereotype, females gave higher ratings than males at two locations, in the U.S. and Egypt (all were $p < .009$ or lower except one, Future, which was $p < 0.02$). There were no significant gender differences in Thailand on these subscales, although there was a trend for females to score higher. Performance on the Travel subscale was a little different. Whereas females were more positive than males in the United States, there was no gender difference in Egypt. However, in Thailand, females were higher than males, but the probability for a Type I error was just less than .05. In light of the many comparisons, this might not be considered statistically significant.

Comparing the different locations on the different subscales at each level of gender also revealed interesting differences. For Culture, Future, Language, and Travel, males from Thailand and Egypt were more positive (all $p < .0001$) than those from the United States but were not significantly different from each other. Males across the three locations for Stereotype were not different.

Females, on the other hand, revealed a different pattern of

responses across location. On the Culture subscale, as well as for Stereotype, there were no significant differences. On the Travel and Language subscales, females in Thailand were between that of females in Egypt and the United States but not significantly different, whereas females in Egypt were more positive than those in the United States on these two subscales ($p < .01$, $p < .02$, respectively). On the Future Orientation subscale, females in Egypt and Thailand did not significantly differ, but both were greater than those in the United States ($p < .0001$).

U.S. vs. Non-U.S. Subjects

A two-way multivariate analysis of variance (MANOVA) was conducted with gender and nationality (Non-U.S. vs. U.S.) as the two independent variables. The six subscales were the dependent variables.

Main Effect for Gender. The MANOVA for the main effect for gender resulted in a significant Wilks' lambda F (6, 780) = 9.108, $p <. 0001$. The following univariate tests on the subscales revealed the same pattern of results as was found in the U.S. sample only data. A comparison of the cell means is presented in Table 10.4. Females were higher in their responses than males on all subscales except Family Relationship, in which no difference occurred. Violations of homogeneity of variance according to Bartlett's chi-square test were found for subscales Language Acceptance, Stereotype, and Travel Orientation. However, extrapolation from Table 13.2 in Hopkins and Glass (1978, p. 258) shows that the observed probabilities for a Type I error are not in danger of exceeding the criterion.

Main Effect for Nationality. The results were a replication of the findings of our earlier study (Gerner et al., 1992a). Non-U.S. internationally mobile adolescents held more positive attitudes in four of the six subscales than did U.S. internationally mobile adolescents (i.e., Family Relationship, Future Orientation, Language Acceptance, and Travel Orientation). Conversely, internationally mobile adolescents from the United States were more positive toward other nationalities than Non-U.S. adolescents based upon the results of the Stereotype subscale. See Table 10.5 for a comparison of the cell means.

Interaction Effect of Gender by Nationality. The overall MANOVA for the interaction between nationality and gender was found to be significant, Wilks' lambda $F(12, 1,560) = 11.74, p < .0001$. The data are provided in Table 10.6. The univariate test showed that the interaction was significant for all six subscales. A more detailed pair-wise analysis of each interaction was done using the Tukey-Kramer procedure. Violations of homogeneity of group variances were noted in Table 10.6, but none were found to exceed the criteria as charted by Hopkins and Glass (1978, p. 256).

Table 10.4. Descriptive Statistics for the Main Effect of Gender Combined across Nationalities.

Scale	Gender		P
	Male n = 386	Female n = 403	
Culture			
M	3.810	4.083	.0001
SD	0.636	0.654	
Family			
M	3.207	3.203	
SD	0.710	0.751	
Future			
M	3.442	3.566	.001
SD	0.540	0.506	
Language'			
M	3.314	3.679	.0001
SD	0.887	0.715	
Stereotype'			
M	3.359	3.513	.001
SD	0.554	0.626	
Travel'			
M	3.678	3.846	.0001
SD	0.655	0.582	

'A significant chi-square for Bartlett's test for homogeneity of group variances

A primary way to look at the interaction is to compare males and females within each location. The simple effect analysis revealed that for the Culture Acceptance subscale, U.S. females scored higher than U.S. males ($p < .0001$), but there was no differ-ence between non-U.S. males and females. In the case of Family Relationship, both females and males were equal for U.S. and non-

U.S. groups. Future Orientation, Travel Orientation, and the Stereotype scale showed similar results to Culture Acceptance, U.S. females outscored U.S. males ($p < .0001$, $p < .0001$, .02 respectively) but no gender differences were found for non-U.S. adolescents. For the Language Acceptance subscale, females gave higher scores than males for U.S. and non-U.S. groups ($p < .0001$).

Table 10.5. Descriptive Statistics for the Main Effect of Nationality.

Scale	Nationality		P
	US n = 270	Non-US n = 519	
Culture			
M	3.929	3.914	
SD	0.693	0.629	
Family			
M	3.113	3.297	.001
SD	0.768	0.704	
Future			
M	3.425	3.582	.0001
SD	0.605	0.468	
Language			
M	3.278	3.490	.0001
SD	0.888	0.741	
Stereotype			
M	3.490	3.382	.02
SD	0.591	0.554	
Travel			
M	3.710	3.814	.03
SD	0.708	0.568	

Simple effects for males also were found between U.S. and non-U.S. internationally mobile adolescents. The former were significantly lower than the latter on four of the six subscales: Family Relationship ($p < .02$), Future Orientation ($p < .0001$), Language Acceptance ($p < .0001$), and Travel Orientation ($p < .001$). No differences were found for Culture Acceptance or the Stereotype scale.

A different pattern was found for females. U.S. and non-U.S. internationally mobile adolescents did not differ on Family Relationship, Future Orientation, or Travel Orientation. However, non-U.S.

females showed less favorable ratings of groups on the Stereotype scale than U.S. adolescents ($p < .04$). Female performance was the same as that of males between nationalities for the remaining subscales.

Effect Size. Another way of assessing these findings is to consider the magnitude of mean differences on a 5-point scale. One example of this is U.S. females living in Thailand or Egypt scored far higher in international career interest (3.5 and 3.6) compared with males (2.9) and females (3.1) who have always lived in the United States. Another example is U.S. females in Thailand (3.4) and Egypt (3.6) rated themselves much higher in openness to learning/communicating in other languages compared with males (2.5) who have always lived in the United States *and* females in Egypt were far more positive than their U.S. male counterparts in Egypt (3.0).

Table 10.6. Comparison of the Mean Scores of All US Internationally Mobile Adolescents with Non-US Internationally Mobile Adolescents by Gender.

	US		Non-US	
Scale	Male n = 141	Female n = 129	Male n = 245	Female n = 274
Culture				
M	3.761	4.097	3.859	3.969**
SD	0.696	0.649	0.597	0.653
Family				
M	3.091	3.185	3.324	3.270*
SD	0.762	0.777	0.665	0.737
Future'				
M	3.298	3.558	3.591	3.574**
SD	0.590	0.593	0.477	0.461
Language'				
M	3.051	3.504	3.578	3.854**
SD	0.945	0.757	0.791	0.667
Stereotype				
M	3.383	3.597	3.336	3.429**
SD	0.567	0.598	0.547	0.632
Travel'				
M	3.558	3.863	3.798	3.829**
SD	0.731	0.648	0.590	0.549

'A significant chi-square for Barlett's test for homogeneity of group variances
*$p < .004$
**$p < .0001$

These differences can be further illustrated by calculating effect size (Gail, Borg, & Gall, 1996). Applied to this study's group differences regarding international career orientation, U.S. females living in Thailand or Egypt showed an *ES* of 1.27 and 1.44, respectively, compared with males who have always lived in the United States. This means that they scored 19 to 22 standard points higher than these males, the difference between a standard score of 100 and one of 119-122, or scoring better than 50% to surpassing 89% to 92%. The difference between females who had always lived in the United States and U.S. females living in Thailand or Egypt in international career interest was an *ES* of .75 to .93 for an average of .84, or moving from the 50th percentile to the 81st, suggesting the experience of living abroad may contribute to greater international career orientation.

Effect size also is useful to interpret more accurately gender differences between U.S. adolescents abroad in either Egypt or Thailand. As stated previously, there were significant differences in favor of females being more positive than males in Stereotype, Travel, Future Orientation to an international career, Cultural Acceptance and Language ($p < .0001$). However, the *ES* associated with these areas are a fairly modest .37, .44, .45, .50, and .53, respectively. This means that females score higher or more positively on these subscales from six to eight standard score points, or the difference from the 50th percentile to the 65th to 69th percentile. It can be inferred that there were significant differences between males and females within the internationally mobile U.S. sample, but these were not as practically meaningful in comparison to whether the male or female had lived abroad in relation to those who had not.

Finally, effect size also helps to explain more fully the extent of differences between U.S. and non-U.S. internationally mobile adolescents. Non-U.S. adolescents scored more positively on certain subscales, among them Travel, Language, and Future Orientation. However, the effect sizes associated with these significant differences were .17, .27, and .30, respectively. This represents a difference of 3 to 5 standard score points or moving from the 50th to the 57th to 65th percentiles (103 to 105 standard scores), not a particularly meaningful or practical difference. The largest and most meaningful differences in this study are between females who had lived abroad and males and females who have not, and between females and males who have not lived abroad. (Note: A weighted standard deviation taking into account unequal sample sizes was used in all *ES* computations.)

DISCUSSION

U.S. Gender Differences

This study supports the impression of gender differences in attitudes between U.S. males and females, whether living in the United States or abroad. In general, females were more positive in accepting other cultures and less stereotypic; they were more oriented toward international careers; and they were more open for travel and being exposed to different languages. It must always be kept in mind, however, that U.S. males who have spent some part of their developmental years living abroad as a function of the international work of their parents also consistently were more positive on these characteristics compared to U.S. males who have never lived abroad. The differences in this study further suggest that the international experience for U.S. males in areas such as Cultural Acceptance moved them closer to the positive ratings of U.S. females, whereas U.S. females tended to maintain their ratings in Cultural Acceptance. However, positive ratings in areas such as interest in a future international career and openness to learning other languages was significantly higher than females who had lived in the United States throughout their lives.

It appears that attitude change associated with international mobility may be more general for males, particularly in terms of the acceptance of other cultures. The experience of living abroad may increase cultural acceptance among males, while females may show a propensity for interacting with different groups whether or not they have lived abroad. On the other hand, the desire to pursue an international career for females seems more robustly related to the experience of living abroad, and United States females living in Egypt and Thailand were more positive about working internationally than females who had always lived in the U.S. . This suggests the possibility that living abroad is a crucial experience to develop female interest in international careers, a potentially important consideration for families who want their daughters to consider diplomatic or international business careers.

The experience of living aboard could not be argued to be responsible for producing the male-female disparity in the data presented in this reanalysis. Consistent differences favoring females as more open to other cultures, languages, national groups, travel, and international careers were found in a group of 9th- to 12th-grade high school students who had always lived within the United States. Males, however, who had the experience of living abroad were more positive in their openness to other cultures, learning languages, travel, and future international careers compared with U.S. males who had always lived in the United States. Females presented a more "mixed" picture, suggesting living abroad may not be as powerful in increasing self-ratings associated with social acceptance, whereas it does in an area such as orientation to a future international career.

Studies of gender role stereotypes may be a pertinent consideration relative to this difference because they suggest females are perceived as more interpersonally oriented and collaborative, while males are viewed as more task-oriented and domineering (Cann & Siegried, 1990). Behavior differences between males and females show marked contrasts at early ages (see Maccoby, 1985 for a review) with girls more socially oriented, open to experience, and concerned for others. In fact, Pratch and Jacobowitz (1996) found that women managers who behaved in the expected manner (e.g., socially oriented and collaborative) were rated more successful as leaders than those who acted in the contralateral management style (e.g., task-oriented and domineering). Whatever the source in the nature-nurture controversy, male-female differences are complex with a history of social reinforcement for gender-specific behavior and this may explain the socially based gender differences found in this study.

The male-female differences within the U.S. sample of noninternationally mobile adolescents are intriguing. It could be argued that without experience of international travel, females who are believed to be socialized to be more accepting of social differences and new experiences may show this influence in their ratings on internationally oriented items that assume social flexibility. Alternatively, females may have been more reluctant to be critical and this could have influenced their self-ratings. Reasons for the gender differences observed in this study are tentative, but there was a general pattern of gender differences that indicates this variable must not be overlooked in future research.

The pattern of male-female attitudinal differences was strong, but it was not universally true for U.S. adolescents living abroad. U.S. adolescents living in Thailand did not show significant male-female differences in most of the areas. On the other hand, U.S. females living in the United States and those living in Egypt gave consistently more positive ratings than their male peers in terms of being open to other cultures, languages and future international careers, and they rated various nationalities more favorably. This introduces the possibility that cultural setting may affect female perceptions; for example, male-female differences may be more self-conscious in societies that define gender roles in sharp relief. To make matters even more complex, whereas females in the United States were much more interested in travel than the males, in Egypt there were no gender differences on the dimension of travel motivation. Generalities about male-female differences may be very difficult when studying specific countries, cultures, and even cities within foreign countries. Important variables to consider are the host cultural context, location within the host country (village, town, city), and degree of cultural contact (i.e., living on the local economy, in segregated compounds, or within an expatriate worker community "bubble").

These exceptions notwithstanding, it is significant that male-female differences were found in a large number of areas and the general direction was that females were more positive on characteristics associated with an internationally mobile lifestyle alleged by exploratory research, interviews, and some data-based studies.

These findings suggest, at least for the U.S. sample, pervasive gender differences among a group of U.S. high school students who had never lived abroad. In addition, there is some evidence of gender differences in internationally mobile adolescents, but the pattern was less extensive suggesting mitigating situational variables or that the experience of living abroad may reduce the extent of these differences in some cases.

Non-U.S. Gender Differences

An interesting finding is that all U.S. internationally mobile subjects and all non-U.S. internationally mobile adolescents taken as a group show consistent differences, with females being more positive in the areas of Cultural Acceptance, Language, Travel, Stereotype, and Future Orientation to an international career. However, the main differences are between U.S. males and U.S. females who are internationally mobile. Males and females from other nationalities do not show a pattern of more favorable female ratings in comparison to males. For example, non-U.S. male and female internationally mobile adolescents from various nationalities combined show no differences in terms of their openness to other cultures, travel, interest in international careers, and how they rated various national groups.

One tentative hypothesis could be that non-U.S. internationally mobile adolescents have a history of being more experienced with other countries because smaller distances can be involved. In Europe, this is especially true where international borders are within easy car and rail access for the majority of the population of a country. It is common for adolescents to travel to nearby nations for shopping, concerts, and school trips as well as yearly family vacations that may last a month. Following this logic, perhaps a shared mutual experience of "internationalism" even while living in one's "home country" reduces many of the differences between males and females. This explanation, however, needs to be viewed with great suspicion considering the limited research on gender differences among internationally mobile children and adolescents. Moreover, there was one notable exception among mixed nationality/non-U.S. adolescents: Females who lived abroad were significantly more accepting and open to learning other languages than males. Because males and females in Europe, Asia, and the Middle East are noted for being more experienced with learning foreign languages, and multilingualism is more common in their home countries, the explanation that historical exposure to internationalism may reduce gender differences on attitudinal variables associated with it does not account for this disparity.

Implications for School Psychology

Currently, there are an estimated 370,000 students worldwide attending international schools registered with International Schools Services (a U.S. -based organization) and the Department of Defense (American Overseas Schools Historical Society, 1998; International Schools Services, 1996). These children and adolescents constitute a very mobile group, often living for a few years in several countries and then returning to their "home" country when the international work of their parents ends. Many expatriate communities abroad average a 30% turnover each year, suggesting that more than 100,000 of these students yearly move to another country or return to their home country. When American students who have lived abroad come back, they return not just to large cities in the United States, but they can be found in school districts of any size in any state. It is likely these children are a completely unknown group for most U.S. school psychologists and an unserved or underserved population.

It has been suggested that this group of students has developed a global collective identity as "world citizens," but the peer group they most identify is an "international mobile peer group" of other adolescents like themselves who have experience living abroad (Downie, 1976; Gleason, 1970, 1973; Pollock, 1989; Useem & Downie, 1976). This research suggests that when they reenter the United States (or another "home country"), they become socially marginal. They feel different from peers who do not have their international experience, and difficulty forming new friendships can result in social alienation and, in some cases, depression. This readjustment process is more stressful for some than others, but interviews with returning adolescents indicate that, for most, it is challenging, and they can benefit from short-term counseling support and the understanding of their teachers and their parents. The school psychologist is in the position to make what is covert, repressed, and perhaps ill-understood a more natural readjustment process by bringing together teachers, parents, and the student to acknowledge constructively the "problem" and work together toward a resolution.

The simple question, "Where are you from?" is an impossible conundrum for these students (Gerner, 1994). Peers who have not lived abroad ask it to get a handle on someone, an understanding of that person. However, if an adolescent from an internationally mobile background tries to answer this innocent query by their most recent city or country, the city or country they liked best, or even more damaging, with a number of foreign cities or countries, they unknowingly offer no relevant information that the home country peer can readily interpret, and they sound evasive and inclined to brag. It cannot be stressed enough that often this simple question begins the process of peers' thinking of the newcomer as "strange," "different," and even "weird."

Pollock and Van Reken (1999) noted that students who return home after a period of living abroad experience the grief of losing a life they have come to love and enjoy. If they talk about their international experience too much, they begin to be treated as "foreigners" in their own country. Many adolescents who have lived abroad recall stressful reentry experiences, and parents, counselors, and school psychologists need to assume an active role in helping them navigate the reentry process. For most returning internationally mobile adolescents, the "going home" process can be painful; yet they also see their own culture with a new awareness they would not have wanted to miss. Acknowledgment of the challenges and ultimate rewards of reentry is crucial for parents and professionals, whereas failing to validate feelings and work through pressures associated with reentry can cause serious stress, a much longer period of marginal adjustment and in a worst-case scenario, clinical levels of depression and alienation.

There are many positive benefits associated with an internationally mobile lifestyle, but school psychologists need to be aware of the pressure points to intervene constructively when international mobility is in a student's background. For school psychologists working abroad at an international school, it is crucial to establish a reentry seminar that is required of all students as a standard part of the curriculum. School psychologists in the United States must recognize that they have children and adolescents in their schools who have returned from a temporary relocation abroad, and this experience has profound effects that in no way can be compared with an extended family vacation. School psychologists working abroad at international schools and those in the public school system in the United States have an investment in preparing children for the "global society" of the future. Internationally mobile adolescents are developing an identity that is transcultural, and the promise of this global identity is too precious to leave to the vicissitudes of inaction or ignorance. Adults need to assume an active role to help the adolescent returning to a U.S. school or college establish contact with other internationally mobile students who have successfully negotiated reentry, explain how to relate to peers who do not have this type of experience, help them craft a course of study or avocation that affirms their interest in things international, and put them in contact with organizations that understand their unique status (e.g., Global Nomads International[2]).

CONCLUSION

Gerner et al. (1992a) showed, with a large sample, that adolescents who live abroad rate themselves as more culturally accepting, more interested in travel, more open to learning other languages, and more interested in an international career in the future compared to United States adolescents who have only lived in the U.S. . Previous exploratory research of U.S. internationally mobile children inspired by the notable work of Ruth Hill Useem was supported in a majority of the areas surveyed (Delin, 1987; Downie, 1976; Gleason, 1970, 1973; Hager, 1979; Olson, 1986; Useem & Downie, 1976). This reanalysis of the 1992 study was necessary because the authors were so focused upon verifying the most basic claims for internationally mobile youth that they neglected to look at one of the most enduring of all potential contrasts, gender differences. It was then both confirming and somewhat striking that U.S. males and females differ consistently in their self-ratings. Females are more positive across several dimensions in comparison to males, and this is true for both internationally mobile and noninternationally mobile females.

This study is the first of a large and geographically diverse sample to suggest consistent and pervasive group gender differences on variables traditionally associated with international mobility during the developmental years of childhood and adolescence. However, a major limitation of this study is that it applies only to internationally mobile/third culture adolescents who are the dependents of parents who work in business and official government agencies as expatriates in the *capital city* of the host country. Internationally mobile adolescents of missionaries and military personnel are very different groups and experience living abroad more enmeshed with the indigenous culture (missionaries) or within a restricted setting (U.S. military bases abroad). The dependents of business and official government agencies who comprise the sample studied in this research are a privileged group who typically attend larger international schools with considerable resources. They tend to be most identified with a peer group of other internationally mobile adolescents at the international school that caters to children of expatriates, rather than adolescents being schooled in the host country public or national school system. It is important to keep in mind that the internationally mobile/third culture population is diverse and includes not only military and missionary dependents who live in vastly different circumstances abroad (military bases vs. small towns and villages), but also the diaspora of Lebanese children who have returned to the "unknown" country of their parents

(Lebanon) from the children's identified "home" country of the United States or Britain after the end of the civil war. Direct comparisons between these children and the adolescents in this study are clearly inappropriate.

On the other hand, this research strongly suggests that gender differences should be routinely examined when any internationally mobile/third culture samples are investigated. Unless this is done, revealing male-female differences may be overlooked. The authors humbly acknowledge that they unconsciously followed the practice of not investigating gender differences because it did not occur to them at the time of the original study (Gerner et al., 1992a). Hopefully, this reanalysis will serve to rectify this omission and call attention to a potentially fruitful line of inquiry in the research with internationally mobile children, adolescents, and adults.

NOTES

[1] The authors wish to acknowledge the valuable contributions of Mark A. Moselle (formerly at the American School of Warsaw, Poland) and Mike Archbold (International Community School/Addis Ababa, Ethiopia), who were coauthors and cocreators of the original research. Address all correspondence concerning this article to Michael E. Gerner, Ph.D., PC, Consulting Psychologists, 3 North Leroux Street Suite 207, Flagstaff, AZ 86001-5537. E-mail: mgernerpsy@aol.com. This article is taken from Michael E. Gerner and Fred L. Perry, Jr., "Gender Differences in Cultural Acceptance and Career Orientation Among Internationally Mobile and Non-Internationally Mobile Adolescents," *School Psychology Review* 29(2):267-283. Copyright 2000 by the National Association of School Psychologists, ISSN 0279-6015. [EDITOR NOTE: Reprint Permission granted from the National Association of School Psychologists. Text in brackets "[ ]" are my changes.]

[2] Global Nomads International is an organization linking people who have lived outside their "home country" during their preadult years. There is a quarterly newsletter, information, and periodic conferences to develop a worldwide community of internationally

mobile persons who can share their unique experience with each other and the world. The address of the organization is P.O. Box 9584, Washington, DC 20016-9584.

REFERENCES

American Overseas Schools Historical Society. (1998). *Historical society databases.* Litchfield Park, AZ: American Overseas Schools Historical Society.

Cann, A., & Siegfried, W.D. (1990). Gender stereotypes and dimensions of effective leader behavior. *Sex Roles, 23,* 413–419.

Cottrell, A., Useem, J., Useem, R., & Finn Jordan, K.A. (1999). *Third culture kids: Focus of major study.* Available online: http://www.iss.edu/pages/kids.html.

Cronbach, L. (1951). Coefficient alpha and the internal structure of tests. *Psychometrika, 16,* 297–334.

Delin, A.S. (1987). *Identity characteristics of seventh through twelfth grade third culture dependents at Cairo American College, Egypt.* Unpublished doctoral dissertation, Michigan State University, East Lansing, MI.

Downie, R.D. (1976). *Re-entry experiences and identity formation of third culture experienced dependent American youth: An exploratory study.* Unpublished doctoral dissertation, Michigan State University, East Lansing, MI.

Gail, M.D., Borg, W.R., & Gall, J.P. (1996). *Educational research: An introduction* (6th ed.). White Plains, NY: Longman.

Gerner, M. (1985). The school psychologist in Saudi Arabia. *School Psychology International, 6,* 88-94.

Gerner, M. (1990). Living and working overseas: School psychologists in American international schools. *School Psychology Quarterly, 5,* 21–32.

Gerner, M. (1993a). A profile of an American international school. *Global Nomad Quarterly, 2,* 3.

Gerner, M. (1993b). Linking your past to your future career: Global nomads as school psychologists. *Global Nomad Quarterly, 2,* 6–7.

Gerner, M. (1994). *Developing skills for consultation with American schools overseas.* Paper presented at the 26th National Association of School Psychologists Convention, Seattle, WA, March.

Gerner, M., Perry, F., Moselle, M.A., & Archbold, M. (1992a). Characteristics of internationally mobile adolescents. *Journal of School Psychology, 30,* 197–214.

Gerner, M., Perry, F., Moselle, M.A., & Archbold, M. (1992b). Moving between cultures: Recent research on the characteristics of internationally mobile adolescents. *Global Nomad Quarterly, 1,* 2–3, 8.

Gleason, T.P. (1970). *Social adjustment patterns and manifestations of worldmindedness of overseas experienced American youth.* Unpublished doctoral dissertation, Michigan State University, East Lansing, MI.

Gleason, T.P. (1973). The overseas-experienced adolescent and patterns of worldmindedness. *Adolescence, 8,* 481–490.

Hager, J.D. (1979). *The schooling of third culture children: The case of the American school of the Hague.* Unpublished doctoral dissertation, Michigan State University, East Lansing, MI.

Hopkins, K.D., & Glass, G.V. (1978). *Basic statistics for the behavioral sciences.* Upper Saddle River, NJ: Prentice Hall.

International Schools Services. (1990). *The ISS directory of overseas schools* (10th ed.). Princeton, NJ: Author.

International Schools Services. (1996). *The ISS directory of overseas schools 1996-1997* (16th ed.). Princeton, NJ: Author.

Kirk, R.E. (1982). *Experimental design: Procedures for behavioral sciences* (2nd ed.). Monterey, CA; Brooks/Cole.

Maccoby, E.E. (1985). Social groupings in childhood: Their relationship to prosocial and antisocial behavior in boys and girls. In D. Olwens, J. Block, & M. Radke-Yarrow (Eds.), *Development of antisocial and prosocial behavior: Theories, research and issues* (pp. 98–125). San Diego, CA: Academic Press.

Maccoby, E.E., & Jacklin, C.N. (1974). *The Psychology of sex differences.* Stanford, CA: Stanford University Press,

Nathanson, J.Z., & Marcenko, M. (1995). Young adolescents' adjustment to the experience of relocating overseas. *International Journal of Intercultural Relations, 19,* 413–424.

Olson, T.N. (1986). *The experiences of third culture children attending a Department of Defense dependents overseas secondary school in the Republic of the Philippines.* Unpublished doctoral dissertation, Michigan State University, East Lansing, MI.

Pollock, D.C. (1989). Being a third-culture kid: A profile. In the *Compendium of the international conference on missionary kids* (Quito, Ecuador, Vol. 1: Understanding and nurturing the missionary family) (pp. 241–252). Pasadena, CA: William Carey Library.

Pollock, D.C., & Van Reken, R.E. (1999). *The third culture kid experience: Growing up among worlds.* Yarmouth, ME: Intercultural Press.

Pratch, L., & Jacobowitz, J. (1996). Gender, motivation, and coping in the evaluation of leadership effectiveness. *Consulting Psychology Journal, 48,* 203–220.

Third-culture Kids. (1988). *The Niler* (Newsletter of the American Embassy in Cairo, Egypt, 25–26.

Useem, R.H., & Downie, R.D. (1976). September/October. Third-culture kids. *Today's Education,* 103–105.

Werkman, S.L. (1986). Coming Home: Adjustment of Americans to the United States after living abroad. In C. N. Austin (Ed.), *Cross cultural reentry* (pp. 5–17). Abilene, TX: Abilene Christian University Press.

Werkman, S.L., Farley, G.K., Butler, C., & Quayhagen, M. (1981). The psychological effects of moving and living overseas. *Journal of the American Academy of Child Psychiatry, 20,* 645–657.

Wilgenbusch, T., & Merrell, K.W. (1999). Gender differences in self-concept among children and adolescents: A reanalysis of multidimensional studies. *School Psychology Quarterly, 14,* 101–120.

Wilkinson, L. (1987). *SYSTAT: The system for statistics.* Evanston, IL: SYSTAT, Inc.

APPENDIX 10.1

The Internationally Mobile Adolescent Questionnaire. The development of the questionnaire was based upon prior exploratory research (Useem & Downie, 1976). A panel of three of the authors (Gerner et al., 1992a) suggested multiple items to measure each characteristic claimed for internationally mobile children and adolescents. This produced a 60-item questionnaire. that was administered to a random sample of 40 students attending an international school in Cairo, Egypt. The students were asked to indicate which items were unclear or problematic; those were eliminated and several other items were reworded or added based upon the comments made by the students in the pilot study. The final questionnaire contained 57 Likert-type items. Forty-seven items consisted of statements to which students indicate their degree of agreement on a 5-point scale ranging from 1 = Strongly Disagree to 5 = Strongly Agree. Ten items ask students to rate their feelings toward 10 nationalities from 1 = Strongly Negative to 5 = Strongly Positive. The final scale consists of seven subscales: Family Relationship (10 items), Peer Relationship (8 items), Cultural Acceptance (6 items), Travel Orientation (7 items), Language Acceptance (5 items), Future Orientation (11 items), and Stereotype (10 items). Thirteen items were added to the beginning of the scale to collect biographical data.

The analysis was organized by first evaluating the reliability of the questionnaire and each subscale is briefly characterized below. The final list of items comprising the questionnaire arranged by subscale is detailed in Appendix 10.1.

Subscale Content

Family Relationship

- 20. I plan to have a career similar to that of my parents.
- 38. I am close to my family.
- 43. When I have a problem, I can go to my parents with it.
- 45. I look forward to the time I can leave home and live on my own.

- 48. My opinion is considered in family discussions.
- 51. If something is bothering me, the first person I would talk to is one of my parents.
- 54. I enjoy spending time with my family.
- 57. I would consider my parents among my "best" friends.
- 59. My parents understand me.

Travel Orientation

- 18. My first preference for a vacation would be to travel to a country I've never visited.
- 22. I do not like to travel.
- 29. I enjoy visiting different countries.
- 35. The more a country is different from my country, the more I would like to visit it.
- 42. I find it easy to adjust to a new place to live.
- 53. I feel I need a changing environment (surroundings) in order to be satisfied.

Language Acceptance

- 17. Learning another language comes easy for me.
- 30. I like learning different languages.
- 36. It is important for me to speak at least one language other than my own.
- 41. Everyone should be required to study another language in school.

Cultural Acceptance

- 28. Some nationalities are better than others.
- 34. I enjoy meeting people from different countries.
- 47. I believe I should do something to help people who have less than I have.
- 55. I am very accepting of people's differences.

Future Orientation

- 19. I would like to attend a college that has an overseas experience as part of its curriculum.
- 23. My plans are to settle down and to establish roots.
- 25. I hope to pursue an international career.
- 31. My grades in school are an important issue in my life.
- 37. I am concerned about what my life will be like in 10 years.
- 40. I plan to spend a large part of my life away from my home country.
- 44. I want to work in a job where I can help people.
- 50. I feel comfortable when I have a schedule or list of things to do.
- 56. I plan to pursue a career exclusively in my home country.
- 58. The idea of living and working in another country is exciting to me.
- 59. When I am out on my own in the future, I plan to settle and stay in one
- place.

Stereotype Scale

- 61. Asians
- 62. Arabs
- 63. Mexicans
- 64. British
- 65. Africans
- 66. Italians
- 67. Thais
- 68. Americans
- 69. Egyptians
- 70. Russians

Note. Some items were included as "experimental" to query a specific claim made in the exploratory literature (e.g., #31, #37, #44, #50; if they did not significantly reduce their subscale's reliability, they were retained in the analysis). The Peer Relationship subscale is not listed, since it had poor reliability and was not used in the analysis. No previous questionnaires specific to internationally mobile adolescents had been published or were available, so the authors had to design their own based upon preliminary, exploratory research mainly from interview data.

11

"OTHER" EXPATRIATE ADOLESCENTS: A POSTMODERN APPROACH TO UNDERSTANDING EXPATRIATE ADOLESCENTS AMONG NON-US CHILDREN

ANNIKA HYLMÖ

INTRODUCTION

Since the beginning of modern civilization, children have accompanied their parents as their families moved due to parental occupation. International mobility was and remains a part of colonization. For a long time, moving across national boundaries was relatively rare, but in the twenty-first century international mobility is increasingly becoming a part of the global organizational landscape. There are two major factors that affect the children growing up in this environment. First, these children grow up as members of an organizational environment that emphasizes local presence in the overseas context while maintaining a sense of home ownership from the sponsoring entity. This in and of itself is nothing new. For example, researchers such as Willis (1977) and Heath (1983) have examined how children are socialized into the particular working context of their parents through language and social norms in the community, the school environment, and through interactions with peers. The second factor is the embeddedness of the children's socialization into an elite international community that serves a particular ideological foundation. This foundation serves as the foundation for sense making and identity construction (Weick, 1995) for the expatriate youth.[1]

This chapter outlines a move toward a postmodernist and post-colonial way to conceptualize the identity formation and sense making of expatriate youth as compared with much previous research. To better understand the strengths and limitations of the present body of research, I have found it to be useful to draw on a framework proposed by Joanne Martin (1992) typically used to examine organizational cultures. Martin uses a tripartite approach of examining cultures as integrated, differentiated, or fragmented to allow for a deeper understanding of the complex processes that make up our cultural experiences. Her approach further allows us to go beyond thin to thick description (Geertz, 1973) of the communicative processes underlying shared experience. The framework of integration, differentiation, and fragmentation leads to a better understanding of the need for a postmodernist and postcolonial perspective on the expatriate family.

INTEGRATED APPROACHES TO THE STUDY OF AN INTERNATIONAL CHILDHOOD AS A CULTURE

The integration perspective to cultures suggests that culture can be considered the glue that connects people together. To that end, cultures can be defined "in terms of clarity, consistency, and consensus" (Martin, 1992, p. 9). All members of the culture share the same fundamental convictions so that the culture provides clarity for its members. Integration perspectives tend to advocate clarity, consistency, and consensus and to propose that the culture is unique to a specific group, characteristics that can be found in much of what has been written about international youth. Many conceptualizations tend to consider the effects of an expatriate youth as consistent across national origins, parental organizational sponsorship, and host country (McCaig, 1996; Pollock & Van Reken, 1999). While examination of the experiences and impacts of an international childhood from an integration perspective is intriguing and opens some doors toward understanding, others are left shut with questions unanswered.

Two Forms of Integration Studies: Organizational and Home Country

Integration studies about expatriate youth can be found in several forms. Two forms that stand out include the organizational cultural context and the cultural contexts of the home country or of the international experience.

From an organizational cultural context, some integration studies might focus on the school as a culture unto itself, such as Burleigh's (1993; 1994) examination of multicultural education at the International School of Berne. Integration studies may focus on the organizational context of the parent's sponsoring organization such as the missionary community (Van Reken, 1996) or the military environment (Ender, 1996; Wertsch, 1991). Each case recognizes that the values, beliefs, and assumptions underlying the organizational environment serve to create a unique integrated community that is communicated through shared rites, rituals, and other activities. As the organization sponsoring the expatriate family becomes a cultural entity unto itself, studies such as these show how the organization absorbs and shapes the experiences not only the expatriate employee but other members of the expatriate family as well.

In other cases, integration studies of expatriate youth focus on the home culture of the children and adolescents, such as Tamura and Furnham's (1993) examination of the reentry processes of Japanese children returning to Japan. This type of study is closely related to the profile type of study as exemplified by Useem and Cottrell's (1996) work summarizing key features of adult American Third Culture Kids (TCKs). It provides a descriptive profile of the "typical" third culture kid.

Interestingly enough, it seems that there are fewer studies conducted across organizational contexts, but within the same host country as a unifying entity. It would be intriguing to see what such an approach would reveal.

Cultural Consensus and Clarity

Integration studies tend to present an image of culture that is filled with consensus. Agreement will typically be described using emotional language filled with emotion and with little room for disagreement (Martin, 1992). In more popular writings about former expatriate youth, emotional language is a cornerstone. For example, McCaig (1996) describes expatriate youth as "citizens of the world" (p. 118) who often "feel forced to disown their valuable heritage for in the name of 'fitting in' lose, as do their communities" (p. 112). Many writers who consider the cultural sharedness of former international youth tend to use similar language, frequently with a combination of a sense of being "lost" without the knowledge of what it means to be a part of the understanding of a shared community as former international mobiles and the sense of being "found" once that knowledge is established (Schaetti, 1996).

Clarity from an integration perspective is achieved by excluding ambiguity. Ambiguity is excluded through the process of sense making by looking back at events to put them into order retrospectively and thereby create meaning (Weick, 1995). When former expatriate youth come together, for example, at the conferences put forth by Global Nomads International (GNI), they are together able to look back at similar events and experiences with a sense of mutual recognition. The initial experience is one of unification and one that tends to be extolled in much of the rhetoric surrounding GNI's activities. This rhetoric attempts to bring former international youth together by assuming that there is a shared culture that stretches across all who have lived overseas while a child or adolescent.

It is through such assumptions of culturewide consensus an underlying objectivist assumption of shared values is revealed (Martin, 1992). In other words, these assumptions reveal an ontological approach to culture that expects there to be one unified "true" culture that is shared by all who have had the experience of growing up overseas. This assumption is clear from several integrationist studies and observations. Pollock and Van Reken (1999) remark about the TCK as a cultural unit:

> Certainly cultural practices are incorporated from the unique aspects of both host and home cultures, but the third culture is more than the sum total of the parts of home and host culture. If it were only that, each TCK would remain alone in his or her experience. (p. 31)

Gillies (1998), upon examining alumni from various international schools, noted that "One thing is certain, they fit in best and relate best to others like themselves" (p. 35). These characteristics are often observed irrespective of home cultures. "Interestingly, these Japanese, Danish, Italian, Swazi, and American TCKs often have far more in common with each other than they do with the peer group of their own individual countries" (Eakin, 1996, p. 61) despite the impression that many TCKs are reared to identify themselves based on the passport on which they travel and to consider themselves as full members of those countries (Schaetti, 1996).

From an integrationist perspective, research on expatriate adolescents is fairly straightforward: a unified group that is brought together through shared characteristics developed through similar experiences. However, the integrationist perspective, while providing an interesting starting point, may in some ways be simplistic. As some individuals who have experienced GNI conferences have commented, they are left with a sense of "Yes, but..." In other words, the integration perspective may cover innate differences of experience by creating a cookie cutter culture that is "shared" only at the surface. For example, the experiences of Namibian expatriate youth may have some experiences in common with the profile presented by the (somewhat) American dominated GNI, but other aspects are more foreign. By peeling back the layers, a more complex and intriguing picture begins to emerge that allows for differentiation among a multitude of experience within the larger whole.

DIFFERENTIATED APPROACHES TO THE STUDY OF
AN INTERNATIONAL CHILDHOOD AS A CULTURE

Like integration studies, differentiation studies define culture as something that is shared. What makes the differentiation perspective distinct is that it considers subgroups within a "culture" rather than the monolithic whole. From a differentiation perspective, a culture may take on the appearance of culturewide consensus while retaining subcultural differences that are embedded in the larger culture. According to Martin (1992), there are three characteristics that define the differentiation approach. First, taking a differentiation approach means recognizing the inconsistency of manifested threads of cultural concern found in stories, practices, and cultural forms. Second, taking a differentiation approach means that consensus from a differentiation approach will only be fully understood within individual subgroups. Finally, the differentiation approach recognizes that clarity will be found within subcultural boundaries while ambiguity exists outside those boundaries.

Differentiation approaches consider culture as conflicted environments where the conflicts are emerging between different subgroups. Espoused content themes are differentiated by the inconsistent interpretations or manifestations provided by each participant group. This is where the differentiation perspective offers deeper insights than would be possible with an integration approach.

Focusing on the Organizational Context

In the current body of research focusing on the expatriate youth population, differentiation studies typically take one of two forms: studies examining the organizational cultural context and studies examining cultural identity.

The first form of differentiation study uses the organizational context, examining one or more of the several organizational contexts in which mobile families are situated, including schools, social and youth organizations, employers, churches, and health and welfare organizations (Cornille, 1993).

One approach to examining the experiences of expatriate youth from a differentiation approach is to examine the role of subgroups in the unified culture espoused by integrationist approaches. Such holistic approaches are rare. More common is the recognition that the subgroups shape the individual experience differently. For example, Useem and Cottrell (1996) argue, based on a long line of research that the sponsoring or employing organization impacted on the international experience of the dependent children. As they point out, "The third culture of the diplomatic community differs from that found on a military base. The third culture of business-people abroad impinges differently on the daily lives of their children than does that of missionaries on their offspring" (p. 25). In other words, the sponsoring organizations serve as interesting foci for examining differentiated experience.

One significant organizational environment that plays a major role in the experience of the international youth is that of the school or educational environment. For example, one differentiation study looked at students' choice of language form at the International School of Berne. The students (and/or their parents) could choose either American or British English as their language of instruction. Each of those two linguistic choices, then, became the basis for two differentiated groups within a larger organizational context (Burleigh, 1993).

Focusing on Cultural Identity

If organizational environments constitute one important cluster of subcultures that have been examined by researchers interested in expatriate youth, cultural identity is the other. There are basically two different approaches to cultural identity that underlie much of this type of work: degrees of enculturation and acculturation on the one hand and cultural marginality on the other.

Pollock (1996) has developed a model that is interesting in its potential for the examination of differential cultural experiences

among expatriate youth. The model essentially argues that there are
four different reactions of expatriate adolescents based on their relative degrees of enculturation (childhood socialization into and adoption of cultural norms) or acculturation (acclimatization toward
another culture) into their home and host cultures (Gudykunst &
Kim, 1984; Pollock, 1996). These four reactions are referred to as
the mirror, the adopted one, the hidden immigrant, and the
foreigner. The mirror is a case where an individual becomes fully
enculturated into the local culture, completely adopting the local
culture and sharing the same physical appearance as the locals. The
adopted one is a case where the individual does not share the same
physical appearance but considers the local culture (that of the host
country or that of the expatriate community) his or her own. When
the individual looks like the majority, typically the host culture, but
acts and thinks differently, the individual falls into the category of
the hidden immigrant. Pollock identifies two forms of the hidden
immigrant: living in another country and experiencing that the
thoughts and values that are expressed are incompatible with the
local community and living in one's home culture with a multicultural identity. Finally, the foreigner is one who Pollock suggests looks
different from the host community and who thinks differently. In a
way, Pollock argues, this individual may become a perpetual
foreigner who never quite fits into any one cultural environment.

Pollock's (1996) model allows for important distinctions when it
comes to examining expatriate youth. Where some children and
adolescents living abroad will be in close proximity to the local
culture, allowing them to be enculturated into it as in the case of the
hidden immigrant, others will remain at a perceived distance, recognizing the need to adapt but remaining culturally their own home
culture as in the case of the hidden immigrant or the adopted one.
Still others will remain culturally fully and only a part of their home
cultures, as foreigners in the host country, but still willing to respect
their differences. Each of these groups of experiences is worthy of
study in greater depth.

The differential experiences of those who fall into Pollock's
(1996) categories of the hidden immigrant, or the foreigner may

further be explored using the idea of cultural marginality. Cultural marginality refers to the tendency of some people not to fit perfectly into any one of the cultures to which they have been exposed but neatly in the margins of each of them (Schaetti, 1996). Among cultural marginals there are two basic responses: encapsulated marginals experience being trapped in their own marginalized experience, while constructive marginals use their marginalization to their advantage. The first group includes those who may give up their internationalized selves in an attempt to assimilate into a particular society, while the second group uses their sense of who they are to create their own community. As Schaetti puts it, "They can finally name a community to which they fully belong, where they don't need to explain themselves, where their experiences are understood and celebrated" (Schaetti, 1996, p. 181). The approach of cultural marginality allows for the examination of differential experiences based on reactions to marginalization following international mobility.

While Schaetti's (1996) and Pollock's (1996) work are more theoretical in nature, there are empirical studies that also examine cultural differences. For example, Willis (1992) examined the Columbia Academy in Kobe, Japan, and its relationship to the larger cultures in which it is embedded, and which are embedded within the school itself: the expatriate community and the local Japanese environment. Other studies may differentiate on the basis of home culture nationality. Some studies have found that there is some degree of cultural similarity between students who are going to home country–sponsored schools and students going to school in the home country compared with those students who do not go to home country schools overseas (Waterson & Hayden, 1999).

The cultural experiences of subgroups of students who attend home schools and those who do not are clearly of interest to the differentiation researcher, yet there is much work to be done. Differentiation studies examining cultural identity have to recognize distinctions between subgroups based on home culture, for example, or cultural sponsorship of the school.

Cultural Ambiguity and Divergence

Differentiation studies recognize that ambiguity is part of cultural life. Ambiguity in Martin's (1992) sense and in the sense of differentiation studies is lack of clarity, not inconsistency between different clear interpretations. It is the subcultures that provide the source of clarity and a clear meaning system for cultural members. In essence, subcultures provide clarity and make complexity coherent.

Many studies have pointed to the need for students to bond with others who share the same language when they first come to a school overseas (Burleigh, 1993; Willis, 1992). Sharing a language means that the students have the capacity to engage in sense making activities in an effort to create meaning. Without that, the students are left with ambiguity (Weick, 1995). Being a part of a linguistic subgroup means that the students can experience clarity and belonging within a small group even if the larger whole is confusing (Martin, 1992). After first, arriving at an international school, lack of or limited English-speaking skills may lead to isolation for a new student (Akram, 1995). The same can also be true in the reverse. As Downs (1990) points out, "When a Japanese student graduates overseas, [the] Japanese can not place him [*sic*] on any recognizable grid; he is truly an outsider in his own country" (p. 42). Without similar others to assist in the channeling of ambiguity to make sense of the experience, differentiation studies recognize that the isolation is complete.

Delving deeper into differentiation studies can help us unmask more of the differences that are inherently a part of the international experience, differences that are frequently masked by rhetoric striving to bring the experiences of former expatriate children and adolescents into a consistent experience with more in common than not. The differences become clearer when one begins to consider the tendency for some parents to choose schools based on instructional language and on the opportunities that the curriculum seems to afford the students.

While American parents choose American-based schools overseas to achieve linguistic and curricular consistency, non-American parents tend to choose American schools because of the opportunities that the English language would afford their children (Wheeler, 1998). The distinction between the groups is at one level simply one of scholastic choice. On another level the distinction is deeper. Non-American parents may have fewer options to choose from. The only other option available to them might be local schools where the language of instruction would be completely different from any other that the children know. For a family continuously on the move from country to country, local schools might not be an option if there is to be any scholastic continuity. Schools with a link to the home country are often unavailable, even for large expatriate communities such as the Japanese (Fukuda & Chu, 1994). Yet the differentiation between the groups is clear: In the one case, home culture norms and values are reinforced; in the other, additional cultural influence becomes part of a mix that already includes home and host culture. Given the importance of the school in the enculturation process of the child, this is no small difference. Indeed, one area of interest to future differentiation studies would be to examine the relationships between the "school home culture" and the home culture of the adolescent in the overall cultural development of the individual, in particular in the case of non-American students.

Cultural Belonging from a Differentiated Point of View

Central to the idea of cultural belonging is the self. From a differentiation perspective, it is the complex nature of the relationships between the different subcultures that will have deep implications for the construction of the individual self-identity. The boundaries of subcultural groups may not coincide perfectly with one another based on, say, parental occupation or national origin. Furthermore, an individual can belong to several subcultures at any one point in time. Each of these subcultures will provide a target of identification for the individual (Martin, 1992).

In essence, the transculturalist expatriate youth has not one, but a multiplicity of cultural identities coexisting simultaneously.

However, not all students at international schools consider themselves to have a mixed culture. Willis, Enloe, and Minoura (1994) found that over one-third of the student body at one international school considered themselves to have a mixed culture. This still means that almost two-thirds did not. Similarly, while over half of the same population was bi- or multilingual, this finding also means that almost half of the population was not. Differentiation studies need to pay more attention to the distinction between those who do perceive themselves to have a blended culture and those who consider themselves to be monocultural, as well as to the distinction between those who are multilingual and those who are not.

However, even with the increased appreciation for the complexities that differentiated group affiliations and the implications for expatriate youth, further appreciation, by looking at the tensions that overlap between affinities, may be created. This is where the fragmentation approach has value.

FRAGMENTATION APPROACHES TO THE STUDY OF AN INTERNATIONAL CHILDHOOD AS A CULTURE

Fragmentation studies avoid definitions of culture. They consider the essence of all cultures to be ambiguous (Martin, 1992). The focus on ambiguity arises out of a recognition that the conflicts and tensions that the members of the culture experience are irreconcilable at best and impossible to articulate at worst. From a fragmentation perspective, examinations of expatriate youth will have to recognize that cultural life is inevitably filled with confusion, paradox, obscurity, tension, and conflicts. In fragmentation studies "ambiguity is perceived when a lack of clarity, high complexity, or a paradox makes multiple (rather than single or dichotomous) explanations possible" (Martin, 1992, p. 134).

Permeability and Fluctuating Boundaries

In fragmentation cultures, the boundaries between the many subcultures remain permeable and fluctuating as they respond to external feeder cultures. In the present context, the feeder cultures are, for example, those home cultures that "supply" new expatriate youth into the existing expatriate culture. Feeder cultures will ensure that the relative salience of the subcultures will change. The British move out and the Japanese move in. Because of this, the fragmentation allows for the recognition that manifestations of culture will be multifaceted and open to a multitude of interpretations that are difficult to decipher (Martin, 1992). Willis (1992) points out that it can be difficult to determine the boundaries of subcultures at an international school since the initial appearance of groupings by national culture were much more heterogeneous than a first glance would indicate. When he observed groups that would appear "American," these turned out to be mixed with Scandinavians; the "Europeans" included a Japanese boy and some Americans. The permeability of experience sets up for fluctuating and dynamic interpretations of realities that are constructed out of relationships yet bounded by larger ideological forces more difficult to contain. Such ideological forces will be expressed through interaction, education, and daily conversation. Through these expressions, the expatriates create their own fragmented interpretations of lived culture and their situatedness therein.

Complexity and Ambiguity

For the expatriate youth, national borders and boundaries are vague and diffuse, characterized by airports and passports rather than by actual political borders to be crossed. The tension between continuous mobility and confinement remains simultaneously ambiguous and extremely salient. The same host country that once welcomed them by allowing them to pass through its borders without travail now sets up barriers backed by legal sanctions to keep them out. In particular, this may be the case for those former expatriate youth who hold a passport from a home country that is not one of the major players on the global political scene. An individual whose passport is Ecuadorian is in many contexts more likely to be limited by visas and border patrols than is an individual from

Britain or the United States, even though the host countries where each has lived might be the same. Ambiguity arises out of national "home" country and the fluctuating relationship between the home and host countries. Similar relationships and effects are found with tertiary cultural interests for those who went to a school sponsored by someone else's home country. The examination of ongoing ambiguity and the sense making process that ensues (Weick, 1995) is an arena of research that is waiting to be tapped.

The experience of ambiguity means that individuals will have multiple interpretations of their experiences. Fragmentation studies focus on expressing that multiplicity. Ambiguity is ever present.

> No two adult TCKs come up with identical ways of putting their lives together, but they are actively creating provisional answers to some of the major and minor problems that face human beings every day in this complex world. (Useem & Cottrell, 1996, p. 28)

Even families can be considered microcultures such that the macrocultures that are made up of familial microcultures often serves as a constellation of conflictual relations (Barter, 1994; Waterson & Hayden, 1999). These multiplex experiences have yet to be explored to their full extent.

Cultural Identity and Fragmentation

From a fragmentation point of view, the culture of international mobility has no clear center: As new categories of relationships among cultural members appear, these categories continue to blur the distinctions between insiders and outsiders. That multiplicity can often be difficult to express. International youth do not like to be referred to by passport because it oversimplifies identity and negates the complex identification processes that the individual has negotiated over the years. Schaetti (1996) identifies herself "as a [sic] American-Swiss global nomad with a very European-influenced international background...a 'cultural marginal'" (p. 178).

From a fragmentation point of view, subcultures overlap, nest, and intersect in individuals so that the individual becomes a subculture unto itself based on the intersections of several subcultures. By taking a fragmented view of the self, researchers are able to recognize the constant fluctuation that exists among diverse and changing identities. Individual identities become fluctuating constellations of partial loyalties (Rosaldo, 1989) expressed as a constant morass of allegiances. An expatriate child may have knowledge of several languages with

> The specialized vocabulary needed to function in each of the three environments, home, school and host country, but not the same vocabulary in all of them, because he does not need the same vocabulary in all of them. (Barter, 1994, p. 36)

Fragmentation studies recognize that effects of pernicious exclusion may be invisible to the members of the dominant groups (Martin, 1992). In other words, exclusion may not be intentional even though it is a part of experienced reality for those who are left out. An important task for fragmentation studies, then, is to detect the viewpoints of those who have had no voice. This includes the viewpoints of those who are typically cast into a category of "other" or "non-American" simply because there are too few of them to be statistically significant in many studies examining a broad rubric of Third Culture Kids. While the homogenization might be unintentional, as a homogenized group of "others," their voices are drowned.

Multifaceted Experiences and Smaller Clusters within the Ambiguous Whole

For all expatriate youth, culture is in the process of becoming while at the same time culture is being, but the being is comprised of many cultural identities existing simultaneously. Their identities are multifaceted, comprised of many factors of which nationality is but one (Schaetti, 1996). Recognizing the existence of the multiple identities and meanings means that interpretation can be reconstructed. Meaning becomes a never-ending chain of interpretations (Guattari & Deleuze, 1987). Cultural manifestations have to be understood in the contexts where they are enacted, experienced, understood, and interpreted (Martin, 1992). In other words, the experience of the Saudi Arabian girl living in Nairobi is understood within the context of her Saudi culture, the Kenyan host country, her American-sponsored school, her parents' employers, and so on. The experience is understood and appreciated as unique and endemic to that particular context, while recognizing that the experience is likely to change by the minute.

From a fragmentation point of view, there does not exist an unequivocal, uniform third culture with a shared set of values (Martin, 1992). While the members of the culture may be looking at a common frame of reference when it comes to important issues, they may not agree as to their relative importance or value compared with one another. From a fragmentation perspective, while many expatriate youth may come to share an overall sense of globalization, what that means and how they view their own role and expectations as a result will be different. For some expatriate youth, globalization may mean increased opportunities for them to work in the corporate sector as expatriates themselves. For others it may mean ideological changes that will affect and possibly disempower the localities where they grew up. For yet another group, globalization becomes a rhetorical mirage that affects those already able to travel and continue their expatriate lifestyle but where their own options are more limited. Fragmentation allows us to question the multitude of meanings of experience and interpretation, thus going beyond both integration and differentiation to provide deeper understanding.

GOING FROM FRAGMENTATION TO POSTMODERNIST, POSTCOLONIAL, AND FEMINIST FRONTIERS

Integrationist and differentiation studies of expatriate youth have paved the way for better understanding of a growing population of current and former expatriate children and adolescents. However, as pointed out, several of these studies tend to focus on groups with specific characteristics. These characteristics are often rooted in a dominant cultural ideology that in turn is embedded in the organizational and national contexts within the expatriate family are situated (Waterson & Hayden, 1999). As members of the expatriate community, expatriate youth are part of the privileged elite (Willis et al., 1994). The expatriate community draws on reified social privileges that its members actively participate in reproducing (Ahmed, 1999). The existing hegemony must be questioned to allow for increased participation by the presently silenced others that are also a part of the expatriate community, as well as those voices on the fringes of it (Shome, 1996).

To begin to examine the voices of the silenced Others it is important to call for "new categories, modes of thought and writing, values and politics to overcome the deficiencies of [...] discourses and practices" (Best & Kellner, 1991, p. 30) surrounding the current conceptualization of the experience of expatriate youth. This means deconstructing current discourse to uncover a different reality, a reality that frequently raises more questions than it answers (Derrida, 1979; 1991). Such research needs to read between the lines to uncover the role and effect of subordination and silencing of women (Martin, 1982; Martin, 1991) in the expatriate context in relation to their children from within a variety of cultural vantage points. Feminist work could serve the present body of research by critically examining the absence of the mother in the lives of American expatriate children in several of the biographical notes of Smith's (1996a) *Strangers at Home*. For example, Ruth Van Reken's (1996) biographical note includes reference to her father, "Her American father was born and raised in Iran, and her three daughters thrived for nine years of their childhood in Liberia" (p. 81). McCaig's biography (1996) makes reference only to one parent, an international business executive. The impact of the silenced parent on experienced reality among all expatriate youth is a question worthy of consideration. Other studies need to examine the relationship of gender to different home and host cultural contexts for non-Americans as well.

Moving forward with research and criticism means recognizing that elitism and expatriatism is rooted in colonialism and that in many ways the expatriate community may serve to reinforce old colonial powers overseas. This means that the expatriate youth must be seen as part of a political context, indeed as political in and of themselves. As Eakin (1996) points out, when children are living overseas they are seen as representatives of their home countries, playing the role of ambassador. From a Foucauldian perspective, these children are part of a panoptic reality where it is never quite clear who sees them step out of an imagined mold of representation (Foucault, 1979). That mold of representation may be even more signified as fewer representatives of a home culture are present to illuminate differences. A single Finnish youth may experience the reality of representation differently than a group of Americans.

For some the apparent role of representation may be more important than for others. For example, many American's experience a deep sense of national consciousness that is a deeply entrenched part of their self-definitions, often to the point of being magnified as expatriates (Smith, 1996b). For others, national boundaries do not carry the same meaning to begin with (Shome, 1996). Examining the cultural context of expatriate youth means having to recognize that cultural hybridity is part of the lives of others as well, not simply a part of the lives of the elite few. Herein lies one paradox of examining expatriate youth: Transnationalism is not a state of being that is reserved for former expatriate youth but rather one that is shared by many postcolonial subjects globally (Shome, 1996).

Moving toward an understanding of the postcolonial context of expatriates means recognizing the inherently Euro-U.S. -centric view of much of the rhetoric surrounding current exposés of the expatriate youth experience. As Ahmed (1999) points out, the language of McCaig's (1996) narrative relies on capitalistic language of the West that serves to commodify the former expatriate youth into a marketable product with uniformity of skill in cultural inter-action. Taking a postcolonial view also means recognizing that privi-lege is variable with varying effects. Expatriate youth in the diplomatic corps from Uganda have a different reality to contend with than similar youth from Great Britain. The youth from Uganda may come from very different social and economic realities, for example. While both families are members of the diplomatic corps, the Ugandan diplomat may have fewer privileges compared with the British diplomat simply due to differences in the two coun-tries' economic status. Yet their children may be educated in the same school, an international school that may enhance the values and ideologies of the West rather than of Uganda even as attempts are made to be "egalitarian" and appreciative of differences. As the child graduates and possibly goes to college, the education received makes it virtually impossible to get a job at home because of overqualification. For many members of the former expatriate youth community, this reality is frequently ignored. For them, the reality is drastically different from that of many former expatriate youth of the dominant, former and present colonial nations. And to add to the questions, not all expatriates fall so neatly into the national boundaries of the existing political denominations. As individuals move and marry across national boundaries, their children embody an intricate reality of continued mobility within organizational contexts that bring out more questions about race, privilege, gender, and colonialism. These are the voices that a postcolonialist approach to studying expatriate youth must seek to uncover.

Most important, a postmodern, postcolonial fragmentation perspective will begin to examine and appreciate the complexity of international mobility as part of a larger diasporic context where mobility and migration is part of a continued discourse. Doing so will allow us to uncover the voice of the other in the emergent context of experiencing an expatriate childhood.

NOTES

[1] Terminology used to describe a given population is never

apolitical. Some refer to the present group as Third Culture Kids (a cultural term), others as global nomads (an economic term, focusing on parental occupation), distinguish between missionary kids and military brats, and so on. I have chosen to use the term 'expatriate' to encompass as many experiences as possible for the purpose of this paper, recognizing that even that term has political implications and is disliked by some (Hylmö, 1999).

REFERENCES

Ahmed, S. (1999). Home and away: Narratives of migration and estrangement. *International Journal of Cultural Studies, 2*, 329–347.

Akram, C. (1995). Change and adaptation: Children and curriculum in international schools. *International Schools Journal, 15*, 39–53.

Barter, R. (1994). Multiculturalism and multilingualism: What it means in practice. *International Schools Journal, 27*, 31–40.

Best, S., & Kellner, D. (1991). *Postmodern theory: Critical interrogations.* New York: Guildford Press.

Burleigh, J.C. (1993). What works: A study of multicultural education in an international school setting, part 1. *International Schools Journal, 26*, 47–55.

Burleigh, J.C. (1994). What works: A study of multicultural education in an international school setting, part 2. *International Schools Journal, 27*, 46–52.

Cornille, T.A. (1993). Support systems and the relocation process. *Marriage and Family Review, 19*, 281–298.

Derrida, J. (1979). *Speech and phenomenon.* Evanston, IL: Northwestern University Press.

Derrida, J. (1991). Letter to a Japanese friend. In P. Kamuf (Ed.), *Between the blinds* (pp. 270–276). New York: Columbia.

Downs, L.D. (1990). The repatriate Japanese student. *International Schools Journal, 20*, 39–44.

Eakin, K.B. (1996). You can't go "home" again. In C. Smith (Ed.), *Strangers at home: Essays on the effects of living overseas and coming "home" to a strange land* (pp. 57–80). Bayside, NY: Aletheia Publications.

Ender, M.G. (1996). Growing up in the military. In C. Smith (Ed.), *Strangers at home: Essays on the effects of living overseas and coming "home" to a strange land* (pp. 125–150). Bayside, NY: Aletheia.

Foucault, M. (1979). *Discipline and punish.* New York: Vintage Books.

Fukuda, K.J., & Chu, P. (1994). Wrestling with expatriate family problems. *International Studies of Management and Organizations, 24,* 36–47.

Geertz, C. (1973). *The interpretation of cultures.* New York: Basic Books.

Gillies, W.D. (1998). Children on the move: Third culture kids. *Childhood Education, 75,* 36–38.

Guattari, F., & Deleuze, G. (1987). *A thousand plateaus: Capitalism and schizophrenia* (Brian Massumi, Trans.). London, England: Athlone Press.

Gudykunst, W.B., & Kim, Y.Y. (1984). *Communication with strangers.* New York: Random House.

Heath, S.B. (1983). *Ways with words: Language, life, and work in communities and classrooms.* Cambridge, England: Cambridge University Press.

Hylmö, A. (1999). *"Where are you from?" Organizing identification and experience among former expatriate children and adolescents.* Paper presented at the meeting of the Eastern Communication Association, Martinsburg, WV, April.

Martin, B. (1982). Feminism, criticism, and Foucault. *New German Critique, 27* (Fall), 3–30.

Martin, J. (1991). A personal journey: From integration to differentiation to fragmentation to feminism. In P.J. Frost, L.F. Moore, M.R. Louis, C.C. Lundberg, & J. Martin (Eds.), *Reframing organizational culture* (pp. 352–355). Thousand Oaks, CA: Sage.

Martin, J. (1992). *Cultures in organizations: Three perspectives.* New York, Oxford: Oxford University Press.

McCaig, N. (1996). Understanding global nomads. In C. Smith (Ed.), *Strangers at home: Essays on the effects of living overseas and coming "home" to a strange land* (pp. 99–120). Bayside, NY: Aletheia Publications.

Pollock, D.C. (1996). Where will I build my nest? The multicultural third culture kid. In C. Smith (Ed.), *Strangers at home: Essays on the effects of living overseas and coming "home" to a strange land* (pp. 202–218). Bayside, NY: Aletheia Publications.

Pollock, D.C., & Van Reken, R.E. (1999). *Growing up among worlds: The third culture kid experience*. Yarmouth, ME: Intercultural Press.

Rosaldo, R. (1989). *Culture and truth: The remaking of social analysis*. Boston, MA: Beacon.

Schaetti, B. (1996). Phoenix rising: A question of cultural identity. In C.D. Smith (Ed.), *Strangers at home: Essays on the effects of living overseas and coming "home" to a strange land* (pp. 177–188). Bayside, NY: Aletheia Publications.

Shome, R. (1996). Postcolonial intervention in the rhetorical canon: An "other" view. *Communication Theory, 6*, 40–59.

Smith, C. (Ed.). (1996a). *Strangers at home: Essays on the effects of living overseas and coming "home" to a strange land*. Bayside, NY: Aletheia Publications.

Smith, C. (1996b). World citizens and "rubber-band nationality." In C. Smith (Ed.), *Strangers at home: Essays on the effects of living overseas and coming "home" to a strange land* (pp. 189–201). Bayside, NY: Aletheia Publications.

Tamura, T., & Furnham, A. (1993). Comparison of adaptation to the home culture of Japanese children and adolescents returned from overseas sojourn. *International Journal of Social Psychiatry, 39*, 10–21.

Useem, R.H., & Cottrell, A.B. (1996). Adult third culture kids. In C. Smith (Ed.), *Strangers at home: Essays on the effects of living overseas and coming "home" to a strange land* (pp. 22–35). Bayside, NY: Aletheia Publications.

Van Reken, R. (1996). Religious culture shock. In C. Smith (Ed.), *Strangers at home: Essays on the effects of living overseas and coming "home" to a strange land* (pp. 81–98). Bayside, NY: Aletheia Publications.

Waterson, M., & Hayden, M. (1999). International education and its contribution to the development of student attitudes. *International Schools Journal, XVIII,* 17–27.

Weick, K.E. (1995). *Sensemaking in organizations.* Thousand Oaks, CA: Sage.

Wertsch, M.E. (1991). *Military brats.* New York: Harmony Books.

Wheeler, K.M. (1998). *Bilingualism and bilinguality: An exploration of parental values and expectations in an American sponsored overseas school.* Unpublished Dissertation, University of Minnesota, Minneapolis, MN.

Willis, P.E. (1977). *Learning to labour: How working class kids get working class jobs.* London, England: Gower.

Willis, D.B. (1992). A search for transnational culture: An ethnography of students in an international school in Japan: Part 1. *International Schools Journal, XII,* 9–25.

Willis, D.B., Enloe, W.W., & Minoura, Y. (1994). Transculturals, transnationals: The new diaspora. *International Schools Journal, XIV,* 29–42.

12

IDENTITY FORMATION AND THE ADULT THIRD CULTURE KID

KATHLEEN A. FINN JORDAN

INTRODUCTION

Since World War II, increasing numbers of persons have become involved cross-culturally and cross-nationally for the purposes of relating segments of society to each other and mediating between cultures. The lifestyles and patterns of relationships that develop in the interfaces between cultures as a result of this participation have been termed the "Third Culture." Children who accompany parents in their overseas roles and grow up in a variety of cultures have been called Third Culture Kids ("TCKs," or later, Adult Third Culture Kids "ATCKs") as a result of the work of Drs. Ruth Hill and John Useem. Third cultures have been broadly characterized as the pattern of behaviors created, shared, and learned by participants of the societies who are relating to each other. These persons generate a composite of values, role-related norms, and social structures that make them a part of, yet, apart from, the first and second cultures that they span yet from which they remain distinct. Many dissertations and studies over the past 20 years have focused on TCKs. A current ongoing research project conducted by Drs. Ruth Hill and John Useem, Dr. Ann Baker Cottrell, and Dr. Kathleen

Jordan provides the source of the newer insights included in this chapter as well as the reporting of lifetime choices and reflections of attitudes and opinions.

Identity formation for the adult third culture person is a complex and intriguing topic.[1] Erikson (1959) describes this process as one formed in adolescence and youth and, while changeable, having a sense of continuity, coherence, and sameness. One's identity is grounded in one's society and culture and related to the historical moment. It is subjectively expressed as a sense of being at one with oneself and recognized by others. A sense of "home" and "roots" is considered essential in this process, providing a familiar space for its evolution.[2] The importance of the struggle between "home" and "roots" and experiences of mobility and change, set in a sponsorship situation that defines the structure of one's personal and family life during the formative years, affects each person in an individual manner. However, some general descriptive patterns can be discerned, and an exploration of these patterns suggests some shared identity elements emerging out of a third culture experience that is unique and characterized by special facets.

The Importance of Sponsorship

The third culture is a culture with a present, a vaguely perceived past, and a tentative future (Useem, Useem, & Donoghue, 1963). Understanding the identity formation of TCKs involves the necessity for competently grasping the nature of sponsorship in general; the sponsorship entity involved in the life of the particular TCK; and the roles, related norms, behaviors, and critical realities to be mastered. The fact of sponsorship provides a modified form of "total institution"[3] for the individuals involved and replaces home and roots frequently considered essential elements in the identity formation process. Sponsorship, in distinction to home and roots, forms the cultural and social matrix that one shares with other TCKs and in which one recognizes and is recognized by others, particularly those significant to one's sense of meaning.

The sponsor is the organization for which the parents worked abroad. Included in the sample for this research were men and women whose parents worked in the military, the state department and federal government, international business, missionary endeavors, and an "other" category for those parents in representative roles in a university or various international projects and services. The sponsor is responsible for sending the family to specific overseas locations; making all interim and continuing arrangements for the stay, providing the environment for work, study, and leisure while the employee is on site; and making provision for home leave at specified intervals. Since all involved are representatives of the sponsor, the employed person's position depends on all family members acting as appropriate role models as that is defined by the sponsor. The rewards for mastering the appropriate role-related norms and acquiring appropriate behaviors result in an "achieved status" for the employed family member within the sponsorship community and an "ascribed status" for the dependents. This ascribed status confers security, privilege, and a type of "specialness" or "elitist" reality that quickly becomes a given or constant as the TCK enjoys mobility, special support, travel, and, generally speaking, a relatively comfortable standard of living abroad. The time of return to the passport country, often erroneously called reentry, though qualified by age and length of time overseas, is difficult to negotiate. This is because, for many, it is really an entry and one must frequently adjust to it without the support of the sponsorship entity or the relationships that form the network of reality for the TCK.

Characteristics of the TCK Identity

The characteristics of a TCK identity emerging from current data are congruent with earlier descriptive studies. They appear to be in a large part:

     * an externalized participant observer self combined with an internal covered or buried self focusing the TCK on intrapersonal rather than interpersonal activity;

* a sense of who one is *not* rather than who one is at the point of reentry and during early transition

* a lack of identification with one's own ethnicity

* a strong base of academic skills combined with an initial deficiency in social skills at the peer level

* a sense of elitism deriving from the ascribed status experienced as a result of living in a sponsorship situation during the early developmental years

* a set of site-specific or role-specific formulas (applied on return and after), which substitute for the self

* a sense of marginality (though it may be constructive), which confers a degree of "other status" to be resolved as formulaic recipes for self become integrated

* a fully conceived sense of networks, relationships, and fictive kin worldwide that serve as extended family

* a certain very strong dependence on, need for approval from, and identification with (even after the childhood years) parents who alone have shared their particular transits

* psychological sensitivity to an internalized sense of otherness and a feeling of less security (when out of the third culture setting) and, in the early reentry years, less optimism about life in general than their peers and

*issues of separation, grief and loss as a result of frequent transition, losing friends, and leaving places in a mobility pattern that was not their own choice.

Third Culture Elements/Third Culture Patterns

The elements of third culture life provide the settings for selves reflecting the aforementioned characteristics. The social construction of third culture reality and the social processes within it are best understood by entering into that matrix at least virtually. An appreciation of this special, complex type of identity, the projected sense of self, the resultant special abilities, and the talents involved might then be defined and better understood. Those who are raised in these sponsored spaces feel special, different, and appreciate the contributions different cultures and different surroundings have made to their lives. The following are some expressions of their sense of this difference:

> As a child I felt very special—living abroad, traveling by ship —I enjoyed being different. Today all my friends travel, but I have lived elsewhere.

> It's hard, of course, to judge how others feel, but I believe I am more restless; my world has always been so immense. It's difficult to limit my focus.

> An appreciation and acceptance of other nations/cultures by one who has lived overseas is very different from one who has not.

> When I went to college I heard people say, "You can tell someone who has been to college" (regardless of length of study or if they complete a degree), they have a different attitude about how they approach things. I think the same is true of travelers. You can tell by their attitudes.

Resolution of Grief and Loss Over Time

The research delineates that TCKs at the time of entry to their passport country relied on a competency base that is knowledge oriented, intrapersonal, and built on observations that they integrate into the network of observational data that has formed the base for past recipes for success. The disorientation that they experience affectively is deepened by feelings of grief and loss. The feelings emerge at this time when they are asked to suppress their third culture identity (it is not recognized by others and no one seems interested in hearing about it) as well as by their lack of social skills with the peer group. They seem to work this out internally and in much less time if they find support. Examples of support include contact with other TCKs, e-mail opportunities to share with members of their third culture past, an occasional reunion where they find the TCK component of the self validated and appreciated, and where experiences of entry can be shared, or some familiar travel. The impact of the grief lessens but it is always a familiar strand. The sensitivities remain but, with proper support, the grief and loss issues resolve over time leaving only painful traces that open the spaces of understanding for future growth.

> I am very much satisfied with the way life has unfolded. It has been good and rich–in spite of, maybe even because of, some times of deepest struggle. It seems there are resolutions if not all the answers.

> I am very proud of my overseas upbringing and of the qualities that gave me. Although it has been a constant struggle to fit into "mainstream America," I have learned and grown considerably.

> Adjusting to and accepting my American experience has been a long and difficult process. The pain of separation from my overseas community made it difficult to touch the cross-cultural needs I had, let alone sort them out. But now I am quite content and excited with their increasing integration into my every day life.

In discussing the protean self, Lifton (1993) outlines a model of identity growing out of restlessness, mobility, and flux, and out of much pain and trauma. The model speaks to the ability of certain persons to transmute the earlier pain in a remembered past of individual history thereby contributing to "grounded imagination." The appreciation for what they have gained in the third culture increases through contact with non-third culture members. They begin to see that the grief occasioned by frequent mobility and loss of friends was a price paid for their particular type of consciousness and the special realizations that are a part of a third culture self. This sense of "gain," as they integrate the third culture self, mediates the previous intensity of the feeling of loss.

> It's difficult to explain to people who have not lived overseas how radically different lifestyles and upbringing can be but you don't realize what you have until you see what others don't have.

The appreciation that "home" in a certain sense is more everywhere than nowhere emerges slowly. The advantage of a strong global sense as well as a far-flung network functioning as an extended family finds a resonance in the local setting. Some comments provide highlights:

> I feel "at home" wherever I am.

> I tend to feel there is no one home but that doesn't mean every place feels equally like home.

> I feel at home anywhere. I enjoy being with and working with people of different backgrounds. I feel because of my experiences I'm maybe a little more tolerant and understanding of differences. My experience abroad makes up who I am, so whatever I do, wherever, I am using some of that which is inherently within.

> I feel special affinity for and enjoy meeting people from other countries. I feel many times that I can have deeper friendships with other people who have lived in other countries. Our perspective is similar.

> I feel more at home in the role of obvious foreigner. I consider myself a foreigner here in the United States, but my foreignness is not readily apparent. I know best how to be a foreigner, a "guest" in someone else's country.

Examination of Third Culture Identity

Berger and Luckmann's (1967) *Social Construction of Reality* discusses identity as a key element of subjective reality that stands in a dialectical relationship with the society. The authors contend that identity is formed by social processes that once crystallized, maintained, modified, or even reshaped by social relations. In examining identity in the third culture context, the realities of sponsorship, mobility, and distance from relations and extended family necessitate a reshaping of our understanding of the elements that form the dynamics of identity formation. From the moment the sponsor sends the employee abroad, the details of family life, the actual transport from site to site, moving arrangements, school placement, location, and frequently choice of housing are proscribed and provided by the sponsor or sponsor's agent. The TCK identity is created and maintained in this environmental bubble. The family as a unit takes its place within the sponsorship network and a hierarchy within the sponsorship defines privilege, benefits, and type of lifestyle accordingly, based on the status of the employed person. The maintenance of those processes once outside the sponsorship entity become complex at best and for a time seem almost impossible. TCKs are required to suppress their complex identity on return because after qualifying the "where are you from" question and noting their transits and mobile history, U.S. peers usually terminate the conversation or become bored or disbelieving and, as a result, the TCKs resort to the observer self to compensate. They apply a series of recipes for survival (attending multicultural functions, writing, arts and music involvement, e-mail, and letter writing to other TCKs) as they seek to transpose their skills to the new setting. The new U.S. setting generally calls for a highly participant self. The TCK's sense of elitism combined with a self that chooses to observe tends to distance the individual TCK from the new setting at a time when support is minimal.

The social matrix structured by the sponsorship entity providing the substitute for home and roots and maintaining a sense of continuity in spite of mobility, change of place, and loss of friends is no longer in place. Sponsorship, because of the rigors of prescription for appropriate behavior, protected the individual from confronting reality for oneself and the environmental bubble that resulted made most significant personal decision making unnecessary. This becomes a difficult area to transit for TCKs in a peer group setting, for they must begin to craft a personal unique formula for that decision making, and the need for adequate support in confronting this challenge is frequently not there. Although novel patterns of behavior were frequently encountered, they were met with observation and related to as "other" but they were not personally tried on.

> However, I suspect that my transnational knowledge, though more than my peers, is still superficial regarding cultural issues of India because we were always separate and observers...we were exposed to superficial levels.

Roles, third culture values, guidelines, rules, and other variables, created in the sponsorship reality to provide structure and stability must be transposed or completely reconstructed. Parents who were once the translators of all these elements become only one of many sources. If return coincides with university attendance, parents are frequently not even in the same country. The sense of historical identity that their social peers have is not accessible to them. Something new must be formulated.

> I feel at home where I grew up. While that is true no doubt for most people, it's far more difficult for the TCK to find remembrances of home. Most U.S. cities have the familiar local sports field, cookie cutter high school, grocery stores, etc. and most people can generally identify with something wherever they live. The TCK has a tough time finding familiar "hangouts" and feeling at home.

Points of Return and Points of Moving On

The fact that the TCK identity is faced upon return with such crisis frequently leads people who meet them in this difficult moment to think that these difficulties cannot be resolved. They focus only on their problems, sometimes writ large in this period, ignoring their special talents and areas of strength. In our sample, we find that the difficulties of these transitional periods, if properly understood, will proceed in due course and that the resolution of the self will involve integrating the parts set aside at the point of reentry and reformulating the self for success in the native land. Workshops that address the realities of the TCK and offer opportunities to share memories, talk about experiences, and model paths to integrate the old into the new, and conferences with like-minded, internationally mobile others are great helps in accelerating the adjustment process.

Adjustments that are made at this time are external. Full adaptation does not occur (Jordan, 1981). Experiences put aside can all be integrated in the best possible sense later. Pursuit of a pattern of successful transition through the presented problems differs from the indulgence of overstating the difficulties (that present on return) as if they were persistent. The basic problem for most individuals at this time is the fact that reentry is really "entry," and "home" is not perceived as "home." It is another new place, but one that has a force about it (because of parents' history) that cannot be relegated to the passing through formula. This new place must be encountered as especially significant and success within it, without the former help of sponsorship, is critical for the future. The future in a third culture reality is only vaguely perceived. One moves on frequently with little notice to yet another place, or one stays and watches others move. On encountering the native country, the future becomes a reality to be confronted, planned for, and participated in fully. The fact that the social skills are not yet in place for that to occur is one of the essential crises of this period. Many, for whom the setting of individual goals had no particular meaning because of the context in which they were previously raised, are confronted with a future that now seems all too real and impinging, immediate. As to goals, overtime, they gain experience in making their own:

I'm not a fanatic about sticking to written goals, but I know what I'd like to achieve and I'm moving toward it.

Parents at this point, for whom return is a reentry, tend to think their offspring are more familiar with the native land because parents are. This is not so, and over time becomes clear to the parents.

I think my parents are beginning to understand the difficulties I had at reentry. They assumed that by telling me I was an American I would be an American. Now they see that this isn't so.

My parents don't understand the importance of the overseas experience to me and why I can't let it go. They don't realize there is no "youth place" to go back to, no "roots place."

The main task for the TCK at this point is the construction of a sense of "home" through the transposition of formulas learned that will assist in the transition. Expectations in this process are key and the age of the subject and the type of support available is also crucial. The TCK, once the assurance of another imminent tour, another mobility, is gone, realizes that at least for a while there will be radical change. Some level of investment in a quasi-permanent reality sets in. A sense of a void past, a conflicted present, and an imagined future are often tied to a dream of returning at some later time to a third culture reality. In earlier studies closer to the actual reentry time, this dream was strongly articulated. In the statements of the ATCKs in this study, the strength of that dream remains but is mediated by the force of the reentry transition and the practical realizations that involve making decisions for oneself and taking on some adult responsibility. This taking of responsibility qualifies the period of "prolonged or extended adolescence" that is part of the TCK's pattern.

The "dream" to return overseas seems to remain but is qualified over time. Frequently, the new feelings of quasi-permanence trigger a profound grief, which surfaces and is connected to a deep sense of loss, a feeling that the scope of life is more limited. The lack of acknowledgment in the new setting of the existence of a third culture reality erodes the only realized sense of self. This strengthens the feelings of grief and frequently enhances a sense of delay, of time lost and many things undone, a sense of lack of readiness for this new essential strangeness. It is important to emphasize that the feeling of "many things undone" rises out of the repression of the former life and the lack of interest in, and recognition of, by those in the TCKs immediate transition environment. TCKs confront peers who seem to have common patterns and experiences and demonstrate social skills in the peer sense that they have not yet mastered. For most, their academic skills, on the other hand, are excellent, and they begin to rely on them as a stronghold as they prioritize the things they need to do in the present situation. It is sometimes easier for the TCK that is the product of a cross-cultural marriage. Some of their differences are at least externalized. But for the person that appears to be monocultural, none of these differences is apparent and they are expected to have all the skills and aspects of their peers without cultural complexity. One cross-cultural American put it very concisely:

> My heart feels mostly South American, my intellect European, my drive from the U.S. and my calm is Asian. In fact it is my love and fascination with other cultures that has fueled my interests in Sociology. I am a musician by trade. I love music most because it can cross cultural barriers with ease and it breathes within me. This aspect of self/identity has allowed me to be a chameleon of sorts.

The Buried Self and Identity States

Many ATCKs do not feel comfortable responding to a question about the "deep self." They respond, rather, with the myriad formulas and conventions that worked country by country or school by school, appropriate configurations, handles. They are rarely caught off guard and maintain a certain poise and presence. They appear to have site-specific identities and often disappoint the ideologically committed. James Marcia (1980), in an article in the *Handbook of Adolescent Psychology*, states that:

> A well developed identity structure...is flexible and open to change in society and changes in relationships. The openness assures numerous reorganizations of identity "contents" throughout the "identity achievement" person's life although the essential identity process remains the same growing stronger. (p. 160)

Years before, Marcia (1966) identified certain statuses of crisis and commitment:

> (i) foreclosure—status indicated by no crisis and a premature commitment, open to parental viewpoints without examining alternatives; (ii) diffused—status indicates a lack of crisis or commitment. The individual in this status drifts without apparent concern; (iii) moratorium—status in which subject experiences crisis during his/her examination of alternatives. Thus, moratorium is in the pre-commitment stage and is close to reaching the identity status; and (iv) identity achievement—status is reached when moratorium makes a commitment after experiencing the crisis of choosing alternatives. (p. 531)

Signs of Identity and "Other Status"

Comments reported in the surveys do not indicate preferences or evidence of many subjects in the foreclosure stage. This occurs despite the sponsorship matrix in the world of the TCK abroad being marked by a type of foreclosure reality. Independent choices were not made unilaterally. The sponsor formally administered the macro schedule while parents made even the smaller day-to-day decisions. The demands of living in a "representative role" meant that behavior was frequently proscribed in the daily situation. TCKs are very close to their parents in many ways and grow closer over the life process compared with many host nationals. But in spite of the unique shared family history and specific pattern of mobility, the subjects studied have not followed in their parents' footsteps, and many comment on the constant exploration of options. Seventeen percent of the sample were missionary but only 2% have a career in religious organizations; 30% were military but only three percent serve, or had their most current job, in the armed forces. Fifty-six percent of all subjects agree that it is important to have an international dimension in their lives.

Some ATCKs give evidence of diffused identity status that lessens over time. In terms of questions about commitment, at the age category 25 to 29, 38.8% of our sample agree that they hesitate in making commitments. Of those in the 40 to 44 age category, 22.3% continue to report hesitation; by age category 55 plus, 17.6% still experience hesitation. Only 16% of the sample report still "feeling adrift." Greater loneliness is reported by respondents between the ages of 25 and 29. It appears many at this age reflect signs of the moratorium stage. As they explore alternatives, more of them begin to make significant life choices. For 11% of the total sample, their first marriage occurs at ages 30 to 41 inclusive. The sense of "delay"[4] that has been noted by other researchers studying this population seems articulated in this instance. The ATCKs of military sponsorship in our sample differ here in the sense that 33.3% of military subjects married by the ages of 20 to 21. As adults, they reported less criticism of the United States and appear to have less interest in international involvement.

Many identity theories, which are appropriate for revealing critical elements for non-ATCKs, are less helpful when applied to ATCKs. Developmental theories based on age/stage levels assume events, shared experiences, historic senses, and a presence of home and roots that the TCKs have not had in a predictable age/stage mode. Fitzgerald (1974) notes that in a bicultural setting, the picture is more complicated as people "participate in separate social and cultural spheres" (p. 1). Referring to his own field studies with

Maoris, he says that they have a diverse number of identity bases, hold a number of identities concurrently, and these multiple identities may be said to enjoy different values or to have different functions. TCKs begin with a different perception of themselves, and others become aware of the distinction, although not always the reason for it, in interactions with them. Contemporary feminist and cross-cultural researchers talk about those that see themselves as "outsiders" or "minorities" in modern social context, and these researchers spend time in discussing marginal socioeconomic status and propose metamodels for identity resolution for individuals who struggle with "other status." Roughly, 41% of our respondents do not identify strongly with their own ethnicity, and 74% see themselves as "outsiders" to the "home" culture or "very different" because of their experience. They perceive themselves as persons having "other status" both at home and abroad. Although marginal socioeconomic status does not apply to most ATCKs, they report feelings of marginality in terms of their idiosyncratic personal histories outside of their own home countries as well as their internationally mobile lifestyles.

Dealing with "Other Status": Reality and Perception of Reality

One respondent states:

Once you've been outside your own paradigm you can never be the same. You come to know an otherness that puts to the question all the certitudes of your first culture. With my multiple cultures I am a real enigma.

Resolving "other status" is a crucial component of identity formation for the ATCK. Root (1990) in looking at resolving "other status" suggests that the intrapersonal and interpersonal conflicts that emerge from themes of race, family, gender, acceptance, difference, and isolation are circular and transitory. They reemerge at different points of development with a chance for greater depth of resolution and understanding with each cycle. The metamodel presented is schematically a spiral where the linear force is internal conflict over a core sense of the definition of self, the importance of which is largely determined by socialization. Different sources of conflict may move the individual forward. It is proposed that in each person's life there are at least one or two significant conflicts during critical developmental periods that move them forward. The circular or system forces encompass the political, social, and familial environments. Resolution reflects the lack of need for compartmentalizing the parts of their ethnic (or, in our case, third cultural) heritage. As an ATCK shares:

> I have had times of feeling at home. I always knew my American home because we went to Grandma's house on furlough. However, after nine years of living in Liberia raising my own family, that became my home. When the war destroyed all that. I found the old confusion and I was thirteen years old again and newly arrived and someone asked: "Where are you from?" At age forty-five, I am not sure again and I thought I'd worked it all out.

For the ATCK, the strength of the relationship with family as well as the sophistication of the "covered self" make the resolution of "other status" a long process. Their camouflaged exteriors and understated ways of presenting themselves hide rich inner lives, remarkable talents, and, sometimes, strongly held contradictory opinions on the world at large and at home. It appears that for many, "work" or, if the desired work is not already found, a "labor of love," or, in some cases, the creation of one's own company assists in providing the stimulus to resolution. Work was always a constant in their lives and provided the source of sponsorship, the structuring variable in creating their third culture identity. The means to the types of sophisticated, international occupations that were needed in the third culture were provided through advanced study and finely honed skills. Further, we find that, in contrast to the U.S. population, 21% of whom have finished a four-year college program, 81% of our sample have earned at least a bachelor's degree. Half of that group went on to earn a master's or higher degree. Their occupational choices reflect this continued love of learning, interest in helping others, and a desire for independence, flexibility, and autonomy.

> As we moved around the world during my childhood, my books and questioning thoughts were my constant companions... I am more comfortable with questions embedded in the mystery, than the answer that leaves no questions...examining shared assumptions cooperatively leads to wider and wider discussion which is always interesting and always opens up new possibilities for understanding and trust.

> I don't like putting myself under group authority. I like freedom to do as I please. It's always a push-pull though, because I miss a community but don't want to be tied down.

In the next chapter, Ann Baker Cottrell discusses the comfort experienced by ATCKs in educational and medical pursuits. They are committed to high educational achievement and look to careers that involve expertise and leadership.

Identity in Relationship: Family and Expression of Values

A small number of respondents continue to report some level of rootlessness or alienation and an inability to make commitments to people or places. However, 67% of the entire sample married or partnered only once; 40.7% at age 25 or older, and 51% had a least one spouse with some international experience when they met. Just over 68% agree that the Unites States is the best place to be living currently but reflect a preference for more cosmopolitan, less insulated areas where there is a multi-ethnic focus.

In following through with an examination of their opinions in the area of values, comments indicate that many transcend what they believe to be "national" values and have differing viewpoints from their U.S. counterparts. On issues that they consider global, such as human rights, the good of the environment, war and peace, and justice, they seem to have very strong opinions. In other matters, they tend to see both sides of an issue and have an ability to argue both sides convincingly. They report, in many cases, that they prefer to take a "due process" approach and write or address petitions, author editorial statements, articles, or think pieces rather than taking more active approaches to protest. This particular behavior seems to be a midway point between "observing" (which they are most comfortable with) and more "active" or public involvement. They also report frequent philosophical examination of the issues in order to take a position on them.

> While I am aware that as a citizen I have definite responsibilities in involving myself in local and national affairs, I am not an activist and tend to have moderate opinions. I look at events more as a historian than as a reformer or builder.

> I feel like a spectator as far as controversial issues.

> I think I've always felt a little separate and baffled by all the unspoken rules and rationalities surrounding the American way of life [but]…I by no means feel isolated or alienated.

> I often feel different. I definitely have an American alternative lifestyle. I live within the boundaries of the United States drawing from different cultures and practices.

> I feel active in American life, however, I feel I have a certain distance and perspective that lends objectivity.

On looking at the United States as the best place for this sample to be living presently, many responded as both agree and disagree and the comments qualified their ambiguity within a decisive "agreed." Some stated they were currently pursuing careers, and others were taking care of parents who were aging. For others, they felt their standard of living was better here.

> I believe I'm supposed to be living here right now for many reasons and at that level I am content and it's best for those reasons. I miss the overseas lifestyle a great deal. Whenever we land in...a foreign country anywhere I feel excited and "at home" in some inner sense, even when it is a strange country specifically to me.

> It's probably the easiest place to maintain my standard of living but not necessarily the best for my personal/spiritual growth.

Making It Home—But It Remains One of Many

ATCKs in our sample make the transition "home." It takes time and calls for a special process of growth and development unique to this population but distinguished mostly in senses of timing and the particular stresses to be expected in a population with a specific history of qualified "representative" mobility. While 74% of our respondents report being overall satisfied with their lives, 32% feel as spectators on American life in general, and 48% do not feel central to any group. Overall, 73% would like to live abroad again. In random comments through the survey, many comment that they feel the experience was enriching and enhancing; 62% always have a passport ready. The stability-mobility stress is consistently expressed by approximately 49% of the group. They remain in a certain sense restless and eager to experience new places and new sites.

In our technological world, where mobility plays an increasingly key role even within the home country, this capacity for mobility and enthusiasm for transition are special skills they can call on. The respondents reflect an existential commitment to the present moment, an increasing appreciation for goal setting as they age but, at all times, there is a sense of qualification, the weighing of alternatives, from a larger perspective. ATCKs very much appreciate the United States and relish many aspects of it that citizens who have not had their experiences take for granted. Their constructive marginality is often reflected in their choice of occupation and in their proclivity for consuming hobbies. Many of them are writers and musicians and keep journals or spend time writing out what they think or feel on many topics even if these pieces are kept to themselves or only shared with close personal friends. Several, in addition, have published works to their credit. Involvement in the arts, writing, and music is considered essential to a large percentage of ATCKs both as a means of expression and a way of nurturing self through the development process.

There are approximately five million[5] American TCKs now and many more TCKs in the world returning to their countries. Although the ATCKs studied know they are Americans, it is through the "reentry process" that they learn how to be Americans and what that means. Our information indicates they do learn to be Americans but constructively marginal ones, less out of sync with peers as they age, but nevertheless still a part of and a part from (Adler, 1974).

A few of the more intense interview comments reveal the deep sense of differences that some have. A respondent from the military sponsorship comments:

> I am accepted by my present culture. I speak the language, am able to move freely; for all appearances, I am part of the dominant super culture. My interior does not show on my face, my skin, my tongue. But I still feel displaced. Perhaps someone needs to come along and declare military children who grew up in other countries a separate ethnic group.

A respondent from the missionary community reflects:

> I may be a citizen of the USA but I'll never be an American at heart. I'll never feel comfortable with the normal American lifestyle, goals, assumptions, attitudes, even normal

American success. I may never again be a true Nigerian, but my heart is more there than here. We Missionary Kids ("MKs") are truly between two worlds.

Some comment on what they call a journey of clarification: a return to the countries of the past after the re entry experience has occurred. Not everyone can do this but it seems most helpful when it is possible and makes the romanticization of the past a more difficult pursuit.

All my high school friends were gone. A good opportunity to see "my country" and its cultures without the "sweetening" of friends, family and security, which MKs and others so often confuse with a love for a place and its people. It's typical when you move out to the next place, to remember the last place with a lot of nostalgia and longing. When you go back as an adult, you often find out that it's very different from what you expected.

CONCLUSION

ATCKs have repertoires of social behavior, are keen observers, and adjust easily but never really adapt. They carry their third cultureness with them, thriving on newness, difference, challenge, and stimulation. The realization that there is a TCK community is, in itself, for some a healthy discovery. As persons who feel outside or at best constructively marginal to groups, many enjoy the opportunity to be loosely a part of a group that is comprehensible in the light of all its diversity. They identify with the communities of childhood within the sponsorship entity but, after that, they do not feel central to other groups. They are central to the third culture and this group, once discovered, provides a certain relief for some. On first hearing the term TCK, one respondent shares:

It was like this enormous thing opened up and I could understand again what was going on...until then I just thought I was an odd ball...then I discovered there's many other odd balls out there and there's a term for it and that it is really an o.k. thing. It gave it so much legitimacy and I really do think of, well, who am I? I'm not an American. I'm not an Indian. What am I? Well, there's this Third Culture.

The third culture is not a blended or hyphenated culture. It is a relating culture, a culture of linkages and networks. Its reality grew out of the need for differing cultures to speak to each other through representatives who had special mediation/negotiation skills and a high competency in a knowledge base in a certain field needed in binational and, now, multinational pursuits. The social identity it spawns is broad and cosmopolite in some aspects (diplomatic, military, business), but it may also be very narrow and focused in others (a local small mission post in a rural international setting). Flexibility, adaptability, and observation are necessary to move between and within diverse cultures. In many ways, the patterns of members of the third culture seem to foreshadow the critical aspects of personality called for in subjects moving into a current technological reality. Like protean selves, their psychological landscapes are fluid and many-sided; their selves make use of bits and pieces carefully integrated: a self only afraid of living a smaller life. The skills that ATCKs possess are necessary skills in a global reality; 91% of them perceive a facility to understand others, while 88% report an ability to handle the unexpected with ease. Continuities maintained through mobility are essential. Tracking how these cutting edge individuals have been able to forge that transit is essential contemporary information. Where change is the only continuity, particular skills are necessary if the foundation of personal identity is to remain intact and growth-oriented. ATCKs have a role to play in a world coming together quickly with ever more need for those who can comfortably and naturally stand in between and relate the differing centers.

NOTES

[1] This study of Adult Third Culture Kids is being undertaken by three sociologists/anthropologists: Dr. Ann Baker Cottrell of San Diego State University and Drs. John Useem and Ruth Hill Useem, professors emeritus of Michigan State University; and by Dr. Kathleen A. Finn Jordan, a consulting educational counselor in Washington, D.C. Some preliminary information from this descriptive study was published in a series of short articles in *NEWSLINKS* (Useem & Cottrell, 1993a, 1993b, 1993c, 1993d) the newspaper of the International Schools Services. The data are from a subgroup of 604 (of the 696) American ATCKs whose child/teen years outside the United States were during the post–WWII/Cold War period and who were living in the United States at the time of the study. Respondents were broadly grouped by sponsor: military (30%), government (23%), missionary (17%), business (16%) and other (14%), where "Other" might include such occupations as educators, employers of international nongovernment organizations, intergovernmental organizations, the media, and foundations.

[2] The concept of "home and roots" by Soddy as discussed in Downie (1976), pp. 131-139.

[3] A total institution, according to Goffman (1961), is defined as "a place of residence and work where large number of like-situated individuals, cut off from the wider society for an appreciable period of time, together lead an enclosed, formally administered round of life" (p. 1).

[4] The "sense of delay" that is reflected in the comments of some of the subjects is addressed in Salmon (1987) p. 45.

[5] Projected from census data and Department of State estimates 1960-1999. The Overseas Schools Advisory Council Worldwide Fact Sheet estimates the number of U.S. dependent school children overseas to be a quarter of a million for the 1999-2000 academic year.

REFERENCES

Adler, P.S. (1974). Beyond cultural identity: Reflections on cultural and multicultural man. In Richard W. Brislin (Ed.), *Topics in cultural learning*, Vol. 2 (pp. 145). Honolulu, HI: East-West Center Cultural Learning Institute.

Berger, P.L., & Luckman, T. (1967). *The social construction of reality*. Garden City, NJ: Doubleday.

Downie, R.D. (1976). *Re-entry experience and the re-entry process for third culture kids: An exploratory study*. Unpublished doctoral dissertation, Michigan State University, East Lansing, MI.

Erikson, E.H. (1959). *Identity and the life cycle*. New York: International Universities Press.

Fitzgerald, T.K. (Ed.). (1974). *Social and cultural identity*. Athens, GA: University of Georgia Press.

Goffman, E. (1961). *Asylums: Essays on the social situation of mental patients and other inmates*. Garden City, NJ: Doubleday.

Jordan, K.A.F. (1981). *The adaptation of third culture dependent youth as they enter college: an exploratory study*. Unpublished doctoral dissertation, Michigan State University, East Lansing, MI.

Lifton, R.J. (1993). *The protean self*. New York: Basic Books.

Marcia, J.E. (1966). Development and validation of ego identity status. *Journal of Personality and Social Psychology, 3*, 531–558.

Marcia, J.E. (1980). Identity in adolescence, In J. Adelson (Ed.), *Handbook of adolescent psychology* (pp.159–187). New York: John Wiley & Sons.

Root, M.P.P. (1990). Resolving "other status": Identity development of biracial individuals. In L.S. Brown & M.P.P. Root (Eds.), *Diversity and complexity in feminist therapy* (pp. 185–205). London: Haworth Press.

Salmon, J. (1987). *The relationship of stress and mobility to the psychosocial development and well-being of third-culture reared early adults*. Unpublished doctoral dissertation, Florida State University, Tallahassee, FL.

Useem, J., Useem, R.H., & Donoghue, J.D. (1963). Man in the middle of the third culture. *Human Organization, 22*, 169–179.

Useem, R., & Cottrell, A.B. (1993a). ATCKs have problems relating to own ethnic groups. *NEWSLINKS, Volume XIII, #2*, 1, 4, & 6.

Useem, R., & Cottrell, A.B. (1993b). TCKs experience prolonged adolescence. *NEWSLINKS, Volume XIII, #1*, 1 & 26.

Useem, R., & Cottrell, A.B. (1993c). TCKs four times more likely to earn bachelor's degrees. *NEWSLINKS, Volume XII, #5*, 1, 18, & 27.

Useem, R., & Cottrell, A.B. (1993d). Third culture kids: Focus of major study. *NEWSLINKS, Volume XII, #3*, 1 & 29.

13

EDUCATIONAL AND OCCUPATIONAL CHOICES OF AMERICAN ADULT THIRD CULTURE KIDS*

ANN BAKER COTTRELL

INTRODUCTION

Martha,[2] was born in China in 1917. Her family lived in a small mission compound where she was home schooled until ninth grade when she went to mission boarding school. Having visited the United States once, she returned to the United States for college while her parents were still in China.

John's dad was a U.S. diplomat. Born in Germany in 1960, John lived with his family and attended schools in the capital cities of Sierra Leone (British Catholic school), Korea (American cooperative), Bolivia (American international), and Switzerland (private international). He lived in the United States from ages 12 to 14.

Alice was born in France. She was in Saudi Arabia with her ARAMCO sponsored family from one to seven years old and in Iran from 10 until after her high school graduation. She attended a local oil company school in elementary

grades. For middle school she was a day student at an American international school. She boarded at a private
international school in Austria for 10th grade and a private
school in New England for 11th and 12th grades.

As an army brat, Susan, lived on American bases in
Germany twice in the late 1960s, attending Department of
Defense Dependants' schools (DoDDs) at ages 8 to 9 and 14
to 16. Including moves in the United States, Susan attended
"11 or 12" different schools.

Larry has lived in San Diego his entire life except for college
and two years abroad. In 1975-76 he attended a village
school in England where his parents were on sabbatical. In
1982-83, his family was in Trieste, Italy, where he attended
the small international school. The family had no contact
with other Americans in either place.

These five Americans have had very different life experiences. Yet,
despite their differences, they are likely to immediately recognize a
transcending bond in the shared experience of the Third Culture
Kid (TCK). TCKs[3] are children who live outside their passport
country because of their parents' work in another country; in other
words, they spend part or all of their formative years in a third
culture environment (Useem & Useem, 1967; Useem, Useem, &
Donogue, 1963; Useem, Useem, Othman, & McCarthy, 1981).[4] As
these vignettes suggest, an American TCK's experience is strongly
influenced by the parents' sponsoring organization and the time in
history the family is abroad. This chapter first provides an overview
of how a family's third culture experience is related to sponsor and
historical period. It then addresses the question of what kinds of
choices adult TCKs make regarding higher education and occupation and how this may reflect their third culture background. In
order to maintain the focus on this research, references to other
research and more detailed explanations are provided in the
endnotes.

Data are from a study of 603 American adult TCKs (ATCKs) whose child/teen years outside the United States were during the post-WWII/Cold War period and who were living in the United States at the time of the study.[5] Respondents are broadly grouped by sponsor: Military (30%), Government (23%), Missionary (17%), Business (16%) and Other (14%). "Other" includes, for example, educators, employees of international nongovernmental organizations, intergovernmental organizations, the media, and foundations. For the first section, describing third culture patterns, this sample is augmented with data from 92 ATCKs whose third culture childhood was prior to the end of WWII: Missionary (66%), Business (16%), Military (10%), Government (4%), and Other (3%).

SPONSOR, HISTORY, AND THIRD CULTURE EXPERIENCE[6]

Before looking at how a third culture childhood has influenced adult life choices, it is important to understand some of the variations in TCKs' childhood experiences. Families in this study had lived outside the United States from 1 to 19 years. Nearly half of these families (45%) were abroad at least 10 years and approximately one-fifth (18%) 15 or more years.[7] Most (60%) lived in more than one country outside the United States, and nearly one-third (31%) had family homes and/or sent children to school in three or more different countries outside the United States. For many families, global mobility involved living not only in different countries but completely different cultural regions; for example, an oil company dependent, abroad for 15 years, lived in Venezuela, Cuba, Indonesia, Italy, Nigeria, Libya, and the United States.

Sponsor

As numerous studies have shown, sponsor is a significant factor affecting a third culture family's experience because the sponsor influences (but does not absolutely determine) how long a family serves overseas, its geographical mobility, and relations with Ameri-

cans and host country nationals.[8] Combining these influences, a
fairly characteristic pattern emerges for each of the five broad
sponsor categories.

Missionary families spent the longest time overseas. The great
majority (85%) were abroad 10 years or more; only two families
were abroad fewer than six years. Missionaries were also the most
likely to have lived in only one country (72%). For most Missionary
Kids (MKs)[9] in this study, then, the United States was a source of
stories and passports; it was not "home." Home was Japan or Nigeria.[10]

Business families were almost as likely as missionaries to be overseas for long periods; 63% were abroad 10 years or more.[11] The
most evenly distributed according to number of countries, business
dependents for the most part would not consider the United States
their childhood home, but fewer would identify with a single
country than missionaries.

Military families were most mobile, but not primarily overseas;
41% were abroad fewer than five years—one or two tours in one or
two countries. For military brats, an overseas posting was business-
as-usual in a highly mobile life, although that business might be
taking place in unfamiliar surroundings.[12]

Government dependents (nonmilitary), especially foreign
service, take the prize for global mobility. Forty-four percent were
abroad at least 10 years, and the same proportion lived in four or
more countries. Nearly all the extreme cases—six or more countries
—were government families. These TCKs are most likely to feel at
home everywhere and nowhere and/or to feel most at home where
they are considered locally to be a foreigner.[13]

"Others," in this study, were most likely to be short-termers
(42% abroad one to two years and 70% less than five), most (59%)
experiencing only one country. For most in the "other" category,
the overseas experience was an exotic interlude in their American
lives. Because in this study two-thirds of the fathers in the "other"
category were university academicians for whom one or two
sabbaticals overseas is typical, this may not be representative of the
diversity of other sponsors. Families with international schools,

United Nations, or nongovernmental organizations were overseas for a longer time.

Historical Period

Historical period also affects third culture experience; a major shift in third cultures occurred with the end of colonialism.[14] Who is abroad, how long they live overseas, and schooling options have all changed over time. Families in the combined samples are classified into four cohorts according to the first year they are recorded as having been outside the United States: prewar (prior to 1946), immediate post-war (1946-59), the 1960s, and the 1970s.[15] None of these respondents was abroad as a child in the post–cold war era. These families illustrate shifting third culture patterns and, in particular, the changes between prewar and postwar third cultures. The dramatic shift in what Americans have been doing overseas is seen clearly in this sample of third culture families. Nearly two-thirds (61%) of prewar families were doing "God's work" in non-Christian parts of the world. Government sponsored families dominated the immediate postwar period (40% military, 21% government).[16] Beginning in the 1960s, the number of ways Americans worked abroad increased, as is seen in the growing presence of the "other" category in this sample (from 3% of prewar families to one-third of the 1970's cohort). Business families have remained a fairly constant 13% to 19% of each cohort.

Schooling options have changed dramatically since the prewar period. TCKs are increasingly able to attend schools near their overseas homes. Suitable local schooling was so scarce before the end of WWII that 80% of families first abroad in those years turned to home schooling or boarding school for at least some of their children's education. In contrast, only 26% of families in the latest cohort made use of those options at any time. This is also related to the historical shift in sponsor representation abroad. Missionaries, declining in prominence, were most likely to send children to boarding schools or to home school their children.

Finally, the length of overseas assignments is steadily decreasing.

Sixty-one percent of the prewar families were abroad 13 years or more, while half of the 1970's cohort were outside the United States for only one to three years. One cannot assume that those who have had a TCK experience, that is, who were abroad for a short time, are less affected by this experience than TCKs whose entire childhood was outside the United States. The effects of their experiences are different. The long-term TCK usually cannot identify with the United States and may develop a strong sense of belonging in their country of residence.[17] But because it is the only life they know, it does not make an impression (at least until re-entry).

> We were just born to it...people always comment on how fascinating it must have been to live in India. It wasn't fascinating, it just was, that was our life. (Mission, female, 16 years)

Those abroad for a short time have the advantage of a comparative frame of reference. Being suddenly catapulted into a foreign setting for a year or two, the third culture experience may create an intensity of excitement unknown by long-term TCKs.

> Those two years changed my whole life. They made me aware of the international dimension and determined to make an international life for myself. (Other, female, 2 years)

ADULT LIFE CHOICES

What kinds of choices do adult TCKs make regarding their place in the world? Does this seem to reflect their international childhood? Do ATCKs from different sponsor backgrounds make different choices? The next two sections look at the higher education and occupation choices of the 603 ATCKs who were overseas after WWII.

Education

Achievement. One of most noteworthy characteristics of ATCKs is their extraordinary educational achievement; 81% had at least a bachelor's degree compared with 21% of the U.S. population over 25 at the same time.[18] An astounding 11% of this sample had completed a doctoral level degree and more were in Ph.D. programs. Although military dependents (the group most representative of the United States population) (Department of Defense, 1995),[19] had the lowest level of educational achievement in this study, the fact that two-thirds had at least a bachelor's degree puts them well above the U.S. population overall.[20]

This very high level of educational achievement reflects considerable cultural capital available to TCKs: parental role models with high education and high expectations, excellent schools, and a wealth of diverse experiences.[21] Because third culture communities are generally communities of professionals, TCKs are raised by highly educated parents in educationally elite communities.[22] Parents' educational levels were as high as the respondents'. At least one parent in 80% of these families had at least a bachelor's degree; nearly half the fathers (46%) and nearly one in five mothers (18%) had a graduate degree. This is related to sponsor, and the more broadly representative character of military personnel is again apparent when parents' educational levels are compared. At least one parent in one-third (36%) of military families had more than a BA, in contrast to the majority of missionary (83%) and "other" (89%) families in which at least one parent had more than a BA.

Parental role models and high expectations are supported by the excellent education provided in the generally small overseas schools.[23] And the experience of living and traveling abroad as a child provides another kind of education, as many pointed out.

I traveled to most parts of the world. I had an outstanding education at an American school and because my father worked for an American company, we [could] take advantage of many opportunities. (Business, male, 18 years)

Ancient history was familiar. I'd been to these places, met these people. (Military, female, 5 years)

I was better prepared as a high school student outside the United States than many of the [other] freshmen...I was more accepting of others, I had confidence of traveling on my own (great distances), so I felt more sure of myself. (Business, female, 10 years)

Influence of Third Culture Childhood. The majority of ATCKs in this study returned to the United States close to the time they would enter college; two-thirds were 16 or older and more than half of them were high school graduates, 18 and older.[24] With overseas experiences so fresh when they entered college, it is not surprising that three-quarters (73%) reported that their TCK childhood affected their higher education, 45% said it affected them greatly. The older they were at return to the United States and the longer they had been abroad, the more likely they were to report an influence.

In response to an open-ended question, these ATCKs described the numerous and diverse ways their third culture background influenced their higher education experience. Adjustment, emphasized in the literature, was the second most frequently mentioned topic (27% of those who acknowledged an effect).[25] However, the most significant impact on higher education, according to these ATCKs, was on what they chose to study (63% of those who acknowledged an influence). Usually this was a decision to study something with an international focus such as international relations, anthropology, foreign languages, or area studies. Close to one-third (29%) of those who had completed at least a bachelor's degree had an internationally oriented major or minor at the undergraduate level, graduate level, or both. The following are typical explanations for choosing an internationally focused major.

Political science, foreign policy, international affairs, also communication . . . I wanted to gain tools so I could preach to others my TCK perspective. (Mission, male, 9 years)

International issues. I have a tendency to empathize/care about others and society, feeling connected to the future well-being of cultures, interest in development. (Other, male, 3 years)

Anthropology, to come to some understanding of my transnational experiences. (Mission, female, 14 years)

Some, such as the son of international school teachers, chose an international major that connected them specifically to their childhood home, often with a goal of returning.

I [majored in] archeology and Arabic hoping to return to the Middle East...I feel I owe it to myself and the world to go back and better the communication between the Middle East and the Western world. (Other, male, 11 years)

For others, the connection between choice of major and their childhood overseas is less obvious. Their majors were not directly international but reflected interests developed while living abroad. One respondent majored in biology in order to go into international wildlife management. Others were influenced by parents' work or needs they saw in the world around them or in themselves.[26]

I used to go to the eye hospital on the mission compound to watch surgeries. I always planned to go back to Africa so [I] wanted to do it as a nurse. (Mission, female, 11 years)

[I] became interested in counseling due to experiences abroad and having to adapt to different cultures. I've desired to help others adjust in whatever circumstances they have. (Military, female, 5 years)

Finally, many chose majors, international or not, less for their interest in the topic than for the likelihood it might lead to work abroad. Teaching, especially English as a Second Language (ESL), was high on this list; business, economics, and nursing were among other fields seen as vehicles to international employment.

The above may suggest that these students entered college firm in their decision about what or where to study and that they carried through with that commitment. While many did so, others changed their minds, sometimes many times. Several, mainly MKs, attributed their difficulty choosing a field of study or making a wrong choice to the fact that, having grown up abroad within the narrow confines of a missionary community and school, they had no idea of career options other than teaching, ministry, or medicine.[27] Others attributed difficulty focusing to their mobile and culturally complex childhood.

> On reflection, I had no focus. Moving constantly never allowed me to focus on what I wanted in life. I loved moving, and still do, but I probably would have done more if I hadn't been so mobile. (Military, female, 5 years)

> Being bicultural causes one to see things differently. Thus, I find myself being interested in almost anything and everything. I absorb information but don't act on it because there are too many variables. I have lots of information but few opinions. I loved being in college but changed majors frequently. (Mission, female, 11 years)

Occupation[28]

Type of Work. Consistent with their high educational achievement, these ATCKs were likely to have careers involving expertise, leadership, and independence. The data in Table 13.1 show that 7 out of 10 in their present or most recent job (if not currently employed) were in the top occupational ranks.[29] (Keep in mind that this includes college students working at less than professional jobs.)

They were executives, administrators, managers, or in professional or semi-professional positions. Over half of the latter group (25% of the entire sample) were in helping professions such as medicine, teaching, social work, clergy, or counseling.[30]

Table 13.1. Current or Most Recent Occupation by Sponsor (percentage distribution).

Type of Work	Mission (n = 102)	Military (n = 176)	Gov't (n = 186)	Business (n = 92)	Other (n = 83)	Total (N = 589)
Executive, Administrator	17	28	35	26	24	27
Professional, semiprofessional	61	34	38	47	53	44
Support (secretarial, technical)	17	27	15	16	18	19
Sales	5	6	7	5	4	6
Other (police, mechanics, etc.)	1	4	5	6	6	4
Total percent	17%	30%	28%	16%	14%	100%

At the time of the survey, the greatest proportion of dependents in each sponsor category were working as professionals. However, comparing ATCKs from different sponsor categories shows a tendency for ATCKs to follow their fathers' general third culture occupational roles (the work done overseas), if not necessarily their specific occupations.[31] MKs and "others," whose parents were most likely to be in the professions, were themselves most likely to be professional or semi-professional. MKs were the most concentrated in a single occupational category; almost two-thirds were professionals including doctors, nurses, teachers, social workers, and clergy. In fact, MKs (17% of the sample) were half of those in medical occupations. This reflects commitment to service, interest, and probably the lack of a variety of role models mentioned above. Government dependents, most of whose fathers were diplomats, were the most likely to be executives or administrators. Although a minority of military dependents were in administrative and technical support occupations, this is more than any of the other sponsor groups and is consistent with the military dependents' slightly lower educational level.

Work Setting. ATCKs were most likely to work in human service settings, as the data in Table 13.2 show. This includes many in administrative support or technical occupations as well as those in the service careers mentioned above. Over one-third (39%) worked in educational, medical, social service, or religious settings. This is not surprising considering that their parents' careers were largely in service, to the country or church, especially. Many parents were also working in service to host nationals, teaching, providing medical services, or working in development programs, for example.

Table 13.2. Employer/Work Setting by Sponsor (percentage distribution).

Work Setting	Mission (n = 102)	Military (n = 175)	Gov't (n = 135)	Business (n = 90)	Other (n=80)	Total (N=582)
Business/Financial	22	32	27	20	17	25
Education	25	23	17	17	28	22
Health/Social Service	24	7	13	23	13	15
Self	11	14	14	14	14	13
Government	3	5	5	7	8	5
Military	2	10	6	1	2	5
Professional'	3	6	12	11	10	8
Arts, Media	0	3	5	4	7	4
Religious	10	0	0	2	1	2
Total percent	18%	30%	23%	16%	14%	100%

'Professional offices or firms other than medical (e.g., law, engineering, consulting, research).

These ATCKs often reported that they were influenced by their parents' work and/or that living abroad sensitized them to issues of need, such as poverty or illness, as well as creating a willingness and interest in working with people from other backgrounds. A doctor who had done refugee medicine with the International Rescue Committee wrote:

Now I don't do much other than to go to Mexico with our group from the hospital...Yes it's related to having lived overseas...in Africa and Southeast Asia. There was a calling, or an obligation, or interest, that I felt I needed to do in that

I was exposed to these people and I was exposed to what they had and didn't have and felt that I could contribute. (Government, male, 13 years)

A relatively small number worked in government bureaucracies (Government employees working directly with clients as social service providers were counted as working in social service settings, not government.). Possibly because expatriates tend not to become involved in local political issues, only two were in the legislative branch of government. Most of the others working for government were in specialized divisions such as human resources, health, or transportation departments at the local and state level or in special federal agencies such as Fish and Wildlife Department, Forest Service, or National Aeronautics and Space Administration.

Although the greatest concentration of these ATCKs in a single occupational setting was in business or financial organizations, from large corp rations to small retail shops, this was a minority (25%). That this is likely to be lower than the U.S. population as a whole may be related to the values imbibed in many third culture communities.

It's hard to want to be a corporate weeny, y'know, because their views...the bottom line is profit, profit, profit. I guess I look at the world in a broader view, I don't know. But its just hard to fit into the American pattern of growing up, getting a business job. (Government, male, 13 years)

For an MK to be a success it is not just a career success. Success doesn't equal money. The number one hallmark is Christian commitment. If you are the richest or most famous and have lost faith you are lost, a failure. (Mission, female, 11 years)

Many may have thought about, or even felt pressured, to follow their fathers by working for the same kind of third culture sponsor. Two foreign service dependents reflected this:

I did take the foreign service exam when I was in grad school. Kind of funny since I was already doing graduate work in [another] area. Something inside you says you have to take it. We all take it. I took it and didn't do well, so that was taken care of. (Government, male, 10 years)

I was...trying to figure out what I wanted to do, where I wanted to live and thought about the foreign service as a place to go, but I didn't really want to repeat *that* experience. (Government, male, 13 years)

These two represent the majority of ATCKs in this study who were not pursuing careers in their fathers' third culture sponsoring organizations at the time of the research, as seen in Table 13.2.[32] The most likely to be working (current or last job) in their fathers' organizational setting were those in the "other" category whose parents were educators; 28% of them worked in educational institutions. Those least likely to have been working in their father's sponsor type were government dependents. Nevertheless, those working in religious institutions or the military were disproportionately from that background; eight of nine clergy were MKs, and 56% of those in the military or military support organizations were military brats. It is very likely that if this sample included American ATCKs living outside the United States a larger proportion would be found in their fathers' sponsor organizations because this choice may have been made with the intention of serving overseas. Supporting this hypothesis is the fact that the dependents least likely to be working in their fathers' sponsor organization were from the sponsors most associated with both overseas experience and a high level of commitment to the sponsor—government (5%) and military and mission (10% each).

A certain independence and self sufficiency is seen in the fact that over 10% did not report to anyone over them in their jobs. These were equally divided between respondents who self-identified as president/CEO/business owner and freelance individuals such as consultants, therapists in private practice, writers, private music teachers, and crafts persons. In addition, many others such as doctors, researchers and professors did work, which was, to a great extent, self-directed. This reflects a level of self-confidence born of continually facing and dealing with new challenges. Another explanation may be the fact that many TCKs grow up with little choice over their lives, constantly having to monitor their own behavior in terms of how it reflects on parents and/or sponsor. Independent careers could be a means of escaping such control. And it may grow from a sense of being different enough to make fitting in difficult. As one respondent noted:

> I always feel outside the mainstream. I would NEVER fit into the 9 to 5 mold. I was being groomed for law school, but I could never work for somebody. I said forget law school and opened a gallery for African art. I did that for five years. Now I have a private investigation firm. I size up people. (Mission, male, 5 years)

Still others may have chosen independent freelance work because it is transportable and can be done anywhere in the world, whether traveling or settled.

> I write technical articles. I kept a journal from an early age. I was always encouraged to write about what I saw. My husband's jobs will determine our location and this is something I can do wherever he goes. I also think it is related to living abroad in that it is independent. My brothers and I all work for ourselves. None of us has an 8 to 5 job. We are all self-sufficient, we all know what else is out there. (Military, female, 7 years)

International Dimensions of Work. Most of these ATCKs desired to maintain a definite international dimension in their lives.[33] The majority agreed that "it is important to have an international dimension in my life" (70%) and "I would like to live abroad again" (88%). Over 90% also agreed that "the U.S. is the best place for me to be living at this time."[34] Both international sentiments were most evident among business and "other" dependents. It is interesting to note that, although only a minority (less than 15%) disagreed with either statement, this relative lack of need for international connections was found most among those who lived abroad the longest, missionary kids, and shortest time, military dependents.

There are many reasons for desiring some international involvement including interest, excitement and challenge, support for one's identity as an international person, opportunities to use cross-cultural knowledge or skills. On the negative side, motivations may include feeling unappreciated, even alien, in the American scene, or not fully understanding nuances of American life, especially work life. Occupation is one place ATCKs can realize a desired international or transnational connection and having this in their work made work life more meaningful for some.

> I have been unhappy with my career and I think that is because it did not have an international dimension. I have just realized this. I feel like something is missing when I don't have the international dimension. (Mission, female, 5 years)

> Now I'm very satisfied with my work life. Finally, all my overseas experiences add up and mean something to others, as well as myself. Since so many others would now like to become "globally competent" as managers, they view me as a role model and I've perfected methods for training them to learn what I know. (Business, female, 10 years)

The following looks at the extent to which ATCKs have incorporated international interests and activities into work at any time since high school. Before proceeding, it is important to stress three points. First, not everyone seeks an international connection through work. For some the experience abroad was not that seminal. Second, some actively seek domestic American work experiences, for various reasons.

I worked as a waitress. I'd never had that experience. Americans I knew all seemed to have worked at a lot of odd jobs like that and we couldn't do that in Peru. Partly also, I just wanted to prove to myself that I could do those kinds of things. (Mission, female, 18 years)

When I got to the U.S. I wanted to fit in. That was most important to me so I just kept trying; I put all that [international] stuff in boxes and put them away. I did not want to deal with that. I married an American girl got an American job and now I have a very American life in a very American suburb. (Other, male, 18 years)

Third, many struggled with the conflict between their desire to find work that would connect them to other places and other peoples, often involving mobility, and the desire to find work that would connect them to one place, one community, and spare their children the rootlessness they experienced. Some chose domestic careers to "protect" their children, although others bemoaned the fact that their children did not have third culture experiences. A diplomat's son found a solution by joining the Navy; his family would have a base and yet he could travel regularly.

My desperate need is to establish [roots here] for my kids. I thought about how I could establish roots but I realize I'll never have it. You never really are [part of the community] 'cause you live with those third culture experiences and eventually that itch comes around again and you're off and exploring. I'm in the military. I don't want [my family] to go overseas. I refuse. I have that option. But the Navy helps [me because] with all the overseas deployments I get abroad. (Government, male, 13 years)

The degree to which, as a group, these respondents have incorporated some international dimension into their work is remarkable, especially considering that most were describing a time when international work opportunities were not as common as they are at the turn of the new century. Respondents were asked to indicate which, if any, jobs had an international dimension and to describe what made them international.[35] Three general indicators of an international dimension in work were derived from these answers: work outside the United States, use of language other than English, and other international aspects to any of the jobs they have held ("other international" in Table 13.3). Table 13.3 shows the distribution of responses for these three indicators.

Table 13.3. International Dimensions of Work (percentage distribution).

Sponsor[*]	Mission	Military	Gov't	Business	Other	Total
Work outside US	46	47	52	59	47	50
Language in work	52	34	52	62	48	48
Other international	46	32	48	59	53	45

[*]No numbers are provided for sponsor groups because these are three different indices and each had a different number of no responses.

Three-quarters (72%) had one or more of these international elements in some job. (Many others cited work with culturally diverse populations in the United States) For some the international element was minimal; for others it was extensive. Work outside the United States ranged from one trip abroad for a professional meeting to working for many years in another country. Language use ranged from translating an occasional letter to working entirely in another language. Nearly half of those who had ever worked cited additional ways in which one or more jobs had an international dimension; responses again ranged from minimal to extensive. The more limited examples include working in a company with a few foreign clients, using examples from overseas childhood in teaching, occasionally translating, or hosting international visitors. At the other extreme are the internationally focused jobs held by nearly one in five (18%) at some time. Examples of internationally focused jobs include cross-cultural training, international student advising, working in government agencies such as Voice of America, State Department Council on International Public Affairs, owning an import-export company, and work with an NGO on an international issue. A good deal of teaching and research is also internationally focused, for example, teaching/translating languages—a foreign language or English as a second language (one respondent taught French to Japanese), or teaching and conducting research on international relations or specific geo-cultural regions.

Although the majority of ATCKs in this study have had at least some international activity in their work history, as just described, it is also important to ask to what extent individuals' career histories reflect international commitment. In order to answer this, participants' career histories were classified according to the centrality and length of international activity. As the data in Table 13.4 show, approximately one-quarter reported no international element in any work role. (It must be kept in mind that this includes the respondents who were in school or were just starting their careers.) A minority were "maximizers," whose work histories have been primarily or entirely in internationally focused careers, such as those described above.[36] This number would undoubtedly be considerably higher if American ATCKs living abroad had been included. Anecdotal evidence indicates, for example, that America's diplomatic offices around the world are filled with ATCKs. Most in this study can be considered "minimalists"; they have had some limited international involvement in their work roles.

Sponsor appears to be related to international involvement in the work life of these ATCKs. Business and government dependents had the highest rate of at least minimal international involvement on the three indices reported in Table 13.3. While military dependents, were not significantly less likely than MKs, or "other" dependents to have worked abroad or to have at some time had an internationally focused job, they were much less likely to report ever using another language in work or to report other international activities in their open-ended responses. This may be related both to the nature of their overseas experience and to their relatively lower levels of education. The relationship between sponsor and career history (Table 13.4) is not as easily described, although again, the military brats were on the low end of the involvement continuum; they are tied with MKs as most likely to have had no international work experience and, like the "other" dependents, least likely to have been internationally focused for most or all of their work history. Regardless of sponsor, the longer one lived outside the United States as a TCK and the more nations one lived in, the more likely one was to use another language in work, to have worked outside the United States, and to have had a work history that was primarily or entirely international.

Table 13.4. International Involvement in Work History by Sponsor (percentage distribution).

International Work History	Mission (n = 100)	Military (n = 175)	Gov't (n = 138)	Business (n = 92)	Other (n = 85)	Total (N = 590)
None	32	84	24	16	25	27
Minimal or limited	29	87	46	48	52	41
Intermediate	26	21	16	23	16	20
Most or entire career	13	8	14	13	7	11
Total percent	17%	30%	23%	16%	14%	100%

Workers for the Global Economy. A popular topic of discussion among TCKs at meetings such as those of Global Nomads International[37] is how well suited ATCKs are to meet the demands of the new global economy. They are not alone in this observation. An academician, himself a British military TCK, writes that specialists needed for this evolving world

> ...not only work outside traditional professional and organizational cultures of the nation-state, they experience the problems of intercultural communication at first hand. This, plus the necessity of moving backwards or forwards between different cultures, various imperfect proto-"third cultures"

necessitate new types of flexible personal controls, dispositions and means of orientation. (Featherstone, 1990: p. 8)

A recruiter for top management positions reiterates this, saying that for jobs in the new economy he looks for individuals who have flexibility and high tolerance for risk. He asks if the person "ever lived or worked in another country, and do they speak multiple languages because that demonstrates an ability to relate to different kinds of people" (Citrin, 2000). Yet another observer writes that "in the corporate world overseas experience ranks ahead of training" as an indicator of international business success (Rabbitt, cited in Fail, 1998: p. 6). All ATCKs have lived abroad, of course, and three-quarters of this sample report having used another language since high school.[38] In addition, ATCKs in this study agreed that they possess a number of the traits often cited as important for various kinds of international work such as flexibility, risk taking, multilingual ability, and so on.[39] The majority agreed with the following statements:[40]

* When I encounter unexpected difficulties I can usually figure out a way to handle them. (97%)
 * I have more understanding of other peoples and countries than most Americans do. (96%)
 * I can find some basis for relating to virtually anyone, regardless of differences such as race, ethnicity, religion, or nationality. (92 %)
 * I welcome the opportunity to meet foreigners. (91%)
 * When I see individuals who look unsure of themselves, I reach out to help them. (85%)
 * I establish relations easily in new situations. (82%)
 * When a dispute arises, I am usually one to play the role of mediator. (79%)

While most felt they had much to offer in this increasingly globalized world, many felt that their ability to contribute and use these talents had been under utilized. Seventy-two percent agreed that they had more knowledge and skills than opportunity to use them. Similarly, less than half (45%) agreed that they were sought out for their transnational/cross-cultural knowledge or skills. These responses, combined with the observations of the academician and the business consultant, strongly suggest that TCKs have been ahead of their time, that they possessed the skills needed in the new global world before the world was fully aware of this need or was even minimally aware of this experienced population.

CONCLUSION

A great deal of research and many autobiographical accounts detail the impact of a TCK childhood on identity and other personal issues. Findings from this research affirm that there is an important and life-long impact. ATCKs never "get over" the experience; it is part of who they are for life. The majority of ATCKs in this study, of all ages, said they feel different from other Americans, and most felt their lives have benefited from their TCK background. One respondent is fairly representative, saying: "My childhood in India is the seminal aspect of my life. It has complicated my life and enriched it too. I wouldn't trade it for anything."

There has been very little research, however, on how ATCKs weave their often complex, multicultural childhood experiences into their adult life choices. Looking only at higher education and occupation, it is clear that ATCKs acquire considerable cultural capital, which is manifest in extremely high levels of achievement in both areas. Although very few follow their parents' specific third culture occupations or work with the same kind of sponsor organization, the influence of their parents' work is apparent in the fact that most, like their parents, are professionals or administrators and careers in service to others predominate. Third culture influence is also seen in the degree to which an international dimension has been incorporated into higher education and work roles. Most would welcome even more international involvement than they have, suggesting that both the ATCKs themselves and others should be made aware of the many ways this population is particularly well suited to the realities of the contemporary globalized world.

It is important to remember that beneath generalizations there are many differences. Parents' sponsor clearly affected the nature of the third culture experience and that difference is, to a degree, reflected in the life choices of adult ATCKs. In addition, individuals respond differently to their experiences; some return to their passport country (United States in this case) wanting mainly to settle in, establish roots, and put the third culture life style behind them. Most do wish continuing involvement with other peoples and places. Still others have acted on this interest by making their adult lives outside their parental country. This population has not been studied and researchers should turn their attention to how it differs, if at all, from those living in their home/passport country.

NOTES

[1*] This research by Ann Baker Cottrell and Ruth Hill Useem with Kathleen Finn Jordan and John Useem was funded, in part, by the College of Arts and Letters, San Diego State University and The International Schools Services.

[2] The histories are true, the names have been changed.

[3] Third Cultures "are created by men who mediate between societies...in the process of representing larger collectivities" (Useem & Useem, 1967, p. 131; see also Useem et al., 1963 and Useem et al., 1981). While third cultures are created by both the foreign representatives and the host national counterparts with whom they work, most research has focused on the foreigners who represent their societies (e.g., diplomats, military, Peace Corps) or particular institutions (e.g., churches, educational institutions, businesses) abroad.

[4] TCKs come from all countries and live in all parts of the world. This study focuses on just one segment of this population, the adult American TCK living in the United States.

[5] In order to focus on adult life choices, 25 years was the

minimal age for participation in this study; therefore, none were abroad in the post–cold war period.

[6] This section uses the combined prewar and postwar samples. Furthermore, to avoid overrepresentation of families with several siblings in this study, data for this section only are based on 493 families rather than individual respondents.

[7] Willis and Minoura's (1989) sample of Canadian and American TCK alumni of the Canadian Academy in Japan had been abroad for even longer periods—69% 10 years or more. Two explanations for the difference are likely. TCKs abroad for only a year, especially in Europe or English-speaking countries, are more likely to attend local host national schools than those abroad for a longer period and/or in countries with non-European languages. The latter are more likely to attend international schools such as the Canadian Academy. The Canadian Academy has few, if any, military dependents who are generally abroad for short assignments.

[8] Studies that look at more than one sponsor group have found sponsor to be an important factor in both overseas experience and in relation to adult lives. See, for example, Gleason (1970), Jordan (1981), Krajewski (1969), Salmon (1987), Shepard (1975), Werkman (1972). Others, such as the American Association of School Administrators (1966), Cohen (1977), Pollock and Van Reken (1999), acknowledge that sponsor communities and cultures may vary markedly. Lambert (1966) devoted a chapter to each of the major sponsors of overseas Americans at that time.

[9] Terms used by the respondents to describe themselves are used in this paper. Missionary children refer to themselves as MKs. Military dependents often refer to themselves as brats, such as "Army brats." While one respondent referred to himself as an "ARAMCO Kid," such terminology is not widespread among other sponsor groups.

[10] A significant literature exists about missionaries and mission communities (e.g., Echerd & Arathoon, 1989; Hersey, 1985; Kingsolver, 1998; Swanson, 1995) and MK childhood (e.g., Alter, 1998; Buffam, 1985; Griffen, 1983; Seeman, 1997; Van Reken, 1988; Van

Reken, 1996). Bibliographies by Austin (1983) and Useem (1998) include many missionary citations.

[11] The business community, per se, is least discussed in the general literature on Americans abroad or TCKs. This may be because, compared with missionaries, foreign service, and military, businesses have not developed a sense of community—including families. Business literature continues to focus on the employee, even when discussing relocation. No autobiographical reports of Americans growing up as business dependents overseas have been located. For some information regarding business families overseas see Gaylord (1979), Harvey (1985), Ross (1985), Wilkins (1966).

[12] For literature about military communities and dependents' experiences see, for example, Allingham (1997), Darnauer (1970), Ender (1996), Paden and Pezor (1993), Tarr (1966), Truscott (1989), Wertsch (1991), Wolf (1969) and, for references, Useem (1998).

[13] Less literature exists specifically about diplomatic communities and dependents than about the military and missionaries. Callaway (1987) gives insight into colonial British civil servants. Bowles (1956), Eakin (1988), Fisher (1966), Hughes (1999), Kittredge (1996), Miller (1974) Schmiel and Schmiel (1998), Wolff (1978) are about diplomatic families.

[14] For elaboration on the characteristics of colonial compared to postcolonial third cultures see Cohen (1977), Useem (1967), Useem (1971) and Useem et al., (1963).

[15] This is an approximation. Some families were abroad before the respondent in this study was born.

[16] The postwar shift is especially clear in data on missionaries. Although in 1966, missionaries constituted the smallest proportion of Americans abroad in over a century, this was the largest number of American missionaries ever overseas (Latourette, 1966). The dominance of military families among United States families abroad in the 1960s is also noted by American Association of School Administrators (1966).

[17] Some adult TCKs choose to remain in their childhood homelands and some become citizens. Because this is a study of Amer-

ican adult TCKs residing in the U.S. this study does not provide information on what proportion make this choice.

[18] *The universal almanac* (Wright, 1993: p. 235).

[19] Eighty-five percent of military personnel are enlisted. (Department of Defense Selected Manpower Statistics, 1995: Table 1.1, DOD Military/Civilian Personnel, September 30, 1995.

[20] Ender (1996), Powell (1998), and Willis and Minoura (1989) all report findings consistent with this study, that over 90% of ATCKs had at least some college education. There is some variation in proportion earning graduate degrees. Ender's predominantly military sample matches the military dependents in this study; 30% and 28%, respectively, had advanced degrees. The nonmilitary ATCKs in this study, like Canadian Academy Alumni (Willis & Minoura, 1989), were more likely to have completed graduate degrees (39% and 40%). There is less consensus regarding adult MKs (AMKs). AMKs in the MK-CART/CORE research (Powell, 1998) were considerably less likely to have completed advanced graduate degrees than MKs in this study (4% versus 17%), possibly because more were in college. The high proportion (33%) in that study who majored in Bible, theology, or Christian education/service fields also suggests they planned careers in which advanced degrees are not necessary.

[21] Cultural capital, "proficiency in and familiarity with dominant cultural codes and practices, for example linguistic styles, aesthetic preferences, styles of interaction" (Aschaffenburg & Maas, 1997: p. 573), is the foundation for success in education and career. ATCKs, overall, have the cultural capital for success in the United States and in cross-cultural environments. The Aschaffenburg and Mass research indicates that cultural participation (which could include the experiences of living abroad) over a long period has a particularly important effect on educational attainment.

[22] Werkman (1986) and The American Association of School Administrators (1966), among others, also note the high educational and occupational level of third culture parents.

[23] Some international schools had fewer than a dozen students

while some Department of Defense schools and international schools had over 1,000.

[24] This is probably not representative of the entire TCK population in terms of age of reentry. Reentry in late teen years is more difficult than in early childhood and therefore late re-entry TCKs may be more likely to volunteer for a study such as this.

[25] Given the dominance of reentry and adjustment in the TCK and ATCK literature, as reflected in Austin (1983) and Useem (1998), one might have expected this to rank higher.

[26] It appears that a great many TCKs use college work to investigate, understand, or try to resolve TCK-issues. Useem (1998) has identified 240 TCK related theses and dissertations.

[27] Werkman (1975) points out that the limited range of careers is typical of American overseas communities regardless of sponsor. Orthner, Giddings, and Quinn (1989) also note the lack of role models, especially for girls, in military families.

[28] Only 2% never had paid employment.

[29] These data report only primary current or most recent work. It is not uncommon for ATCKs to have nonlinear career paths, some making quite radical changes in their line of work. Also, at the time of the research, a number had more than one paid job, which were sometimes quite disparate. For example, a college professor was also a state legislator and an engineering firm's scientist/vice president, taught quilting, and worked in a quilt shop. Participants were coded for this study, however, by primary occupation.

[30] Mason (1978) found that her sample of pre-WWII China MKs worked in education, social service, churches, or the State Department.

[31] Only 25% of the respondents reported mothers who worked overseas. The vast majority were missionaries because missions expect wives to be working partners. The other mothers who worked while the family was abroad were nearly all in education or worked as secretaries.

[32] Consistent with these findings, Bowen (1986), Ender (1996), and Truscott (1989) all note that a very small proportion of military dependents make a career in the military. Some data on AMKs

suggest that, although most have not pursued Christian vocations, the proportion who have may be significantly higher than among AMKs in this sample (Powell, 1998; Van Reken, 1987; Van Rooy, 1998). The difference may reflect the fact that these samples included AMKs currently working abroad, supporting the suggestion that those who follow in their parents' sponsoring organizations are more likely to be found among ATCKs living outside the United States. Wrobbel's (1988) AMKs were more likely than respondents in this study to be in religious occupations, but less than found in the studies noted above. Mason's (1978) AMKs, on the other hand, had rejected the evangelical aspect of their religious heritage but retained the values of social service.

[33] Most of the TCK college students in Downie's (1976) and Jordan's (1981) research expressed a strong interest in finding work abroad. Gleason's (1970) TCK students were asked more pointedly where they wanted to establish a home; MKs (33%) were most likely to say outside the United States.

[34] Data regarding the respondents' attitudes and feelings are based on a series of questions to which they responded "agree," "disagree," "both" or "no opinion." Figures reported in this paper represent the percent who answered agree and both to a statement; in all cases, the vast majority agreed without qualification (i.e., without "both"). Providing the "both" alternative was done to accommodate TCKs who are comfortable with ambiguity and frequently hold oxymoron opinions. Although this creates an analytical nightmare, respondents appreciated the choices. As one explained: "I particularly appreciate the both agree and disagree response choice because it reflects the paradoxical nature of this lifestyle, the 'both/and' or 'yes/but' aspects. I think not allowing that (in terms of reactions) has forced many TCKs to make either/or choices that lead to overprotection of the background or complete rejection of it. Thanks." (Mission, female, 11 years).

[35] The definition of international is somewhat subjective; for some it is apparently limited to being in or working with individuals from another country, for others the definition is very encompassing. For example, some claimed international activity based on

rarely interacting with someone from another country or rare use of another language, while a Spanish teacher and Asian literature professor saw no international dimension in their work lives. To simplify the questionnaire, we used the term "international" rather than the broader "cross-cultural," which can be applied to a great range of cultures including class and gender cultures. The professors may well have agreed that their work was cross-cultural. Anyone who used another language in working with culturally diverse Americans was included in "uses another language in work."

[36] "Maximizer" and "minimalist" are terms used by Carlson, Burn, Useem, and Yachimowicz (1990) to describe levels of international involvement among adults who have studied abroad.

[37] Global Nomads Inc., founded by Norma McCaig, a business dependent, is a national organization with some local chapters. For more information see http://globalnomads.association.com.

[38] Although no effort was made to assess language proficiency, it is noteworthy that this many have enough knowledge and lack of fear to make some use of other languages.

[39] Pollock and Van Reken (1999) identify and discuss TCKs' special cross-cultural, observational, social and linguistic skills, all of which are useful in international work.

[40] These questions also asked for agree, disagree, or both answers. Data are those who said agree and both. The number who said both is relatively small.

REFERENCES

Allingham, G.E. (1997). *Growing up in khaki: Life as a service brat.* Fuquay-Varina, NC: Research Triangle Publishing.

Alter, S. (1998). *All the way to heaven: An American boyhood in the Himalayas.* New York: Henry Holt & Co.

American Association of School Administrators. (1966). *The mission called O/OS.* Washington, DC: American Association of School Administrators.

Aschaffenburg, K., & Maas, I. (1997). Cultural and educational careers: The dynamics of social reproduction. *American Sociological Review, 62,* 573–587.

Austin, C.N. (1983). *Cross-cultural reentry: An annotated bibliography.* Austin, TX: Abilene Christian University Press.

Bowen, G.L. (1986). Intergenerational occupational inheritance in the military: A reexamination. *Adolescence, 21,* 623–629.

Bowles, C. (1956). *At home in India.* New York: Brace and World.

Buffam, C.J. (1985). *The Life and Times of an MK.* Pasadena, CA: William Carey Library.

Callaway, H. (1987). *Gender, culture and empire: European women in colonial Nigeria.* Basingstoke, UK: MacMillan.

Carlson, J.S., Burn, B.B., Useem, J., & Yachimowicz, D. (1990). *Study abroad: The experience of American undergraduates.* Westport, CT: Greenwood Press.

Citrin, J. (2000). *Profile of Patricia Fili-Krushel.* Interview by Snigdha Prakash, Morning Edition, National Public Radio, April 5.

Cohen, E. (1977). Expatriate communities. *Current Sociology, 24,* 5–129.

Darnauer, P.F. (1970). *The adolescent experience in career Army families.* Unpublished doctoral dissertation, University of Southern California, Los Angeles, CA.

Department of Defense. (1995). Selected manpower statistics. Total Department of Defense Personnel, Table 1.1 DOD Military/Civilian Personnel, September 30, 1995 (http://web1.whs.osd.mil/mmid/m01/fy95/smstop.htm).

Downie, R.D. (1976). *Re-entry experiences and identity formation of third culture experienced dependent American youth: An exploratory study.* Unpublished doctoral dissertation, Michigan State University, East Lansing. MI.

Eakin, K.B. (1988). *The foreign service teenager—at home in the U.S.: A few thoughts for parents returning with teenagers.* Washington, DC: Overseas Briefing Center/Foreign Service Institute, Department of State.

Echerd, P., & Arathoon, A. (1989). *Understanding and nurturing the missionary family.* Pasadena, CA: William Carey Library.

Ender, M. (1996). Growing up in the military. In C. Smith (Ed.), *Strangers at home* (pp. 125–150). Bayside, NY: Aletheia Publications.

Fail, H. (1998). Global nomads at work. *Global Nomad Perspectives,* 5, 6–7.

Featherstone, M. (1990). Global culture: An introduction. M. Featherstone (Ed.), *Global culture* (pp. 1–16). Newbury Park, CA: Sage Publications.

Fisher, G.H. (1966). The foreign service officer. *Annals of the American Academy of Political and Social Sciences, 368,* 71–82.

Gaylord, M. (1979). Relocation and the corporate family: Unexplored issues. *Social Work, 24,* 186–190.

Gleason, T.P. (1970). *Social adjustment patterns and manifestations of worldmindedness of overseas-experienced American youth.* Unpublished doctoral dissertation, Michigan State University, East Lansing, MI.

Griffen, W.M. (1983). *Separation from parents: An inquiry pertaining to missionary children.* Unpublished doctoral dissertation. International College, Los Angeles, CA.

Harvey, M.C. (1985). The executive family: An overlooked variable in international assignments. *Columbia Journal of World Business, 20,* 84–92.

Hersey, J. (1985). *The call.* New York: Knopf.

Hughes, K.L. (1999). *The accidental diplomat: Dilemmas of the trailing spouse.* Putnam Valley, NY: Aletheia Publications.

Jordan, K.A.F. (1981). *The adaptation process of third culture dependent youth as they re-enter the United States and enter college.* Unpublished doctoral dissertation, Michigan State University, East Lansing, MI.

Kingsolver, B. (1998). *Poisonwood bible.* New York: Harper Collins.

Kittredge, C. (1996). Growing up global. In C. Smith (Ed.), *Strangers at home* (pp. 6–21). Bayside, NY: Aletheia Press.

Krajewski, F.R. (1969). *A study of the relationship of an overseas-experienced population based on sponsorship of parent and subsequent academic adjustment to college in the United States.* Unpublished doctoral dissertation, Michigan State University, East Lansing, MI.

Lambert, R.D. (ed.). (1966). Americans abroad. *Annals of the American Academy of Political and Social Sciences, Volume 368.*

Latourette, K.S. (1966). Missionaries Abroad. Americans

Abroad. *Annals of the American Academy of Political and Social Sciences, 368*, 21–29.

Mason, S.R. (1978). *Missionary conscience and the comprehension of imperialism: A study of the children of American missionaries to China, 1900-1949.* Unpublished doctoral dissertation, Northern Illinois Univer-sity, De Kalb, IL.

Miller, R.F. (1974). Where do you come from? Growing up in the foreign service. *Foreign Service Journal* (April), 21–23.

Orthner, D.K., Giddings, M., & Quinn, W. (1989). Growing up in a military family. In G. Bowen & D.K. Orthner (Eds.), *The organization family: Work and family linkages in the U.S. military* (pp. 117–142). New York: Praeger.

Paden, L.B., & Pezor, L.J. (1993). Uniforms and youth: The military child and his or her family (pp. 3–24). In F.W. Kaslow (Ed.), *The military family in peace and war.* New York: Springer Publishing Company.

Pollock, D.C., & Van Reken, R.E. (1999). *The third culture kid experience: Growing up among worlds.* Yarmouth, ME: Intercultural Press.

Powell, J.R. (1998). *MK research: Notes and observations.* In Joyce M. Bowers (Ed.), *Raising resilient MKs: Resources for caregivers, parents, and teachers* (pp. 433–444). Colorado Springs, CO: Association of Christian Schools International.

Ross, C.W. (1985). *Americans abroad: A study of the factors which influence the adaptation of American employees and their families to a foreign culture,* Unpublished doctoral dissertation. The Fielding Institute, Santa Barbara, CA.

Salmon, J.L. (1987). *The relationship of stress and mobility to the psychosocial development and well-being of third-culture-reared early adults.* Unpublished doctoral dissertation, Florida State University, Tallahassee, FL.

Schmiel, G., & Schmiel, K. (1998). *Welcome home: Who are you?* Putnam Valley, NY: Aletheia Publications.

Seeman, P. (1997). *Paper airplanes in the Himalayas: The unfinished path home.* Notre Dame, IN: Cross Cultural Publications.

Shepard Jr., F. (1975). *An analysis of variables of self-perception and personal ambition in overseas-experienced American teenagers: Implications for curricular planning*, Unpublished doctoral dissertation, Michigan State University, East Lansing, MI.

Swanson, J. (1995). *Echoes of the call: Identity and ideology among American missionaries in Ecuador*. New York: Oxford University Press.

Tarr, D.W. (1966). The military abroad. Americans abroad. *Annals of the American Academy of Political and Social Sciences, 368*, 31–42.

Truscott, M.R. (1989). *Brats*. New York: E.P. Dutton.

Useem, J. (1971). The study of cultures. *Sociological Focus, 4*, 3–25.

Useem, J., & Useem, R.H. (1967). The interfaces of a binational third culture: A study of the American community in India. *Journal of Social Issues, XXIII*, 130–143.

Useem, J., Useem, R.H., & Donoghue, J. (1963). Men in the middle of the third culture: The roles of American and non-western people in cross-cultural administration. *Human Organization, 22*, 171–179.

Useem, J., Useem, R.H., Othman, A.H., & McCarthy, F.E. (1981). Transnational networks and related third cultures: A comparison of two southeast Asian scientific communities. *Research in Social Movements, Conflict and Change, 4*, 283–316.

Useem, R.H. (1967). *The student third culture*. Council on International Educational Exchange, Occasional Paper on International Educational Exchange #10.

Useem, R.H. (1998). *Third culture kid bibliography*. East Lansing, MI: privately published. (May be ordered through Dr. Ruth Hill Useem's page on TCK World at http://www.tckworld.com)

Van Reken, R.E. (1987). *Preliminary results of adult missionary kid survey*. Paper presented at the International Conference on Missionary Kids, Quito, Ecuador, January 4–8, 1987.

Van Reken, R.E. (1988). *Letters never sent*. Elgin, IL: David C. Cook.

Van Reken, R.E. (1996). Religious culture shock. In C. Smith (Ed.), *Strangers at home* (pp. 81–98). Bayside, NY: Aletheia Press.

Van Rooy, S. (1998). Career developments: Woodstock class of 1968. In J. M. Bowers (Ed.), *Raising resilient MKs* (pp. 141–145).

Colorado Springs, CO: Association of Christian Schools International.

Werkman, S.L. (1972). Hazards of rearing children in foreign countries. *American Journal of Psychiatry*, *128*, 992–997.

Werkman, S.L. (1975). Over here and back there: American adolescents overseas. *Foreign Service Journal, 52*, 13–16.

Werkman, S.L. (1986). Coming home: Adjustment of Americans to the United States after living abroad. In C. N. Austin (Ed.), *Cross cultural reentry* (pp. 5-17). Abilene, TX: Abilene Christian University Press.

Wertsch, M.E. (1991). *Military brats: Legacies of childhood inside the fortress*. New York: Harmony Press.

Wilkins, M. (1966). The businessman abroad. *Annals of the American Academy of Political and Social Sciences, 368*, 83–94.

Willis, D.B., & Minoura, Y. (1989). Growing up in Japan: The transcultural experience of Canadian Academy alumni. *The Alumni Review of the Canadian Academy, 1*, 2–4.

Wolf, C. (1969). *The garrison community: A study of an overseas American military colony*. Westport, CT: Greenwood Publishing.

Wolff, J. (1978). *Children of the golden ghetto: Growing up in the foreign service*, Unpublished senior thesis. Merrill College, University of California, Santa Cruz, CA.

Wright, J.W. (1993). *The universal almanac: 1994*. Kansas City: Andrews and McMeel.

Wrobbel, K.A. (1988). *Study of psychosocial development of adult MKs*, Unpublished masters thesis. Wheaton College, Wheaton, IL.

ABOUT THE EDITOR AND CONTRIBUTORS

EDITOR

MORTEN G. ENDER, Ph.D., is Associate Professor of Sociology in the Department of Behavioral Sciences and Leadership at the United States Military Academy at West Point. He completed his B.A. in Sociology with a minor in German Language from Sonoma State University and his M.A. and Ph.D. in Sociology from the University of Maryland at College Park. He is a 1994 recipient of the *Phi Kappa Phi Award for Distinguished Faculty Mentor* and a 2000 *Apgar Award for Excellence in Teaching* at the United States Military Academy. He was the *Østfoldakademiet Professor*, American-Norwegian Institute for Education, Island of Jeløy, Norway, in 1998. He is the coeditor of *Teaching the Sociology of Peace and War: A Curriculum Guide* in 1998. His most recent academic publications have appeared in the journals *The American Sociologist, Teaching Sociology, Armed Forces and Society, Journal of Political and Military Sociology,* and *Death Studies.* Dr. Ender spent many of his childhood summers in Germany and, in an effort to hold off adulthood responsibilities, he traveled throughout Europe, the Middle East, and North Africa before returning to the United States to complete his undergraduate studies. UPDATE: Morten is now Professor of Sociology at West Point, taught thousands of cadets, and has written numerous books including his *Army Spouses: Military Families during the Global War on Terror* based on hundreds of interviews. Follow him: https://mortenender.com.

CONTRIBUTORS

ANN BAKER COTTRELL, Ph.D., is Professor of Sociology at San Diego State University. She completed her B.A. at Miami University (Ohio) and M.A. and Ph.D. from the Michigan State University. Her primary teaching areas are Global Systems, Ethnic and Racial Identities, Social Change, and Qualitative Research Methods. Her major research projects include three studies of South Asians married to Westerners following a two-year Fulbright Research Grant to conduct research on Indian Western couples in India and a comparative study of reentry female university students in the United States and Italy. Her publications include *Women and World Change: Issues in Development with Equity* (1981) with Naomi Black and *Mobilization of Collective Identity: A Comparative Perspective* (1980) with Jefferey A. Ross, Philip Rawkins, and Robert St. Cyr. Her articles have appeared in *The Diaspora Potrezebe, Newslinks: The Newspaper of the International Schools, The Newspaper of the International Schools Service, International Education Forum, Journal of Comparative Family Studies.* Dr. Baker Cottrell is the Former Assistant Director International Programs at San Diego State University. She has presented results from her studies in the United States and abroad. Dr. Baker Cottrell spent her junior undergraduate year at the University of Edinburgh, England.

KAREN CACHEVKI WILLIAMS, Ph.D., i s Assistant Professor of Child and Families Studies in the Department of Family and Consumer Sciences at the University of Wyoming. She earned her B.A. in English from the University of Illinois at Urbana, B.S. in Family and Consumer Education Services from the University of Wyoming, M.A. in Human Development from Pacific Oaks College in Pasadena, California, and Ph.D. in Curriculum and Instruction from the University of Wyoming. Dr. Williams has published a book on early childhood research ethics, as well as a variety of articles in such professional journals as *The Journal of Early Childhood Teacher Education*, *The Researcher*, and *Young Children*. Karen has studied early childhood education in the People's Republic of China and is currently conducting a study in Mongolia and France.

KATHLEEN A. FINN JORDAN, Ph.D., completed her doctoral dissertation, *The Adaptation Process of Third Culture Dependent Youth As They Re-Enter The United States And Enter College: An Exploratory Study*, at Michigan State University. In addition to her research work with Adult Third Culture Kids, presentations, and consultancies on a variety of cross-cultural and intercultural topics, she works independently as an NBCC certified counseling therapist, collaborates with Navy personnel as part of the Navy Intercultural workshops, volunteers part-time as an HIV therapist at the Whitman Walker Clinic, and engages in legal proofreading for an international law firm in their Washington, D.C., office. She has taught in private and public schools in the United States and in international private schools in Italy, Israel, and Iran. Her most recent publication, "Third Culture Persons" appeared in *Culture, Communication and Conflict: Readings in Intercultural Communications* (Simon and Schuster) in 1998. She is currently preparing a series of children's books with an illustrator in London for Third Culture Kids and their traveling friends. She received the Dr. Ruth Hill Useem research award in 1998 conferred by The Washington Global Nomads Association. She is a first generation American born in New York City holding passports from the United States and the Republic of Ireland.

MICHAEL E. GERNER, Ph.D., is a consulting school psychologist who has lived and worked in Saudi Arabia, Egypt, and among the Hopi and Navajo of the American Southwest. He is President of Consulting Psychologists, a professional association of psychologists and counselors who provide services for educational institutions in the southwestern United States and on-site consultation for international schools throughout Asia and the Middle East. Dr. Gerner specializes in understanding the challenges and opportunities of an internationally mobile lifestyle, personality development in Third Culture Kids (TCKs), the evaluation of culturally/linguistically diverse people, and applying contemporary advances in cognitive science to learning differences and learning disabilities. Dr. Gerner has been selected as "School Psychologist of the Year" by the Arizona Association of School Psychologists, and he is an internationally recognized presenter on the education and development of internationally mobile children and adolescents. He has served as psychologist and coordinator of special services for two international schools, psychologist for the Community Services Association in Egypt, the British International School, and Saudi Arabian Airlines. Dr. Gerner has consulted with the Jakarta International School, the Near East/South Asia Council of Overseas Schools (NESA), the East Asia Regional Council of Overseas Schools (EARCOS), and schools and agencies on the Hopi and Navajo reservations in the American West as well as metropolitan school districts throughout the United States. His daughter, Anna, was born in Egypt and inspired the article that appears in this book by her intrinsic interest and sensitivity toward other cultures. Both father and daughter look forward to many more visits to the country of her birth and traveling and living in faraway places.

ANNIKA HYLMÖ, Ph.D., is an Assistant Professor at Loyola Marymount University in Los Angeles, California. She earned her Ph.D. from Purdue University in Communication Studies. She completed her B.A. degree at Lund University, Sweden, and her M.A. at the American University in Washington, D.C. Her research interests include the study of Third Culture Kids, organizational identification, social support, telecommuting, and changing organizations. She is herself an Adult Third Culture Kid who retains her Swedish passport while remaining internationally mobile. She lives with her two dogs while retaining close contact with the rest of her family, wherever they may be. UPDATE: Dr. Hylmö, like many adults with an international childhood, continues to explore cultures and identity through her work as a documentary and fiction film-maker with Los Angeles as her base. She enjoys spending time with her horse and traveling for work and fun while retaining close contact with the rest of her family, wherever they may be. Follow her at www.annikahylmo.com.

MICHELLE L. KELLEY, Ph.D., is an Associate Professor of Psychology at Old Dominion University in Norfolk, Virginia. She received a B.S. and M.S. from the University of Oklahoma (1983 and 1985, respectively) and a Ph.D. in Psychology from the University of Houston in 1988. Her research interests include the effects of military-induced separation in traditional and nontraditional military families, social policy and parenting, and parenting and child development in at-risk families. Previous publications include "The effects of military-induced separation on family factors and children's behavior," *Journal of Orthopsychiatry*, *64*:103-111; "Military-induced separation in relation to maternal adjustment and children's behavior," *Military Psychology*, *6*:163-176; and "The Effects of military-induced separation on the parenting stress and family functioning of deploying mothers," *Military Psychology*, 6:125-138. She recently completed a longitudinal study of the effects of deployment on Navy mothers with young children as a part of the Defense Women's Health Research Program. She was motivated to study deployment by numerous students, both military dependents and active-duty service members, who questioned the impact that lengthy periodic separations have on military members and their families. UPDATE: Dr. Kelley is Professor of Psychology and Eminent Scholar at ODU and continues her focus on the effects of deployment and military life on active-duty members, veterans, and their families.

LISAMARIE LIEBENOW MARIGLIA, M.S., completed a B.S. in both Sociology and Psychology in 1995 and a Master of Science degree in Family and Consumer Sciences from the University of Wyoming in 1997. She is a Certified Family Life Educator through the National Council on Family Relations. Her M.S. thesis is titled

The Emergence of Associations for Adults Who Were Children in Military Families. Ms. Mariglia has been a military brat in both the United States and overseas, a dependent wife, and has a daughter who is a military brat. She is currently a Training & Curriculum Specialist Trainer at Ramstein Air Force Base and lives in Ramstein, Germany, with her family.

ROBERT S. MCKELVEY, Ph.D. is Professor and Director of Child and Adolescent Psychiatry, Oregon Health Sciences University, Portland, Oregon. He is the author of *The Dust of Life: America's Children Abandoned in Vietnam* (University of Washington Press, 1999). Dr. McKelvey is a former marine who served in Vietnam in the late 1960s. UPDATE: Dr. McKelvey is Professor Emeritus of Psychiatry, working in part-time private practice, and a member of Oregon's Psychiatric Security Review Board.

RICHARD L.D. PEARCE, is currently registered for a Ph.D. at the Department of Education, University of Bath, United Kingdom. He completed his B.A. in Natural Sciences at Trinity Hall, Cambridge, England. After a brief career as a museum curator, he taught in the United Kingdom independent (private) schools. He later joined the International School of London as the Head of Science and assumed many responsibilities including Director of Admissions. He also has taught at St. Paul's School, Brooklandville, Maryland, and the Southbank American International School, London, England. He has written and presented on international education and cultural issues for a number of years. He taught in a M.A. program in International Education at Oxford Brookes University and at the University of Bath, both in the United Kingdom. He also consultants on national and international education. His Ph.D. research involves adjustment of relocated children in international schools. Mr. Pearce was born in Kent, England, on Battle of Britain day and currently lives in England.

FRED L. PERRY, JR., Ph.D., is an Associate Professor at the American University in Cairo, Egypt, where he teaches research methodology and testing and measurement in their graduate program in applied linguistics. He has spent more than 30 years overseas and has partnered with his wife in raising three internationally mobile children.

PHOEBE EVELYN PRICE, B.S., completed her Bachelor of Science degree in Psychology from the United States Military Academy, West Point, New York in May 2000. Her thesis is entitled "Behavior of High School Students in Movie Theaters" and received a paper award in the 16th Annual Hudson Valley Undergraduate Research Conference. She is currently a Transportation Lieutenant in the United States Army and is stationed at Fort Bragg, North Carolina, where she serves a Detachment Commander in the 18th Airborne Corps.

BARBARA F. SCHAETTI, Ph.D., recently completed her graduate studies in Intercultural Communication with a focus on Multicultural Identity Development at The Union Institute, Cincinnati, Ohio. She holds a B.A. in International Political Science from Trinity University, San Antonio, Texas, and an M.A. in Intercultural Conflict Resolution from Antioch University West, Seattle, Washington. She is the Principal Consultant of Transition Dynamics, a consultancy serving the international expatriate and repatriate community. Ms. Schaetti is a contributing author to several books and professional journals, regularly presents at international conferences, and has been interviewed for such publications as *The Guardian* [U.K.] and *The Washington Post*. She holds a dual nationality (U.S. American and Swiss) and had lived in 10 countries on 5 continents by the time she was 18 years old.

MARY P. TYLER, Ph.D., is currently a psychologist with the United States Office of Personnel Management, Office of Work/Life Programs. She provides consultation and other services to Federal agencies concerned with traumatic incidents, workplace violence, and organizational stress. Internationally known as a researcher on the impact of traumatic incidents on organizations, she has published widely in American and European journals and has addressed numerous scholarly and professional organizations in the United States and abroad. She has provided extensive, on-site support to federal organizations responding to such situations as the Oklahoma City bombing, the Northridge Earthquake, and Hurricane Andrew and has also assisted in numerous situations involving violence and threats in federal workplaces. She has developed guidance for Federal agencies on such topics as preventing workplace violence, responding to domestic violence in the Federal workplace, managing after traumatic events, and supporting employees working on Year 2K issues. Her previous positions include Traumatic Incident Program Manager, Internal Revenue Service; Research Psychologist, Walter Reed Army Institute of Research: Assistant Professor, Florida State University; and visiting lecturer, University of Vienna (Austria). She was educated at The University of Chicago, The University of Texas at Austin, and Duke University Medical Center. Dr. Tyler is a member of the American Psychological Association, the International Sociological Association, the Association of Threat Assessment Professionals, and the International Society for Traumatic Stress Studies, a Fellow of the Inter-University Seminar on Armed Forces and Society, and a guest scientist with the Walter Reed Army Institute of Research.

INDEX

A

Adolescent behavior, and media violence, 55. *See also* Military teenagers' behaviors

Adult children of military families, 115-30; adjustment problems of, 80; atypical socialization of, 129; demographics and social history of, 118-21; family life attitudes of, 108-9; geographic mobility/foreign residency of, 122-23, 124-26, 128; and military lifestyle stress, 123-24, 128; military service of, 121; research study, 115-16; second-language acquisition of, 125; social movement of, 115-16, 125; sponsorship and, 271-72, 275; voluntary group association of, 97-98, 108-109. *See also* Adult Third Culture Kids (ATCKs)

Adult Third Culture Kids (ATCKs), 294-327; educational achievements of, 121, 300-01; educational choices of, 301-03; gender-based research on, 214-16; global economy and, 313-14; independence and self-sufficiency of, 308; international careers and involvement of, 308-09, 310-12; marriages of, 283, 285; and need to establish roots, 309-10; occupations of, 284-85, 303-12; research study of, 118-19; use of term, 270

www.ingramcontent.com/pod-product-compliance
Lightning Source LLC
Chambersburg PA
CBHW050331270326
41926CB00016B/3400